BEYOND CAMP DAVID

Emerging Alignments and Leaders in the Middle East

PAUL A. JUREIDINI
R. D. McLAURIN

SYRACUSE UNIVERSITY PRESS
1981

Library of Congress Cataloging in Publication Data

Jureidini, Paul A
  Beyond Camp David.

  (Contemporary issues in the Middle East series
;   )
  Bibliography: p.
  Includes index.
  1. Near East—Politics and government—1945–
I. McLaurin, Ronald D., 1944–   joint author.
II. Title. III. Series.
DS63.1.J79   1981   327'.0956   80-27406
ISBN 0-8156-2235-X
ISBN 0-8156-2236-8 (pbk.)

Manufactured in the United States of America

Contents

FIGURES

MAPS

PAUL A. JUREIDINI is Vice-President of Abbott Associates, Inc., Alexandria, Virginia, and a specialist in Middle Eastern political and security affairs. He has been involved in numerous studies of the Middle East, particularly of Lebanon and the Fertile Crescent, for the U.S. government. He is co-author of *The Palestinian Movement in Politics*.

R. D. MCLAURIN is Senior Research Scientist with Abbott Associates, Inc., Alexandria, Virginia. He is co-author of *Foreign Policy Making in the Middle East: Domestic Influences on Policy in Egypt, Iraq, Israel, and Syria* and author of *The Middle East in Soviet Policy*.

Preface

IN A REGION AS TUMULTUOUS AS THE MIDDLE EAST, descriptions of events and trends as well as forecasts of developments to come are overtaken by new facts with dizzying and humbling swiftness. The observer and the analyst alike find it more comfortable to *discuss* the challenges of the present and future but to *write* only about the past. We have experienced the frustration of attempting to look ahead and running afoul of some *deus ex machina* just as others have, and we trust that unforeseen variables will continue to complicate the job of looking ahead in this complex and troubled region.

For reasons made clear in the Introduction, we believe the Camp David agreements and regional changes coincident with (but in some cases unrelated to) them constitute major changes that demand regional analysts' attention. It is the purpose of this book to give some consideration to the forces at work in the Middle East today, the alignment patterns that have evolved over the last few years, the emerging regional leaders (both individuals and countries), and the interrelationships of these factors to the extent they give us clues as to the future behavior and directions we may see in the Middle East.

We have divided the text into an introduction; a discussion of the actors and forces within Middle East states that influence their attitudes and behaviors; an analysis of the external (bilateral, multilateral, and regional) pressures on these same states; an assessment of emerging alignments within the region; a description and forecast of changes in the leadership within the Middle East; and, finally, a brief suggestion of some of the implications of the analysis for American foreign policy in the years ahead.

The organization we have adopted requires some repetition between chapters, but we have tried to keep this redundancy to an absolute minimum. The alternatives preserve logical and chronological presentation at the expense, on the one hand, of sensitivity to the nature of issue linkages, and, on the other hand, of a clear focus on the substantive changes we are seeking to highlight. This book is by no means an exhaustive study of the diplomatic history of the Middle East in the mid-twentieth century. Rather it is an attempt to consider and forecast emerging alignment and leadership patterns. We hope we have not made the task of the reader too difficult.

In the preparation of this book the authors were assisted by many individuals with a similar interest in and concern about the pattern of international relations in the Middle East.

We would like to express our gratitude to our colleagues, Preston S. Abbott, Edward E. Azar, Kurt Karsten, Mohammed Mughisuddin, Emile Nakhleh, Lewis W. Snider, and, especially, James M. Price who actively assisted us throughout the preparation of the manuscript, and Cathie Love who typed what appeared to be frequently illegible.

While there is insufficient space to acknowledge the intellectual and factual contributions of all those who supported this effort, we would like to extend particular thanks to His Royal Highness Hassan Bin Talal, Crown Prince of Jordan; His Excellency Yassar Askari, Arab League Ambassador to the United States; Nancy Bearg, principal deputy assistant secretary, U.S. Department of the Air Force; Peter A. Gubser, president of American Near East Refugee Aid (ANERA); W. Nathaniel Howell, U.S. Department of State; Renee Joyner, Office of the Assistant Secretary of Defense (International Security Affairs); Dr. Sami Khoury, health officer, US/AID, Jordan; the Honorable Robert K. Murray, Undersecretary of the Navy; and Colonel Paul Slater, chief of doctrine, U.S. Army Field Artillery School, Ft. Sill.

The counsel of each of these people and of many others has been invaluable. We, of course, are solely responsible for the final product which presents our own perceptions and projections, even if it has benefitted greatly from those of others.

Summer 1980   PAJ
                                                       RDMcL

Introduction

T HE MIDDLE EAST AFTER WORLD WAR II has been the setting for a complex drama in which several major themes have been interwoven—nationalism, the consolidation of political and economic independence and security, competition for regional power, and, finally, the rivalry of external states for influence over Middle East governments and their resources. While each of these factors has been extremely important, another—too frequently neglected—has also subtly but significantly shaped government behavior: the nature of the regimes and the political culture of the Middle East.

In this chapter we establish the background against which new regional alignments and leaders are emerging with an overview of the Middle East since 1967, the patterns of regional relations, and the new forces driving regional developments. The focus of this necessarily retrospective introduction will be the key actors of the 1967–77 period—Egypt, Jordan, Lebanon, Saudi Arabia, Syria, and the Palestine Liberation Organization (PLO).

ALIGNMENT PATTERNS IN THE MIDDLE EAST— STABILITY AND CHANGE, 1967–73

Observers are often wont to choose wars as the chronological markers for new eras, but alignment patterns usually fit poorly war or interwar periods if the conflicts themselves are not decisive. In many respects *both* the June (1967) and October (1973) wars *were* decisive, but neither achieved the long-term political goals of any of the parties. This is not to argue that wars without total victory are unimportant: the 1967 and the 1973 conflicts, for example, were the single most important factors in bringing about fundamental changes in Middle East politics and alignment structure. We argue only that inconclusive wars produce delayed effects rather than immediate ones.

The June War laid to rest all remaining doubts that Israel was able to defend itself against any combination of Arab states. While Arab military analysts and others tried to explain away the magnitude of the Israeli victory on the basis of "surprise," no one seriously gainsaid the potency of Zahal, the Israeli Defense Forces. The military results of the war included the virtual destruction of the Egyptian, Jordanian, and Syrian armed forces; and the political results of that destruction included the serious weakening of the political control and security of those three governments. This weakening, in turn, gave rise to the growth of a new force inside territory under the nominal sovereignty of Egypt, Jordan, and Syria—Fatah and other Palestinian commando organizations.

In the aftermath of the war, too, the politics of Egypt and Syria were turbulent. Gamal Abdel Nasser, Egypt's president and charismatic leader, reorganized both the political and military structures of his country and, as if the June War were a personal humiliation, allowed himself to lose the flexible approach to regional politics that had characterized his behavior before the war. Moreover, the defeat reduced, at least temporarily, the margin of Egypt's preeminence over the other Arab states of the eastern Mediterranean.

Syria, never fully integrated as a nation-state, was governed by the Arab Socialist Renaissance Party—the Ba'th—which had, despite several internal schisms and changes of leadership, been more or less in control since 1963. However, by 1967, the Syrian Ba'th (and the army as well) had come to be dominated by a minority religious sect, the 'Alawis. Resentment in Syria against the poor showing of the armed forces during the war and specifically for the loss of the Golan Heights to Israel had the potential of taking on an anti-'Alawi cast. Moreover, during the tumultuous and brief political history of independent Syria, coups and political violence generally had become expected and almost sanctioned forms of political behavior. In the wake of the war, when government-army and party-army relations were almost anarchic, no force emerged to effectively control or guide Syrian politics.

Indeed, no direction reemerged in Arab politics as a whole until about 1970, an extremely important year in Middle East history.[1] In Jordan, the Bedouin army, which had increasingly chafed under restrictions on its interactions with Palestinian groups on Jordanian soil, finally forced King Hussein to authorize a military strike to eliminate once and for all PLO power in the kingdom and to reestablish the primacy of the throne and its security forces. In Syria, Salah Jadid, the strongman who had lost much of his power to fellow 'Alawi Hafez Assad, head of the Syrian Air Force, decided to move against Assad only to lose out in a quick turn of events. Between Egypt and Israel sporadic firing across the Suez Canal gave way to the War of Attrition, which in turn led to an influx of unprecedented numbers of Soviet advisors, and within Egypt, near the end of the year, Nasser died.[2]

The civil war in Jordan resulted in the kingdom's quarantine by the rest of the Arab world. Meanwhile, the PLO, driven from Jordan and under increasing control and restraints within Syria, mounted a strong campaign against the Hashemite monarchy. Indeed, Jordan became perhaps more of a political target than Israel. Amman's relations with Syria, however, quietly improved: Assad was intent on ending Syria's isolation and did not see the boycott of Jordan as functional to his goals.[3] Syria's interaction with Lebanon took on a very different tenor, as Assad's ties to some of the leading Maronite figures were good, quite in contrast to the period when Jadid ruled Syria.[4] Taking Syria away from the Rejectionist camp, Assad accepted Resolution 242. Notwithstanding some initial questions about Anwar Sadat, Nasser's successor, Assad and Hussein both found relations with Egypt more stable. Sadat, after extricating himself from the War of Attrition, pursued two tracks to achieve movement in the stalemated Arab-Israeli situation.[5] The first consisted in a variety of initiatives designed to reopen negotiations at some level. Recognizing the importance of the United States as the only outside power able to mount effective pressure on Israeli policy-making, Sadat endeavored to demonstrate a new Arab (read Egyptian) openness to America and to encourage the United States to take an active role in reopening and conducting negotiations. The second Sadat path, admittedly less desirable, was that of war. In case movement could not be sparked through the first approach, Egypt's new president concentrated as well upon the preparation of the Egyptian armed forces for a limited-objective military operation that would likely *compel* U.S. involvement.[6] Such a strategy required cementing relations with other Arab regimes, especially Syria (since Syria's participation was critical to the plan), Jordan, Libya, and Saudi Arabia.

What had happened by the early 1970s—and this was a result of the 1967 war—was that the reality of Israel's existence *and ability to ensure* that existence had gained acceptance by the political elites of the Arab world. What we call "rejectionism" or the politics of the Arab irreconcilables—that is, the rejection of Israel's right to exist and, specifically, of UN Security Council Resolution 242 which states this right—were believed to be required by domestic political exigencies and by the necessity to maintain *some* bargaining leverage in a situation in which Israel had a sufficient margin of military superiority to guarantee its security. Arab leaders had by the early 1970s come to grips with reality and recognized the need for a *modus vivendi,* but a *modus vivendi* that met some of their needs, too. They had, in other words, reached the stage long sought by Israel—readiness to accept a negotiated settlement including recognition of Israel's existence—at the same time that Israel was no longer willing to spend much political capital to achieve only this end.

Thus Egyptian policy focused on overcoming the rivalries and enmities that plague the Arab world, while preserving the appearance of "business as usual." Egyptian planners, believing the magnitude of the Israeli victory of 1967 to be attributable to the effect of surprise, recognized the importance of this element in their own plans. Consequently, elaborate alliance structures and threat patterns were eschewed. Yet, a retrospective appraisal of the prewar period shows that attentive fence-mending and uncharacteristically vigorous exchanges of visits were effective Arab—especially Egyptian—tools for the construction of a utilitarian wartime Arab coalition. By late 1972 and early 1973 there remained no insuperable obstacles to a broad Arab participation in the war.

THE OCTOBER WAR AND POSTWAR CHANGES, 1973–77

The October 1973 war was the symbolic "end of an era" in the Middle East. This conflict is the only one of the several Arab-Israeli wars that did not erupt after a period of building tensions. It was a "planned" war, preceded by a careful and effective deception campaign and coordinated at the strategic level by the two principal allied Arab governments of Egypt and Syria. The war can be viewed as the result of realism and consequent frustration in the Arab world. Before and after the October War, Israeli military superiority was accepted, but the parameters of that superiority changed significantly. Until 1973 Israeli regional power seemed limitless and without cost. After 1973 Arabs and many Israelis as well recognized that Arab forces could at least exact a high price for a political stalemate.

The importance of the October War can be viewed in three contexts—military, domestic political, and regional political.[7] In this section we shall consider the first and third of these contexts only. The second, domestic political impact, is limited to Israel—where the war produced political scapegoating, hastened the decline of the Labor Alignment,[8] created a new determination to retain high degrees of military readiness,[9] resuscitated the credibility of the Arab threat, and breathed new life into the desire for a general settlement[10]—and Syria, where poor military performance also led to scapegoating, in this case to buttress the legitimacy of the minority-dominated Assad government.

The military results of the war were more clear cut, at the strategic level, than many observers have suggested.[11] Israel remained the only confrontation state capable of sustained offensive operations. Both Syria and Egypt showed their capacity to defend fixed, fortified positions. Air defense suppression and the combined arms teams were more important than Israel had recognized, but warfare of this intensity demanded too much of Arab command, control, and communications (C^3) as well. The military *outcomes* of the war are associated with resupply. Once again, Israeli inventories have received material one or more generations in advance of that of the Arab states, and the war resulted in U.S. approval for the transfer to Israel of numerous high-technology systems theretofore embargoed. Even without the Egyptian-Israeli peace treaty, Israeli regional military superiority is clear.[12]

More complex are the regional political results of the conflict. The apparently[13] effective application of the petroleum embargo ended the low profile Saudi Arabia had maintained with regard to its increasing influence in the Arab world. Principal financial source for the Arab confrontation states, and the only major oil producer with immense, untapped reserves the leadership was prepared to exploit, Saudi Arabia is also the only Arab oil exporter consistently providing substantial quantities of oil to the United States. Yet, Saudi foreign policy on major issues continued to be a function of the views of King Faisal until his death in the spring of 1975.[14] Following the succession, decision-making became more complex, with the views neither of the princes nor of King Khalid always "winning" in family councils. Still, in spite of a less firm hand at the policy helm, the resources supporting Saudi diplomacy made the country central to regional politics, a frequently reluctant, high-visibility actor.

Sadat's strategy of war had been designed to lure the United States into a more active role in the Arab-Israeli situation. The pressure and threat implicit in the Arab oil embargo, the orchestration and moderation of stated Arab goals, and the personal attitudes of the new foreign policy team conduced to the realization of Sadat's objective: the United States actively inserted itself into the confrontation even before the guns of October fell silent. The cease-fire left Arab and Israeli forces dangerously interlocked in dispositions from which continued firing seemed assured. Fearing the reignition of general hostilities, U.S. Secretary of State Henry Kissinger initiated intensive negotiations designed to disengage opposing forces, first on the Sinai front, then on the Golan.[15]

The discussions on disengagement were conducted separately on each front. Kissinger hoped that from these tactical talks could emerge a trust that might in turn lead to momentum toward a general settlement. The preliminary and discrete nature of the process, as well as the nature of its relationship to the ultimate objectives, resulted in the term "step-by-step" diplomacy.

Few would take exception to the necessity of disengagement. By contrast, the applicability of the approach to the general settlement issue is highly questionable given the complex interrelationships involved. Predictably, separate negotiations led to heightened inter-Arab conflict, and the second-stage agreement on the Sinai played a major role in regionalizing and broadening the Lebanese civil war. Syrian President Assad sought to ensure the solidarity of Lebanon, Jordan, and the PLO under Syrian influence, so he intervened politically to help promulgate a new national pact that would restore substantial power to the established political leaders and forces. When this accord proved unacceptable to the leftist/Palestinian alliance, Syrian military forces intervened. From the inception of Damascus' engagement in Lebanon to the present, Syria's objectives have been as constant as its alignment has been inconstant. Yet, partly because of the threat of Israeli counterintervention, Syrian forces have been unable to wholly control the conflict with the result a stalemate.[16]

Syria's other partner proved much more dependable than any of the Lebanese antagonists. After the opening to Damascus was established, Jordanian policy placed substantial importance on the maintenance of high-level coordination with the 'Alawi leaders of Syria. Jordan served as Syria's window to the West, especially until 1976. Military strategy was evolved tying in the defense of the Irbid Heights (a corridor to Syria that would outflank the Golan defenses) to overall Syrian military preparations.[17] After 1974, when the Rabat Conference stripped Jordan of any claim to represent West Bank Palestinians (in favor of the PLO), Hussein's acceptance of the Rabat decisions and improved ties with Syria cleared the way for Jordan's return to widespread Arab good graces.

The confrontation states were then divided—Egypt on the one hand, Jordan and Syria on the other—over the approach to and acceptance of a major U.S. role in the negotiations for a general settlement. Hussein, optimistic, felt Jordan had little role until invited to participate; he also felt such an invitation to be inevitable. Assad, pessimistic after late 1975, saw little point in step-by-step for Syria. Sadat, optimistic, felt—in contrast to his two counterparts— that Egypt and the Arab world had much to gain from throwing in their lot with the United States, in trying to encourage the latter to become a full and active partner in the settlement process.[18]

Odd man out in the Arab world was Iraq. Challenged on the east by Iran and on the west by Syria, viewed with distrust by both Kuwait and Saudi Arabia to the south and Jordan to the west, Iraq was perhaps the most isolated Arab state. Although the central government seemed to be making slow but marked progress against the continuing Kurdish insurgency, resources allocated and dissension exacerbated by this problem sapped Iraqi strength. In 1975, however, an agreement with Iran cut off the insurgents from their principal source of external support and led the way to a quick and decisive conclusion of the internal conflict. Although never close, relations with Iran stabilized at a reasonably cooperative level. By contrast, Iraqi-Syrian rivalry was exacerbated by Syrian behavior in the Lebanese civil war. Troop movements and other threatening gestures never led to war, however, and eventually Iraq was forced to recognize and accept Syria's determination to maintain its preeminence in Lebanon.

As we have indicated, Saudi Arabia's regional role increased enormously after 1973, because the kingdom's financial power brought influence, because Saudi Arabia was the strongest single member of OPEC (one whose production decisions could single-handedly go a long way toward determining the success or failure of OPEC pricing initiatives), and because Saudi Arabia became a more and more critical supplier of petroleum to the United States. Thus, after 1973, Saudi Arabia was courted by virtually all regional powers: Egypt, Jordan, and Syria looked to Riyadh for subsidies; Iraq and Iran sought Saudi support for increased OPEC prices. Moreover, the smaller Gulf states looked to Saudi Arabia for defense support, Egypt found close Saudi ties to be excellent credentials in the attempt to improve communications with the United States, and Syrian leaders feared the potential influence of Saudi Arabia within Syria (cf. Chapter 1).

The newfound Saudi power inevitably broke down the insulation between the eastern Mediterranean and Persian Gulf subregions of the Middle East with the result that Israel and Saudi Arabia for the first time figured directly in each other's strategic planning. The only direct external threats to the Saudi monarchy had been seen in Baghdad and, over a longer term, in Iran. Suddenly, Israel, which since 1967 occupied two Saudi islands (Sanafir and Tiran), was the single greatest military threat to Saudi Arabia in Saudi eyes.[19]

Israel, too, was a country in change after the October War. Once the initial shock of the war had worn off and scapegoats had been identified, Israeli leaders determined to maintain a posture of military readiness higher than previous levels. In particular, military force modernization and training efforts were upgraded and extremely ambitious procurement plans developed. Economic constraints meant that procurement programs would depend upon unprecedented levels of American grant military assistance.[20] Notwithstanding the greater degree of military readiness and the substantial technological development in post–October War Israel, disenchantment with national leadership under the Labor-led coalition grew apace with catastrophic rates of inflation. Economic stagnation and a series of political and financial scandals cast a cloud over the coalition, but even more fundamental processes were eroding Labor's attractiveness to the electorate. The result of these processes was the defeat of the Alignment and its replacement as government plurality by the *Likud* coalition led by Menachem Begin who became prime minister. The Begin government took a more "hawkish" position vis-à-vis the Arabs and began to move away from some of the socialist measures of its predecessors. Yet, faced with a staggering military budget, the influx of significant amounts of capital and goods from overseas, widespread inefficiency, and extensive social dislocation resulting from changes in the demographic composition of Israel, the Israeli economy continued to look bleak.[21]

Israel was not alone in suffering through inflation, although its inflation rate was several times that of other Middle East countries. Yet, the boom economies of the oil producers were regionalized to an extent. In addition to the subsidies (to which we have already adverted), the oil producers extended development loans and paid for military hardware.[22] Equally important in some cases was the employment offered in the oil producers' economies: one of the largest sources of capital in countries like Jordan rapidly became the receipts from expatriates working in the Gulf. Moreover, many Western firms viewed all Arab markets as vehicles for the penetration of the oil producers' markets, so substantial amounts of technology were transferred, and significant numbers of commercial visits were common across the region.[23]

Each of the major oil producers developed ambitious plans for economic development. That these plans embodied greatly increased interactions with the West followed naturally from their authors' understanding of the economic development process and preference for Western values and goods. Thus pressures from both oil suppliers and consumers drove the steady increase in human and material resources transferred from Europe, Japan, and North America to the Persian Gulf and, to a lesser extent, the eastern Mediterranean. The great influx of Western nationals and Western capital had pronounced and predictable impacts on the traditional societies of the region. For development, however, all the oil producers of the Middle East looked West.

THE SHADOW OF AN EGYPTIAN-ISRAELI PEACE, 1977–78

Seeking once again to break the stalemate into which the Arab-Israeli situation had devolved, Egyptian President Anwar Sadat made a direct and personal plea to Israeli Prime Minister Menachem Begin in November 1977, volunteering to go to Jerusalem if that would contribute to a settlement. After several exchanges, Sadat did in fact visit Israel, initiating a new era in the Arab-Israeli dispute and fundamentally affecting inter-Arab relations. Syria and the PLO, fearing the conclusion of a separate peace that might remove Egypt—the most powerful Arab state—from the anti-Israel coalition, undertook with the support of the extremists (Iraq, Algeria, Libya) vitriolic attacks on Sadat's new approach.

The Egyptian strategy left more than adequate time for a constructive Arab alternative; but none was forthcoming. Sadat's opponents seemingly could agree on nothing save opposition to his policies.[24] Even opposition was to some extent muted by Sadat's insistence that he would never settle for a "separate peace." Thus Saudi criticism was centered not so much on the nature of the Egyptian approach as upon the fact that it was undertaken without prior consultation with and among the Arabs. Two monarchs—King Hassan of Morocco, much at the periphery of the Arab-Israeli problem, and King Hussein of Jordan, just as much at its core—seemed to offer limited support, although Hussein was increasingly skeptical concerning Israeli intentions.

The new Egyptian strategy fundamentally altered Middle East relations. The most important changes occurred between Egypt and its erstwhile allies, Iraq, Jordan, and Syria; between Jordan and the PLO; between Iraq and Saudi Arabia; and temporarily between Iraq and Syria. These and other changes are graphically portrayed in Figures 1.1 and 1.2 (and described in Chapter 3). The discontinuity of the two figures results from the distinction between Arab perceptions of Egyptian strategy before and after the Camp David summit meeting[25] and the subsequent Egyptian-Israeli peace treaty.[26]

Ultimately, and predictably, the other Arab states were unable to act to effectively counter Egypt's new strategy.[27] However, events in the Middle East in late 1979 and early 1980—the seizure of the U.S.

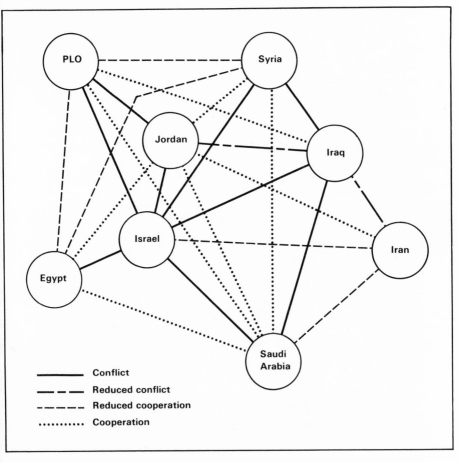

FIGURE 1.1 Key Middle East Relationships, 1975–78

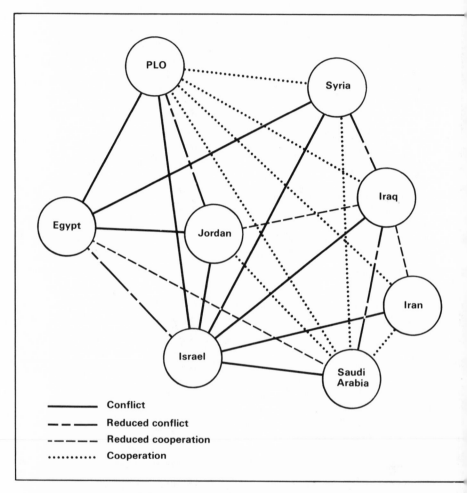

FIGURE 1.2 Key Middle East Relationships, 1978–79

embassy in Tehran,[28] attacks on Americans and American property and embassies elsewhere,[29] and especially Soviet military intervention in Afghanistan[30]—rekindled U.S. strategic fears and submerged what had been widespread public and congressional opposition within the United States to overseas commitments and to U.S. military action abroad.[31] The fact that Camp David and its "peace process" roughly co-occurred with the Iranian revolution and the events of 1979–80 further reduced the ability of the Arab states to respond effectively by *diminishing* the relative importance of the Levant vis-à-vis the Arab/Persian Gulf, and by *increasing* the salience of the Arab countries only insofar as they cooperated with new Washington views on a U.S. military presence in the region.

After all, Israel continued to be the strongest military power in the Middle East, secure from attacks by any combination of Arab states and doubly so now that a peace had been concluded with Egypt. In the Arab view only the United States, as Israel's principal supplier of military hardware and technology, could mount sufficient effective pressure on Israel to bring about more conciliatory policies. The United States could in turn be pressured by Arab governments and the PLO through manipulating the superpower rivalry, through threatened oil embargoes, and through petroleum price escalation. However, such a strategy was based upon the relatively reserved behavior of the United States during and after the Vietnam War and on the tendency of both superpowers increasingly to react to regional events in terms of regional interests rather than their global competition. When American attitudes abruptly changed in 1980 after the Soviet intervention in Afghanistan, it appeared that local governments might once again be seen as useful only in terms of their contribution to U.S. global strategy. While this attitude may not endure, Middle East governments have already been forcefully reminded of how little control they have over regional developments when the superpowers determine to act.

The result of the foregoing has been a deemphasis of the Egyptian-Israeli "peace process," as other Arab governments:

• (in the Gulf) recalled how peripheral the Arab-Israeli conflict was to them; or

• recognized the degree to which they sought American support as well as the degree to which their opposition to Camp David had weakened that support; or

• realized that their security under the new circumstances was much less assured outside than inside the peace process; or

• in the face of their inability to affect Egypt and Israel came to the conclusion that limited benefits within the Camp David formula might be preferable to being left behind by the developments issuing forth from it.

An important result, then, of the various developments in the late 1970s and early 1980 has been to move toward a return to the previous insulation between the various subregions of the Middle East. As the countries of the Gulf have felt the repercussions arising from the Iranian revolution, their governments have been too concerned with internal and Gulf problems and issues to further subdivide attention and resources to address the Levant. Similarly, political changes in the eastern Mediterranean and the domestic impact of regional (including Gulf) developments have had such fundamental and far-reaching ramifications on Levantine states that their governments have tended to be less concerned with the Gulf than at any time since 1973. It is with this new phenomenon in mind that we turn to consider in more detail the principal actors in both those subregions of the Middle East.

BEYOND CAMP DAVID

Actors and Forces

WITH THE RISE OF MIDDLE EAST OIL as a paramount consideration in international politics, the number of Middle East countries that can be viewed as important has grown apace. The key countries now include not only the traditional political and military powers— Egypt, Iran, Israel, and Syria—but, as well, two states with new-found substantial weight—Saudi Arabia and Iraq. In this chapter we discuss in some detail the importance and role of each of these states and of Jordan (which is a marginal regional actor in most respects but which may play a central role in the evolution of the West Bank issue) and the principal factors governing their decision-making. The Palestine Liberation Organization (PLO) and other states are treated more cursorily in the final part of the chapter.

EGYPT
Objectives and Interest Groups

For much of the period between 1967 and 1973, Egypt appeared to have relinquished its role as leader of the Arab world. Even during the War of Attrition,[1] Egypt's impotence seemed at least as much in evidence as its power. Indeed, it was the influx of unprecedented numbers of Soviet advisors into Egypt during and after the War of Attrition that led to renewed external interest in and concern about Egypt's direction.[2] Notwithstanding the early impression Anwar Sadat made on the world,[3] however, his policies, decisions, and actions since 1970 have once again placed Egypt in the position of leadership. By suggesting Egypt is a leader once more, we are not prejudging the outcome of Sadat's current policies. Rather, we refer to the fact that Sadat is marshalling Egypt's own not inconsiderable

1

resources to determine Egypt's fate instead of behaving as if the Arab world as a whole will determine Egypt's destiny.

It is important to note that Egypt's people constitute more than 30 percent of the population of the Arab world. The GNP represents a substantial share of the aggregate gross product of the Arab world, and despite overwhelming, demographically caused problems in education, employment, housing, sanitation, and other areas of the economy and society, Egypt's manpower constitutes a disproportionate share of the skilled and unskilled labor base and of the educationally and technically sophisticated manpower reservoir of the Arab world. Without Egypt, there can be no meaningful military threat to Israel from any combination of other Arab states.[4] Thus Egypt's political, economic, and military role is unique. Moreover, Egypt alone among Arab states can limit its sphere of responses to stimuli arising from within. Egypt can disregard the Arab world; the Arab world cannot disregard Egypt.

The principal ingredient in Egyptian decision-making at this time is the development of a new economy and new economic style for Egypt.[5] Egyptian demographic pressures have figured prominently in Anwar Sadat's thinking since he took over the helm of the country.[6] Recognizing that fundamental structural changes in Egyptian economic realities were required to avoid social disaster on a massive scale, recognizing that such a change was impossible with the crushing burden of military outlays necessitated by the struggle with Israel and while domestic dissent might be generated against a policy that seemed to acquiesce in the continued occupation of Egyptian territory, Sadat has pursued several approaches designed to bring the conflict with Israel to an end, to terminate the Israeli occupation of Egyptian territory, and to establish the conditions prerequisite to foreign support for fundamental, structural change in Egypt.

We have discussed elsewhere the principal interest groups in Egyptian society and their roles in the decision process.[7] Clearly, the Arab Socialist Union, though still a force to be reckoned with, has lost much of its strength over the last few years. Sadat's own National-al Democratic Party, however, will not have the benefit of the charismatic leadership the ASU enjoyed with Gamal Abdel Nasser. Rather, in place of the ASU there is widespread popular support behind Anwar Sadat as a national leader. Sadat has succeeded, against substantial odds, in conveying to the populace a hope for the future and a belief that it can be achieved. By taking several unexpected initiatives, by acting outside the expected and traditional parameters of Egyptian politics, Sadat has been able to persuade the Egyptian nation that the constraints imposed by age-old problems may, too, be overcome.[8] The result is a surprisingly strong support for him—surprising because it is so new.

Three other interest groups enjoy some power in Egypt—the military, the left, and Islamic religious elements. If they were united against the president, there is no question that the armed forces could remove him. Yet, apart from the Young Officers' movement that deposed King Farouk, the Egyptian military has shown much less inclination to intervene in politics than have the military forces of many other states. Moreover, it appears that Sadat enjoys general armed forces support, although dissidents (including some relatively prominent officers) certainly do exist.[9] Leftist groups retain much less influence in Egypt today than they did some years ago, even though the individuals involved are frequently nationally known figures.[10] Justifiably or otherwise, much of the Nasserist ideology and infrastructure have been discredited,[11] with the result that his leftist supporters choose their words and platforms carefully. A resurgence of the left cannot be discounted, but such a development would definitely require alignment of the left with some other groups such as the military. Finally, there can be no doubt that considerable power remains in the hands of the Muslim right.[12] Sadat has chosen to work with, and at times co-opt, Islamic elements, recognizing as he does their considerable influence in Egypt.[13] Like the military, and unlike the left, the Muslim right definitely places constraints on Egyptian policy and behavior.[14] Although they cannot be compared with the Iranian Shi'a clergy, who can construct leadership under the banner of Islam, Egyptian Islamic groups can only exert real *opposition* power and could crystallize and mobilize dissent.

Thus only two domestic groups—the military and the religious right—are major factors in Egyptian policy-making at this time. It should be noted that Sadat's background and personal ties provide him credibility, access, and roots in both these groups. Consequently, although armed forces attitudes and those of the Muslim sector carry some weight and suggest certain parameters within which policy objectives should be articulated, it is equally true that Sadat is able to exert a very substantial influence on the policies and views of these two groups, or, at least, on the official positions of their institutional representatives. Under these circumstances, and operating in an environment and political culture that do not favor subversion,[15] President Sadat has a degree of flexibility unusual for a Middle East leader.

IRAN

Under Shah Mohammed Reza Pahlavi, Iran's behavior derived from the clear-cut objectives of the Peacock Throne. Although the objectives or means of achieving them might have been questionable, the shah embodied and used national power. Only partially responsive to his immediate environment, he tended to act much more in accordance with his own views and beliefs; the shah saw little benefit in accepting policy parameters other groups articulated.

For twenty-five years the shah's style of governance was successful.[16] So numerous, so diverse, so cacophonous were the ethnic, bureaucratic, military, religious, class, economic, political, and other voices either suggesting or demanding their own preferred approaches to perceived problems that there seemed little likelihood these divergent elements might coalesce effectively against the regime. Although Mohammed Mossadeq supplanted the shah for a brief period in 1953, even Mossadeq, a relatively popular politician, was unable to mobilize or unify a substantial portion of the populace, a fact recognized by the handful of conspirators who restored the shah to the throne.[17]

Shah Mohammed Reza Pahlavi did succeed in bringing social change to Iran, though change has only begun to affect the deeper element of Persian culture. Ironically, several of the newly introduced elements of change were directly or indirectly responsible for the diposition of the shah. More important, these elements in combination with the numerous natural schisms that separate the many political, ethnic, linguistic, religious, and economic groups that make up Iran bode ill for political stability or power in that country. Each of the cultural and ethnic minorities, each of the political groups, and a number of the religious elements—all are beginning to organize, to mobilize their members, to identify and marshal their forces, and to amass and coordinate their arms. Iran has undergone sufficient westernization to ensure effective *within-group* communication, with a concomitant increase in the effectiveness and likelihood of resistance to centralized authority.[18]

The result of the emergence of multiple centers of power and submergence of central authority is the weakness of specific themes and objectives as explanations or driving forces behind Iranian behavior. Similarly, no one element in the complex amalgam that is Iranian politics today can be viewed as decisive over the next twelve to thirty-six months.

The elaboration and implementation of an Islamic republic are the policy themes articulated by the coterie of followers of Ayatollah Khomeini and by the ayatollah himself. That the nature of these processes is itself far from self-evident is shown in the conflicting paths pursued by various Khomeini followers. Moreover, the reaction of the Persian people against the speed and breadth of at least some important elements of the shah's modernization program does not necessarily mean the opponents of the program will any more comfortably accept Khomeini's concept of an Islamic republic. There is little coherence or clarity to the principal policy theme espoused by the government in Tehran, and even some evidence to suggest that increased understanding may mean greater opposition. Without an acceptable theme and in the presence of rapidly accelerating centrifugal forces, reunification of Iran as a national actor will be extremely difficult if not impossible in the short run.

Over the next five years the potential political futures for Iran are difficult to forecast with certainty but most likely will be one or some combination of the following:

1. *Continued centrifugation.* Without an effective armed force to execute national decisions, and faced with strong desires for autonomy by groups and regions in all parts of the republic, Iran will be hard pressed to arrest the power of these centrifugal forces. Thus de facto devolution or decentralization may lead to almost complete autonomy in Kurdistan, Baluchistan, or Azerbaijan. Khuzistan, whose peoples have also been restive, may be a uniting factor to other Iranians, however, since oil revenues from Kuzistan are anticipated by all the other provinces. Continued centrifugation might conceivably leave Ayatollah Khomeini in power in Tehran (though such a prospect is unlikely), but Tehran will have little to do with the remainder of Iran.

2. *Political instability in Tehran.* By instability we mean the rise and fall of several regimes. While the peoples of Iran are conservative and traditionalist, not radical, in their political and social beliefs, a leftist take-over is possible because of the greater organization of the left by contrast with the several rightist groups. Such a totalitarian government, however, would be as (or more) hard pressed as (than) the current regime in securing real control over the country in its entirety over the next five years. Only the intervention of very substantial numbers of foreign military personnel could probably provide a semblance of stability for the central government. We see political instability as a very likely concomitant of any political future for Iran.

3. *Partition.* The most extreme, multifaceted, and unlikely possibility is partition of the current geographical unit of Iran into two or more polities. Partition could grow from the centrifugation presently underway. Alternatively, it could arise as a result of intervention by Iraq (in Khuzistan), the Soviet Union, or the Soviet Union and the United States.

One of the few issues on which Iran has taken a clear stand is the Palestinian problem. The Khomeini government, and many of its opposition elements as well, have strongly supported the PLO and have placed Iran firmly in the "Arab" camp.[19] If Iran took an active military role in Middle East issues, and if the new position had been seen before the purge of the Iranian armed forces, such a change might have had some important implications for the Arab-Israeli balance. In the event, the significance has been largely limited to the economic plane, where Israel has been forced to shift its oil procurement.[20] With the cancellation of many of the shah's planned arms purchases, the likely deterioration in the condition of equipment already deployed, large scale problems in the motivation, morale, and leadership of the Iranian armed forces, and the probability that Iran's new government will restrict its military operations to locations inside Iran's borders, Iran will not play any major military role in the Arab-Israeli situation.[21]

Indeed, Iranian foreign and defense policies generally can be expected to remain more reactive under the new regime than they were under the shah. Notwithstanding the conflict with Iraq and troublesome relations with several other Arab countries, the Khomeini government will be unable and unwilling to undertake strong initiatives. (This may not be true of a successor government should it be secular and totalitarian in nature, but the disarray of Iranian security forces has reached such an extent that it will be difficult for any government to restore complete order and control, return equipment to operable status, and develop politically dependable as well as militarily effective command, control, and communications— C^3—in less than five years.[22])

Perhaps no single issue exemplifies the paralysis of government in Iran more clearly than that government's inability to come to grips with the problem of more than fifty U.S. diplomatic hostages captured by Islamic student militants when they seized the U.S. embassy in Tehran on November 4, 1979. By the spring of 1980 the hostage situation had become an institutionalized captive of chaotic Iranian domestic politics, a pawn in the ambitions of the many centers competing for power.

The current and impending instability in Iran render meaningless serious attempts to forecast specific policies. The direction of Iran's foreign relations will certainly be more independent and neutralist than it was under the shah, but the drive to increase petroleum prices will be even less sensitive to the economic stability of the industrial world. Domestic pressure from the ideological left will be much more pronounced than at any time in the last quarter century, and the need to unify the country is certain to dominate all other needs as the motive force behind both international and domestic policies. Latent hostility against the United States, Israel, Iraq, Saudi Arabia, and the Arabs in general may be exploited in attempts to evoke Iranian nationalism and thereby bring greater national unity behind whatever regime is in power.[23]

ISRAEL

The state of Israel has occupied a critical place in Middle East affairs since its creation in 1948. Inter-Arab relations and extraregional relations as well have been fundamentally affected by Israel's presence, policies, and power. The interrelated issues of occupied territory, stable and normalized intergovernmental relations (including recognized boundaries), and the Palestinian problem are all inextricably linked to Israel.

The leadership of Israel, like that of Iran, has fundamentally changed since the October War of 1973. The Likud coalition, which assumed power after the May 1977 elections, itself tenuously unites several schismatic factions of Israeli political life. Policies are articulated differently today from the past, and the nature of policy support has changed. Moreover, the social perspectives of the Israeli public have evolved consonant with demographic change in the origin of the Israeli population.[24]

Over the years, the role of the Oriental Jew, including those Jews who have emigrated from Arab countries, has grown in relation to the earlier dominance of Ashkenazi or European Jews. The latter have tended to be more conciliatory toward the Arabs, more politically ideological and liberal, and, economically, more comfortable. The Labor Party, or Alignment, symbolized moderation (by Israeli standards) on the Arab-Israeli issue, liberal democracy and socialism, and industrial development. The Alignment was also characterized by close ties to the United States. Yet, these values and directions ran counter to increasingly prominent portions of the Israeli populace. Moreover, the defection from Alignment ranks of credible "establishment" figures, such as Yigael Yadin, increasingly legitimized the act of voting against Labor—an act many earlier felt was virtually unpatriotic.[25] Several scandals emerged prior to the 1977 elections that accelerated the spread of this legitimacy as it cast the shadow of corruption and venality over Labor.

It should not be inferred from the foregoing that Israel's foreign policy was uncontroversial or lacking in salience. Yet, until 1973 there was no requirement to come to terms with the prerequisites of settlement. Even after 1973, the inherent conflict between territorial annexation and settlement has not been placed in a clear-cut situation of choice, despite the private efforts of many Israelis to do so. Some argue that the current Egyptian-Israeli negotiations based upon the Camp David and subsequent accords will bring about precisely such an environment; others disagree. Without outside pressure from the United States it seems unlikely that the question can evolve dichotomously in any short term, and developments in Jordan could at least conceivably moot such an evolution over the longer term.[26] Thus for the present, the Israeli public wants security, including continued control of the West Bank, *and* settlement. The strong autarchic (in the political more than the economic sense) impulse in Israeli political culture, which amounts to a great (and understandable) distrust of any foreign power and (equally understandable) skepticism concerning its resolve, means that any difference between Israel and the United States can be employed by the incumbent regime in the former to rally nationalist support.

Relations with the United States, then, and the nature of Arab-Israeli interaction are prominent international issues. Their salience—viewed as nothing less than the survival of Israel—and the regional psychological isolation of the Jewish state have tended to unite most Israelis behind the broadest outlines of national policy on the Arab-Israeli issue. By contrast, economic factors have been more divisive and have played an increasing prominence in Israeli politics.

Israel's economic situation has worsened rather continuously since the October 1973 war. Inflation, balance of payments problems, and inefficiency in management and state-run enterprises are the major economic problems Israel faces. With one of the highest inflation rates in the world, Israel is still pursuing a guns-and-butter economic policy that has forced the central bank to print large sums of money to finance the resulting deficit. There appears to be little sympathy for reducing defense or social expenditures, partly because the United States is defraying a substantial share in public and private assistance.[27]

The primary interest groups in Israel are ethnic groups, labor, the military, and *kibbutzim*. Jews of different origins, while not organized per se into competing interest groups, are intensely aware of the ethnic origin of their leaders, and survey data clearly demonstrate that aggregate interest articulation is directly related to ethnic origin on many issues. Social and economic classes are becoming more pronounced in Israel, and attitudes are frequently affected by class which is often in turn a function of ethnic origin. It must be noted, however, that virtually all attempts to organize political parties along ethnic lines have failed, suggesting that ethnic affinity will probably not lead to effective interest group formation.

Labor is certainly the largest interest group in Israel today. It consists of a constellation of institutions, but the Histadrut (General Federation of Labor) is its central organ. Most laborers in Israel are Histadrut members, and a high proportion of the country's social services are provided by the organization.

Another key interest group is the military. Yet, the Israeli military draws so broadly from the population as a whole that is constitutes a microcosm of the Israeli people. Thus attitudes within the Israel Defense Forces (IDF) are not identifiable as "military." To the contrary, retired military leaders are active at or near senior positions of leadership of all parties and groups, including peace groups. The IDF is an important socializing institution in Israel, as Lustick has pointed out:

> The Israeli Defense Forces . . . is by far the single largest and most important organization in the Israeli Government. . . . Regular service, three years for men and somewhat less for women, is mandatory for all Jews. From the time of their release from regular service Jewish citizens are required to serve annually in the Reserves for 30–60 days. Thus, for the average Israeli Jew, participation in the military becomes a regular part of his annual schedule. For Israeli society as a whole, Army service has been a dominant factor in the gradual integration of Sephardic and Ashkenazic Jews, in the creation of a strong sense of Jewish Israeli solidarity, and in the transmission of a wide assortment of mechanical and technical skills.[28]

> Simply the possession of veteran status is a prerequisite to a wide variety of jobs and public programs. The personal associations a soldier establishes in the course of his regular service and his reserve duty, as well as his rank and service record, are among the most important elements in the determination of his future career in Israeli society—the officer corps being . . . the primary conduit for administrative and managerial personnel in all branches of Israeli industry, commerce, and Government.[29]

Yet, if we seek uniquely military perspectives, the search will be fruitless. There appears to be something closer to a similar point of view among the career staff of the ministry of defense, but it is limited to the most general issues of national defense. The military, including the ministry of defense, is inclined to put military security ahead of all other questions and to constantly seek new and more advanced weapons and weapons technologies.[30]

A smaller but disproportionately influential group consists of kibbutz members. Although there are clear-cut processes of urbanization and industrialization (the kibbutz is still symbolic of the agricultural theme of early Israel) underway in Israel, kibbutz members continue to be overrepresented in government and especially in the military. Kibbutz members tend to advocate an Arab policy based on the use of force but have traditionally operated through existing parties.[31]

SYRIA

For almost a decade Hafez Assad has ruled Syria with unwonted stability. His tenure is unprecedented in Syria's history as an independent state and is the more remarkable for Syria's diversity and lack of national integration.[32] We and others have pointed out that a sense of Syrian nationalism was growing.[33] But nearing their quindecennial of control by a relatively small, ethnic, minority group, the majority of Syrians—Sunni Muslims—is growing increasingly restive, and primordial or subnational loyalties are taking the place of national allegiance once again. Syrian foreign policy initiatives have traditionally been greatly affected by domestic considerations and will continue to be hostage to these factors. The religious disintegration of Syria is potentially one of the most important developments in the Middle East, even if it has attracted little interest outside Syria.

Syria's central role in the Middle East is assured by virtue of its leadership of the anti-Israel Arab coalition. While not a rejectionist state,[34] Syria will not agree to a settlement without Israeli withdrawal from the Golan Heights and a resolution, acceptable to the PLO, of the Palestinian problem. Because Assad has remained convinced that Israel will not withdraw from the Golan, he has maintained a relatively hard-line stance since late 1975. Syria's regional strength and weakness have been demonstrated in Lebanon, where Damascus became a principal factor, and fought on different sides, in the internal conflict devastating that country; and Baghdad, where the conferees opposed to the Egypt-Israel peace treaty accepted Syria on Assad's own terms and where Iraq has quickly realigned itself with Syria when its internal problems increased (only to change course again in late 1979); in Amman, where Jordan was induced to Baghdad Conference leadership and to unprecedented levels of opposition to U.S. policy at least partially as a result of loyalty to Syria; and in Cairo, where Egyptian media have concentrated their anger on Syria for its role in the coalition opposed to Sadat's policies.

From 1973 to 1976, and to a lesser extent in 1977, Syria was among the most dynamic countries in a dynamic region. During this period, many outside observers believed the Assad government unstable and short lived. They failed to understand the nature of and techniques employed in Assad's grip on Syrian power.[35] As a result, with the new regional financial resources and Syria's claim on them as a front-line Arab/Muslim state, with Syria's apparent stability and Assad's policy of (relative) economic liberalization, with a clear-cut movement to improve relations with the United States and an equally evident end to Syria's regional isolation, capital—and development—came to Syria. The country was moving and the mood upbeat.

Syria's involvement in the Lebanese conflict and Egypt's initiative for a separate peace have now begun to take their toll on Syria and on Syria's role in the Middle East. In Lebanon, the Syrian army has been unable to bring either the Palestinians or the Maronites to heel, and in place of the Syrian-oriented, unified but weak Lebanon Assad had sought to create, there emerged a Lebanon partitioned into (1) a virtual Israeli protectorate in the south, (2) a Maronite Mt. Lebanon-East Beirut, and (3) a rump Lebanese entity controlled only marginally and unevenly by Muslim/leftist forces, the central government, and the Syrian army.[36] The Egyptian peace initiative reduced Syria's leverage vis-à-vis Israel by removing Israel's principal military threat from the Arab coalition. By forcing Syria to the sidelines, Sadat has shown the weakness of Syria alone, and yet joining the rejectionists would be at odds with Assad's foreign policy objectives.[37]

Syrian government is run by a competent bureaucracy, but all major policy decisions and foreign policy are made by Hafez Assad (often in consultation with others, especially his brother, Rifaat). Policy is tightly controlled and monitored by Assad, and his intimate advisors are few. While the Syrian foreign ministry exists, and even makes some decisions, it is without great importance. Syrian foreign policy is Assad's policy based on the interests of Syria, generally, and the 'Alawi minority, in particular.[38]

There are a multitude of interest groups in Syria, but they have played little *direct* role in policy in the post–October War period while Assad has had very effective control of Syria. We have described and analyzed these groups elsewhere,[39] but since their role has diminished we shall discuss here only the three that retain substantial importance for the future course of Syria—one political party, the Ba'th; and two religious groups, the 'Alawis and the Sunnis. Officially, Syria's is a Ba'thist government. For matters of international politics, this Ba'thist identity is of little importance: Assad is the consummate pragmatist, and no ideology will distract him from pursuing the course he believes to be in Syria's best interest. Government policies are legitimized through the Ba'th, are given ideological clothing, and a certain degree—a strictly limited degree—of internal dissent is permitted. The party is an active participant in political socialization, in political mobilization,[40] and in socioeconomic and political development. Socialist polemic and ideals remain, but the senior and emerging leaders are rewarded if and as they follow the guidance of the Assad brothers. Thus the party has been a real but manageable constraint on foreign policy. It has been of no importance in the formulation or initiation of policy.

Certainly the most important consideration in Syrian foreign or domestic policy is 'Alawi confessional identity. The 'Alawis as a group, the reasons for their prominence in contemporary Syria, and the process by which they achieved this role are adequately described elsewhere.[41] Because they constitute but a small (c. 12 percent) part of the Syrian population, and have been traditionally looked down upon and discriminated against by the Sunni majority, the 'Alawis have tenaciously held onto the power they acquired in the late 1960s as the dominant group of the secret military committee that in fact controlled national power in Syria. Hafez Assad carefully installed 'Alawis in key positions throughout the government and armed forces and ensured that these 'Alawis had a direct line of communication to the leadership in order to alert Assad and others of dissension or conspiracy. Rifaat Assad was placed at the head of a special army command unit staffed with loyal personnel (many 'Alawis) and designed to protect the regime against plotters or attempted coups.

The principal aim of Assad's government has been to maintain 'Alawi rule in Syria. To accomplish this objective, Assad determined to bring about real economic progress, liberalize political discourse, and end the isolation into which Syria had fallen under his predecessor's control.[42] All of these interim objectives have been met, but 'Alawi control is less firm today than at any time in the recent past. The control *mechanisms* remain intact and indeed are as thorough and ubiquitous as ever. Yet, a small minority such as the 'Alawis cannot indefinitely dominate a larger majority when the latter feels unified in its resentment of the minority in power. Communication links and determination among the anti-'Alawi Sunnis have increased, and numerous assassinations of 'Alawis and other violent incidents[43] are the symbol of the growing Sunni consciousness, the sense that an end to their powerlessness is at hand. Of course, the 'Alawi leadership is also alert to this evolving phenomenon.

At the visible level both sides are marking time, both are waiting for the next development, and both are convinced there will be further developments. While this process is domestic in nature, the ramifications on foreign policy are extremely important. Assad is by Syrian standards moderate with respect to the Arab-Israeli conflict. He favors a peaceful settlement in accordance with Resolution 242 and therefore accepts Israel's statehood and "right to exist." On the one hand, increasing Sunni unrest will compel a more uncompromising *political* stand, for the 'Alawis have already been accused of "selling out" to Israel. On the other hand, fears about 'Alawi ability to maintain control within Syria will require a provocative but less firm *military* stand. Assad needs the Syrian army in Syria. This fact inevitably affects not only policies toward Israel and Lebanon but, as well, Syria's regional role as a whole. To the extent the Assad brothers and the 'Alawis as a group sense their grip on Syrian society slipping, Syria's regional power must inevitably decline, even if a premium is placed as a result on high visibility *actes de présence,* drama without substance, "sound and fury" calculated to be insufficient to ignite a situation that might get out of hand.[44]

Continuing pressure on the 'Alawis had by the spring of 1980 brought the regime to the edge of collapse. Security controls—which had eased after the overthrow of Salah Jadid by Hafez Assad and especially during the period of Syria's greatest power in the mid-1970s—once again reached a level that justified calling Syria a police state. The *mukhabarat* having failed to apprehend those responsible for the constant assassinations of 'Alawis and their supporters, the Syrian army was called upon to perform police duties. Traditionally, use of the army in a police role is a sign of desperation in the Arab world and a precursor to regime change. Other such signs include Syria's virtual total isolation in the Arab world and recourse to assassination of overseas Syrian opposition leaders. In spite of all these efforts, however, domestic violence continues to increase.

IRAQ

At the crossroads of the Gulf and Levantine Arab subregions, Iraq boasts a history that is at once inseparable from and unique in the course of Arab history. On the one hand, Iraq is buffeted by the winds of the Arab world; on the other, its leadership has perhaps been more intensely inward looking than that of any other Arab state.

It is not that Iraq is so different in governance and the problems of governance from many other third world countries. Here, as elsewhere in the developing world, administrative institutions are new and fragile and have shallow roots in society. Thus their legitimacy and longevity would be questionable in the best of circumstances. Yet, also like many other third world states, sociopolitical circumstances are far from ideal. "Iraqi" consciousness competes—often unsuccessfully—with other claims on individual loyalties, claims of region, religion, tribe, and ethnic group.[45]

In the face of challenges to the legitimacy of the country and its government, Iraqi politics manifests two dichotomies—first, that between rhetoric and reality; second, that between the internal and the external. It is hardly surprising, then, that observers mistake both internal rhetoric for external realities and external rhetoric for internal realities. While we believe postmonarchic Iraq has relied much more heavily upon this tactical schizophrenia than did the Hashemite regime that preceded it, such an approach to Iraqi government is, as Claudia Wright has recently pointed out,[46] a tradition reaching back into antiquity. The approach is a function of the shallowness and irrelevance of government in the face of the competing loyalties and conflicting identities of the Iraqi peoples.

Given the absence of political legitimacy attaching to governments in Iraq, their principal objective has generally been regime survival. It is this objective that has necessitated the dichotomies to which we have already adverted. Justifiably or otherwise, the self-styled "revolutionary" regimes in Baghdad since the overthrow of the monarchy have perceived public support to be associated with the social and economic *bona fides* of the regime. Thus governments in

Baghdad stress ideological directions that suggest Pan-Arabism, socialism, and national unity. That the Middle East has left behind the era of ideology has until very recently seemed to escape the Iraqis. Ba'thist ideology must, however, be seen as a tool of political legitimization rather than as a meaningful set of social symbols. If Ba'thism was begun as a social movement,[47] it has devolved in both Iraq and Syria (though clearly more in the latter[48] than in the former) into a political party in the most parochial sense.

The Iraqi Ba'thist regime is narrowly based in ethnic, regional, ideological, and sectarian terms. Moreover, although the Syrian government is even far more narrowly based on all these dimensions,[49] Iraqi leaders have been unable to secure the tight control over the armed forces that their Syrian 'Alwi counterparts have.[50]

A multiethnic state, Iraq's principal culture groups are Arab (approximately 80 percent) and Kurdish (approximately 15 percent), and it is from and against the Kurds that the major political violence inside Iraq has been sporadically directed for decades. Kurdish secession and autonomy struggles have been supported by force of arms in Iran, Syria, and Turkey, as well as Iraq, because this non-state people has a cohesive sense of national consciousness forged in the course of its many struggles with the governments of the countries in which the Kurds constitute significant minorities.[51] One of the factors greatly increasing the salience of the Kurdish problem is that Iraqi oil fields are primarily in Kurdish areas. Following an agreement in 1970, the Iraqi government began to unilaterally implement provisions of the accord.[52] Moreover, Arabs were resettled in Kurdish areas, Kurds in Arab sectors. The combination of tactics largely defused the theretofore explosive situation.

Notwithstanding the general effectiveness of Baghdad's recent approach to the Kurdish problem, Iran and the United States directly supported a Kurdish insurgency against Iraq in order to weaken and divert the government in power there.[53] When in 1975 Iraqi leaders finally conceded a number of important political and strategic points to the shah—including prominently the redrawing of the Iraqi-Iran border in the Shatt al-'Arab[54]—Iran withdrew its support for the Kurds, and the insurgency promptly collapsed.[55]

The Kurdish issue continues to be a major consideration in Iraqi politics, influencing the nature of administration and generally constraining Iraqi leaders to secure the Kurdish flank before embarking on new initiatives. However, the magnitude of the Kurdish problem is significantly reduced since the 1975 agreement, the spirit of which both parties seriously tried to honor. Certainly, the Kurds will continue to remain aloof from many of the foreign policy issues facing Iraq and will retain their discrete identity. At the same time, to the extent they are allowed to participate in decisions affecting them and to maintain a certain degree of autonomy, the Kurds will probably not actively work to undermine Iraqi political development or foreign policy initiatives.

From a regionalist point of view as well, Iraqi national integration is still an objective rather than a reality. The country's boundaries are, like those of most third world states, largely arbitrary: they bring together in one polity three distinct historical territories—the lower river plains (Tigris and Euphrates rivers) around the Gulf; the upper river valley (Tigris and Euphrates) area; and the western steppes.[56] The first of these is dominated by the tradition of the marsh Arabs and is oriented in history, values, and perspectives toward the Gulf, while the second is indistinct from Syria in tradition, orientation, and heritage.[57] The western region is culturally akin to the Arabian Peninsula, and indeed is inhabited by tribes that stretch from Jordan through Saudi Arabia to some of the smaller Gulf sheikhdoms.[58]

It may be argued that regional loyalties have never played as prominent or divisive a role in Iraq as they have in, for example, Lebanon,[59] Syria,[60] or even Saudi Arabia.[61] While this observation is accurate for modern Iraq, regional differences do affect the Iraqi leadership in terms of elite recruitment, individual loyalties and alliances, and issue area salience (competing preference schedules relative to issues).

The leadership is drawn to a disproportionate extent from the region of Tikrit, a small village on the Tigris. While this regional limitation reduces the *national* legitimacy of the key group in Iraqi politics, it has at times facilitated communications and trust within this group.

In ideological terms, too, the current government faces problems. Although Ba'thism is built on symbols meaningful to most Arabs—"Arabism" and (secularist) Islam[62]—it integrates them into a doctrine at once alien and anachronistic. True, Ba'this ideology is Arab—it is not alien in that sense. Still, the values, dogma, and socialist content are in many respects foreign to the experience and tradition of most Arabs. (Note the limited and particularist appeal of Ba'thism in Lebanon, Syria, and Iraq.) Also, at a time when the Arab world has largely left ideology behind, Ba'thism and the rhetorical excesses to which its adherents are given seem singularly antiquated.

In yet another respect is the Iraqi leadership minoritarian. While the precise proportions of membership in religious sects are unknown,[63] we have pointed out that the Sunnis who govern and have traditionally led Iraq are a minority in that country. Sectarian divisions have always had serious implications in Iraq, but rarely have these differences constituted a real, immediate threat to incumbent security. Challenges to the leadership have generally been based upon other grounds.

A new upsurge in Shi'a consciousness following the recent revolution in Iran has swept the Islamic world.[64] In Lebanon, the Gulf, and even east Asia, Shi'as have raised the banner of protest with greater fervor and cohesion than at any time in the recent past. One of the first countries to recognize and feel the results of this renascence was Iraq, where Shi'as have traditionally been left outside the corridors of power.[65] In government crackdowns before and after the attempted coup of July 1979, Saddam's security forces singled out and punished Shi'as.[66] Moreover, the coup itself seems to have been based at least partially upon sectarian unrest.[67]

As Iranian-Iraqi relations continued to deteriorate after Ayatollah Khomeini's accession to power in Iran, Tehran made a conscious effort to play upon the political and social conditions of Iraq's Shi'a majority.[68] However, the destabilization potential of this issue is far greater, and thus the issue is far more sensitive, than the Kurdish problem, which was after all limited to autonomy and secession threats—not challenges to the legitimacy of the government of all of Iraq. Indeed, it is an issue so sensitive that even the shah largely refrained from exploiting it. While it is true that the territorial differences and some problems in the implementation of the 1975 border treaty between the two countries both contributed to the Iraqi invasion of Iran in 1980, the provocation implicit in appeals to Iraqi Shi'as must be considered a basic *casus belli,* too.

SAUDI ARABIA

Saudi Arabia is entering a period of social and economic dynamism. Many observers are—correctly—quick to point to differences between Iran under the shah and the present Saudi Arabia. While not denying the distinctions between these very different countries, we simply wish to note that many of the social challenges Iran has recently confronted will also face Saudi Arabia, though in different degrees and contexts. The profound Saudi desire to preserve much of the ethos of the old order is far deeper than in most societies and may accentuate the clash of old and new.

In the 1970s, Saudi Arabia has become one of the key regional actors in the Middle East, wielding its substantial financial power as a weapon or lever. Content with low visibility before this decade, Saudi leaders have found what others before discovered—greater power means more interests, more decisions, and more responsibilities. Yet, inevitably, broader definitions of interest mean a larger number of vulnerabilities. And thus Saudi Arabia is a factor in the domestic and foreign affairs of Egypt, Iran, Jordan, Kuwait, Lebanon, Oman, Qatar, Syria, Sudan, Turkey, and the United Arab Emirates. It is the key member in the Organization of Petroleum Exporting Countries (OPEC) and the Organization of Arab Petroleum Exporting Countries (OAPEC). In regional issues such as Palestinian autonomy, the status of Jerusalem, and resolution of the Lebanese conflict, and even in matters of global concern such as restructuring the international financial system and identifying strategies for dealing with international terrorism—in all these areas Saudi views are considered important; in some, critical.

It is hardly surprising that the institutions of Saudi foreign policy formation have not kept pace with the country's new and greater role. Even though the king is the ultimate decision-maker in foreign policy, his power is far from absolute, since the king's position depends upon the acquiescence of the royal family, a large and complicated group that must be viewed as a discrete institution.[69] Indeed, the royal family did depose King Saud, the late King Faisal's predecessor, when his personal habits and judgment were deemed unsuitable for the country's needs.

Notwithstanding the power of the royal family—which in fact must be considered a *constraint* upon decision-making rather than an alternative center of power—the king's authority is paramount if he seeks to use it. (Another constraint, far less powerful in the short term, is that of the *ulema* [religious leaders]). King Faisal had such prestige and authority that his views were virtually unquestioned. His successor, by contrast, does not carry the same degree of respect and deference. Thus views and policies are debated now among some of the senior princes, and many decisions seem to be contradictory. Frequently, they are: an issue presented in two or three contexts or in terms of specific problems has resulted in contradictory decisions where different coalitions have formed to address these different problems.[70]

The domestic considerations in Saudi foreign policy have not been significant. The Saudi leadership did not perceive significant internal dissension or unrest before 1979 and even now sees such unrest as an unlikely major problem. The reasons for this confidence are several. While there are rivalries within the royal family they are just that, *within* the family. That the Saudis are somewhat concerned about the number of foreigners entering their country is clear[71]—but there appear few alternatives to the importation of skilled and semi-skilled labor in a country with so small a manpower base, if Saudi Arabia is to move toward development. Saudis feel that the situation in Iran bears little resemblance to their own country, so far as social unity is concerned. There are tribal differences, to be sure, but none of these is particularly salient. The large number of Shi'as in the eastern province[72] practice dissimulation and are certainly not going to engage in any conspiracy to achieve greater representation for their minoritarian views. Despite the substantial total of Palestinians working in Saudi Arabia, they are not believed to constitute a significant constraint upon foreign policy decisions. The Saudis and the Palestinians need each other: the latter are a valuable source of needed labor, the former a major source of funds for the Palestinian cause. Neither group wishes to alienate the other, but Saudi leaders have usually acted more out of personal or group conviction than out of fear.

In late 1979 during regional turmoil that began when the American embassy in Tehran was seized and its occupants held hostage, a group of dissident Saudis and some foreigners seized the

Grand Mosque in Mecca. Although this act was portrayed by the Saudi government as the insane behavior of a small but well-armed group of religious fanatics, there is substantial evidence that is was part of a much larger conspiracy that stretched well beyond Mecca.[73] Saudi leaders will certainly give greater attention to the domestic front as a result of the Mosque episode. Whether they will be able to adequately address the major changes that are taking place in the perspectives of Arabian Peninsula tribes and their relationship to the royal regimes remains to be seen.

JORDAN

The Hashemite Kingdom of Jordan has played a role in the Middle East out of all proportion to its size and resources but very much proportionate to the political skill and personal courage of King Hussein bin Talal. More than even Egypt or Syria, Jordan's foreign policy is the foreign policy of one man—the king. Foreign ministers are selected for various domestic or external reasons, but always their mission is to implement the foreign policy guidelines of King Hussein, and the king's virtually exclusive role in this regard is widely recognized and generally accepted within Jordan.

In assessing Jordan's options, King Hussein has never limited his view to domestic or foreign requirements. That Jordan's foreign policy has in general been more responsive to external than to internal developments should not be construed to mean the king faces only minor domestic constraints. Quite to the contrary, the monarch and Jordanians as a group represent a national minority, the majority of the East Bank's population being Palestinian. The presence of so many Palestinians within Jordan by itself constitutes a constraint, for this group is politically aware and highly sensitive to political change. However, Palestinian political activity does not equal political consciousness: the middle class Palestinians are interested primarily in commerce, and the lower class Palestinians eschew open political activity because they want to remain in Jordan (though they retain strong Palestinian nationalist consciousness).

Jordan's king has been uniquely able, then, to construct and revise foreign policies based upon the external issues and Jordan's national rather than subnational interests.

OTHER STATES

In addition to the countries discussed above, Libya, Algeria, and Kuwait also bear mention within a discussion of Middle East alignments after Camp David. Although these states are not actors of the scope of Syria, Iraq, Jordan, or Saudi Arabia, their policies have affected the Middle East's political conditions more than many realize.

Libya

Libya is perhaps the most boisterous of these three countries in its policy pronouncements due to the personalities of its leader, Colonel Muammar Qaddafi, and his chief aide, Staff Major Abdul Salaam Jalloud.

Colonel Qaddafi's outspokenness and freedom of action are the result of his having had until recently little internal opposition. Libya had for a long time been considered the world's poorest nation, especially in the 1950s. With its extremely low level of literacy, almost static economic development, and sparse population, Libya experienced virtually no political development until the last decade. As a result, interest groups, whether they be based on ethnic, tribal, economic, or ideological grounds, never really developed in Libya during the first seventy years of this century.

On the other hand, about the same time Colonel Qaddafi assumed power[74] in 1969, Libya began to develop its oil export capabilities and has now vastly increased its economic wealth and prosperity, radically altering the nature of Libyan society and creating two potentially troublesome interest groups besides the army: the middle class and the intellectuals. Many individuals in both of these groups increasingly question the quality of Qaddafi's leadership and its directions.

The educated class,[75] for example, is shocked by Libya's involvement in Uganda[76] and frustrated by Qaddafi's effort to keep them out of the government and his "heavy handed efforts to keep them on the sidelines"[77] in general. Libyan managers and entrepreneurs, moreover, have been severely disturbed by Qaddafi's efforts to give the people more power,[78] which among other things is beginning to eliminate managers and middle men. Furthermore, those who still own their businesses expect to lose them at any moment.

On top of the dissension building up within the civilian sector, army leaders have also become disgruntled with Qaddafi, specifically over the Uganda issue.[79] While the civilian population itself may not be able to engineer a coup, military coups d'etat cannot be ruled out in the Middle East.

Notwithstanding the growing domestic opposition to his regime, Qaddafi's foreign policy moves, with the exception of military operations such as in Uganda and Chad, are generally not limited by domestic constraints. As will be discussed in Chapter 2, Libya's policies are far more affected by external than by internal forces.

Algeria

Despite the sophistication of Algeria's political elite,[80] domestic limitations have not played a major role in Algerian foreign policy-making. The military remains far and away the most highly organized group in the country.[81] In fact, it was largely due to Algerian President Benjedid Chadli's relationship with army leaders that he was elected president.

The current leadership in Algeria directly beneath Chadli consists largely of the military and civilian elites who were close to former president Houari Boumedienne. This elite group, along with the president, has a very free reign in their foreign policy choices and appear to be following Boumedienne's policies vis-à-vis the third world and the Arab-Israeli conflict. However, due to widespread domestic discontent over food and other shortages, which many Algerians view as the result of Algeria's involvement in the conflict over the Spanish Sahara,[82] the current leadership is engaged in an effort to bolster the agrarian sector in the economy and is seeking a way to peacefully settle the Saharan dispute.[83] At the same time, Chadli has introduced measures to ease the intensity of his rule.[84]

At present, it appears that Algeria's domestic situation will not pose important constraints on Algerian foreign policy-making, but the country may well concentrate on domestic and Maghreb issues until the position of the new leadership is solidified.

Kuwait

The major internal pressures on Kuwait's foreign policy-making result from the fact that Kuwaitis are a minority in their own country. Approximately 47 percent of Kuwait's one million people are natives. The other 53 percent are Palestinians, Iranians, Egyptians, Yemenis, Omanis, Pakistanis, Indians, Syrians, and Lebanese. The largest alien population in Kuwait is Palestinian. Approximately 250,000 Palestinians currently live in Kuwait.

The Sabah dynasty, which has ruled the Kuwaiti region since 1756, has traditionally exercised a large amount of authority unhindered by domestic interest groups.[85] However, the preponderance of aliens within the country, especially Palestinians and Iranians, has affected the public face of Kuwaiti policies.

The large Palestinian population is the key domestic factor behind Kuwait's relations with the Arab world. Partially in order to placate its Palestinian population, Kuwait has publicly and financially supported the Palestinian cause and remained publicly faithful to the Baghdad Conference resolutions. Kuwait's significant Iranian population has been a source of concern for Kuwaiti leaders since the Iranian revolution. However, this concern has been translated into discussions concerning domestic rather than foreign policy.

THE PALESTINE LIBERATION ORGANIZATION (PLO)

PLO "foreign policy" operates under considerable constraints both internal and external to the organization. In this section we shall briefly discuss internal pressures only, meaning by "internal" inter-Palestinian as well as intra-PLO.

The principal handicap of the PLO has always been the diversity of its constituent organizations and their members. This diversity has resulted in a rigidity of the institutions and organic documents of the PLO not unlike the rigidity of the Lebanese political system. PLO leaders, such as Yasser Arafat, and the larger and more powerful PLO groups, such as Fatah and Saiqa, have shied from imposing too much of their own will upon the PLO in order to maintain the affiliation of the other groups, thus preserving the legitimacy of the PLO as the representative of *all* Palestinians.[86]

Differences between the major Palestinian groups are both strategic and tactical. On the strategic level, they disagree about objectives; on the tactical, about means to achieve even those objectives they share. The effects of this pluralism are often embarrassing to the PLO, but the meaning is that the organization is little more than the institutional symbol of Palestinian nationalism. "Organization" is a misnomer: the PLO is able to make few important decisions.

The largest and most important of the PLO groups,[87] Fatah and Saiqa, are certainly the key decision forces. Fatah is a relatively moderate, well-staffed, independent, and nonideological organization. Saiqa is the Syrian-sponsored group, also quite large, and closely related to both the Syrian government and the (Syrian) Ba'th Party. Both Fatah and Saiqa are pragmatic at the top leadership levels, though the latter is much more tightly controlled and more nearly monolithic (largely because it is responsive to Syrian policy needs). Fatah and Saiqa have worked cooperatively most of the time—except when Syrian leaders were at odds with Fatah (as in 1976, when Syrian forces and Saiqa took on the Palestinians and Lebanese Muslim/leftist forces during Syria's intervention).[88]

Because of the diversity of Palestinian views on the one hand and, on the other, the importance placed by PLO leadership on maintaining Palestinian unity under the PLO, policy initiatives by the organization are generally limited to unofficial statements or to announcements by secondary PLO officials, posing a serious credibility problem. The senior leadership appears to be willing to support a new approach only if its success is assured so that the costs the organization bears will have been worthwhile. Since the component groups of the PLO are or have been unable to agree on a realistic set of objectives or options relating to the political future of the Palestinian people, the PLO finds its consensus limited to responses to others' initiatives and, in effect, limited to negative responses. Thus while the PLO can undertake humanitarian and other constructive initiatives in nonpolitical domains, the only actions and policies possible in the political realm are "negative"—rejection, sometimes employing violence (terrorism, sabotage, and the like).[89] This symbolic role is crucial, for it is the focal point of their diverse political aspirations.

Though Palestinian attitudes concerning individuals, policies, and objectives differ, the sense of national identity is strong—stronger than that of most Arab countries, and incomparably stronger than in 1948.[90]

2

Bilateral, Multilateral, and Regional Pressures

D ISINTEGRATIVE FORCES resulting from social change in countries of ethnic diversity[1] have rendered domestic considerations paramount for states such as Iran and Syria. In other countries, particularly those where the peoples are more homogeneous, social change has not proved so potent a force of disunity. In these nations—e.g., Egypt, Jordan, and Saudi Arabia—foreign policy is more clearly a function of the leadership's perception of external issues and variables, although domestic considerations are of some importance throughout the Middle East. In this chapter we identify and assess the most significant external pressures on the defense and foreign policies of each of the states covered in the previous chapter.

EGYPT

Egypt's international orientation has undergone significant changes since the Nasser period, and while the country's fundamental vulnerabilities, strengths, and interests may not have changed, they have certainly been interpreted differently by Sadat. Egypt's concurrent roles in the African, Middle Eastern, and third world contexts were emphasized by Nasser,[2] but Nasser played the leadership role, while Egypt itself was viewed as an integral part of the three areas. In reality, Egypt had an advantage relatively rare in the third world— invulnerability to its neighbors. The only contiguous country militarily stronger than Egypt was Israel, a neighbor separated from the Nile Valley by the Sinai and the Suez. The two countries had few national conflicts with respect to their own national interests or territory. All Egypt's other neighbors are and have been far weaker than Egypt itself. Thus Egypt's defeats (other than against Israel) have

27

come in conflicts away from the heartland of Egypt when Nasser or Sadat tried to project power.[3] No Arab country can expect to "conquer" Egypt.

Egypt is part of the Arab world by will. It is set off from other Arab countries to the west and east by desert, and while the Egyptian people are an Arab-Nubian mixture, their Arab consciousness has not always been high. This isolation from the rest of the Arab world ramifies on far more than the military realm: the Egyptian public has a sense of national identity and can afford to disregard other Arab peoples. Subversion (other than assassination and sabotage) cannot easily be systematically undertaken within Egypt by other Arab leaders nor a false "popular rebellion" mounted. Egypt's size, isolation, and diversity permit more real and psychological independence from the Arab world than that felt by any other Arab state.

The most important external constraint on Egypt lies to the south. The Nile River is popularly perceived by Egyptians as a vital national resource. True, this concept is rooted in culture—history and tradition that may no longer apply to politico-military realities. Nevertheless, the fact that the Nile—and therefore the Sudan—is believed to be important by the Egyptian populace *makes* the politics of the Nile important to an Egyptian leader seeking popular support.[4] The critical bilateral relationship for Egypt's leaders, then, is with the Sudan. Iraq and Syria are felt to be part of the Arab world, but distant and inscrutable to most Egyptians.

The second most important regional Arab country to Egypt in recent years has been Saudi Arabia which provided significant amounts of economic assistance.[5] This relationship is fundamentally different from the links between Egypt and the Sudan. Historically the latter countries have retained a close, sometimes integral, association, while the Arabian Peninsula has never had greater meaning or attraction for Egypt than for other Arab peoples or countries. It is Egypt's crippling population problem,[6] and the related poverty of the country, that made Saudi Arabia and other Gulf donors important sources of budgetary support. Although Sadat—who was the target of major food riots in 1975—did not underestimate the importance of the revenue provided by Saudi Arabia, he also recognized that by themselves the Saudis and and other Gulf Arabs neither could nor would provide the answer to Egypt's basic problem. He believed and continues to believe that Egypt must develop by importing technology through commercial arrangements with the industrial West. No Arab country is in a position to supply such technology, although Saudi financial support *was* used to begin the definitive move toward a serious commercial relationship with the United States.[7] And Sadat was careful to ensure that in the event of a break with the Saudis Egypt would be in a position fully supported by Washington. Such a strategy both complicated Saudi decisions, giving the strongest disincentives to a policy of cutting off Egypt's financial infusion, and enhanced Sadat's image in American public opinion and government policy-making.

Other Arab states are much less salient to Egypt. Libya is geographically large but demographically small. The Libyan "threat" is a convenience for Sadat, nothing more. Muammar Qaddafi is not seen as dangerous by Egyptian elites except in subsidizing assassination or sabotage attempts. Although Sadat may point with alarm to the substantial Libyan inventory of modern Soviet weapons, no informed Egyptian official, certainly including the president, views Libya as anything more than a nuisance. Indeed Egypt, which could certainly use Libya's oil revenue on an immediate basis, is far more of a threat to Libya than the converse. Neither Qaddafi nor Libya as a whole represents a significant influence on Egyptian policy-making strategy.

Toward the eastern Arab world, Egypt's traditional rivalry with Iraq for influence over Syria is in abeyance at present. Since the late 1960s competition over influence in Damascus has proven futile, as Syrian policy has responded largely to domestic rather than external needs, and Syrian relationships have been largely tactical and limited in nature.[8]

Sadat's personal antipathy toward King Hussein—reciprocated by the Hashemite monarch—has adversely affected relations with Jordan, but Jordan's only real importance for Egypt derives from its potential role regarding the West Bank. To the extent Jordan follows a divergent policy on West Bank issues the personal relationship of Sadat and Hussein can only aggravate a basically conflictive situation.

Iraq is increasingly a central factor in the Persian Gulf and a factor in the eastern Mediterranean equation, but a marginal factor in Egypt. Hobbled by internal problems of importance and by major external conflicts of potentially explosive magnitude on all its borders, and saddled with a regime distrusted by most of its Arab neighbors, Iraq has been unable to exert its power in such a way as to affect Egyptian interests. Baghdad is far from Cairo, and Iraq's interests are far removed from those of Egypt. Iraq's role in the anti-Sadat coalition has been less important than that of erstwhile Egyptian allies such as Syria, Jordan, and Saudi Arabia. Thus although Iraq's political power has undeniably grown, especially in the last few years, Baghdad has not been and will not be able to use this power effectively against Egyptian interests.

By contrast, Israel is more central to Sadat's objectives and policies for the present. If for whatever reason Israel is induced to permit real autonomy on the West Bank and to return all of the Egyptian territory now occupied, and if Israeli leaders indicate a real willingness to negotiate resolutions to the Golan and Palestinian issues, Sadat and Egypt will be welcomed back to the Arab world. If, on the other hand, Israel forces through an unadulterated version of its own concept of autonomy and demonstrates its lack of interest in meaningful negotiations over the Palestinian and Occupied Territories issues, it will be more difficult for the Arab world to accept Egypt's separate peace. In their attitudes toward Sadat, Israeli leaders can also affect (though not control) U.S. policy toward Egypt which is critical to the realization of Sadat's objectives.

Since he came to power following Gamal Abdel Nasser's death in 1970, Sadat has moved Egypt closer and closer to the United States and further and further from its once intimate relationship with the Soviet Union. This process is today seen as a fact but unfolded as a series of major and minor acts over a period of years. Today it may be said without exaggeration that the United States is Egypt's most important ally. Sadat has in effect staked his political future on U.S. support and dependability. At this stage it would not be possible for a Sadat-led Egypt to secure renewed Soviet support at adequate levels: Moscow will certainly not trust Sadat again. If, therefore, it begins to appear as if Egyptian policy has failed—i.e. the United States does not provide and encourage sufficient financial assistance, does not undertake the level of commercial and technological transfer that Egypt expects, and does not assist in providing Cairo military capabilities adequate to meet defensive requirements as seen in Egypt— Sadat is not in a position to alter his course quickly. Rather, he will be forced to undertake another gradual shift or to resign in order to permit Egypt to move more flexibly among the great powers and the Arab world. Anwar Sadat is capable of either of these approaches.

Sadat's understanding of the relative independence Egypt enjoys vis-à-vis the Arab world and of Egypt's central role in Arab identity has underwritten his policies. However, Sadat is a realist; he knows well that Egyptian isolation from the rest of the Arab world cannot last indefinitely. The Arab world needs Egypt in the short run; but in the long run Egyptians must sense themselves a part of the Arab world, too. It is in this context that one must place Egypt's quiet support of Iraq (behind a public criticism of both parties) during the 1980 Iran-Iraq war. Anwar Sadat is facilitating the bridge-building between Egypt and the rest of the Arab world.

IRAN

For Iran under the shah, key rivals were clearly defined. The shah's rivals were almost "selected," for he sought major, identifiable threats in order to justify procurement of numerous advanced weapons systems from the United States. When these threats seemed no longer credible, the shah pointed to the Soviet "threat," even though his relations with the USSR after the early 1960s were relatively stable. Yet, Iraq—the most commonly cited threat—never was a real threat to Iran, as the shah well knew. In spite of numerous provocations in the Shatt al-Arab, in Iraq itself, and within Iran,[9] Iraqi leaders, recognizing the limitations of their highly politicized, inadequately trained, poorly led, and inexperienced army[10] as well as the vulnerabilities of Iraq itself, never responded to Iran's bellicosity with more than verbal ripostes and sporadic gunfire.[11]

Iran exists as a socially isolated nation in the Middle East. Considering themselves superior to Arabs, Persians have neither the strong cultural links Arabs feel on a transnational basis nor the kind of historical bonds experienced by Turks and Arabs. The arrogance, aggressiveness, and "non-Arabness" of the shah and his foreign policy alienated most Arab states and threatened (i.e. were perceived as a threat by) Iraq, Saudi Arabia, and the smaller Gulf countries. While the Arabian monarchies took comfort in Iran's ideologically "conservative" international orientation and close ties to the United States, they were distrustful of the Persians, uneasy at the ambitions they imputed to the shah, and concerned about Iran's weapons acquisitions.[12]

U.S. policy following the departure of the British Navy from the Gulf envisaged the development of both Iran and Saudi Arabia as the heirs apparent to Britain's policeman role,[13] a policy and perspective Iraqi leaders did not share, given their significant ideological and social differences with the two monarchies and their poor relations with both.[14] Nor did the shah believe Iran should share the mantle of Gulf leadership with Saudi Arabia: he saw Iran as the preeminent power of the subregion and, eventually, as a global great power.[15]

The deposition of the shah was accompanied by the general collapse of Iran's armed forces.[16] No longer is Iran in any position to assert a credible claim to Gulf leadership, much less to exclusive leadership. While the Islamic government under Ayatollah Ruhollah Khomeini clearly expects to enjoy better relations with many Arab states, it was Iran's economic and military power that led to its political puissance.[17] Absent the economic and military sources of power, which Khomeini appears unlikely to mobilize, Iran will not enjoy much influence in the Middle East. The early days of the Islamic Repbulic saw Iran using its religious credentials—Iranian mullahs, including Khomeini's son, travelled to Arab countries with Shi'a populations—the Gulf states, Iraq, and Lebanon, for example. And Shi'a consciousness clearly *was* awakened by Iran's revolution and its subsequent proselytization—but at the *expense,* not to the benefit, of Iran's relations with other Middle East governments. The relative social, economic, and political position of the Shi'as outside Iran is a poor foundation for the exercise of Iranian leadership.

A little known but interesting exception to Iran's poor relations with the Arab world after the overthrow of the shah has been Syria, whose 'Alwi leadership, as Shi'a Muslims, developed a quietly cooperative relationship with the Islamic republic. While religion was the justification and the vehicle, it was their common enemy, Iraq, that gave the link vitality.[18]

Pakistan—ironically, a devoutly Sunni country—has been Iran's closest regional ally in recent years. Despite some shared interests, Pakistan can expect to receive little additional assistance from Iran, and will, therefore, become peripheral. By contrast, the Palestinians may continue to work closely with Khomeini and receive Iran's international support. Again, however, a sick and dis-united Iran can have little significant influence over the success or failure of Palestinian objectives.[19]

The Iran of Khomeini will not last. It is too early to foresee a successor regime, since coalitions remain fluid at this time (see Chapter 1). It is possible that Iran will be much more actively involved in and more closely identified with developments in the Arab world in the future; but it is extremely unlikely that any government in Tehran will be able to significantly *affect* the nature of those developments in the next five years when Iran is condemned to impotence. The hurdles to reorganization and reconstruction are already formidable and will probably grow with time as competing dissident groups organize, mobilize, and sink roots. Sucessor governments must confront above all the central issues of reunification, integration, and reconstruction inside Iran. Questions of manpower—already straitened by dint of the speed of earlier development and the brain drain—must be dealt with in legal, ethical, social, and political, as well as economic contexts. Too, the psychological factors that have driven highly trained Iranians to emigrate in large numbers to the West for over a quarter century have been amplified; it will take years to halt and then adequately reverse this flow.

ISRAEL

Israeli foreign policy and international relations have been dominated since independence by several objectives and characteristics that continue in their primacy. Since 1948 Israel has existed in a sea of hostility. Every one of the new state's borders was hostile, and the establishment of the Jewish State long remained unrecognized—even implicitly—by a single Arab government. Yet, Israel faced not only hostile neutrality at the hands of its neighbors but, as well, the verbal threat of physical extinction. Israeli nationalism, highly imbued with the lessons of Jewish history, rejected the concept of *dependence* on any foreign power, even while, cognizant of the forces aligned against Israel, it embraced *succor from* any source. The objectives were and remain basic: to establish Israel's security such that the idea of destroying Israel is inconceivable and the possibility unattainable; to establish a legitimate and accepted role in the region for Israel as a Middle East power in the economic, political, and social domains.

These objectives are more basic than those of most countries, even newly independent countries, which usually take them for granted, but the nature of Israel's creation has made of these goals very real problems and indeed has resulted in a conflict between the two of them. So deep has been the hostility against Israel[20] that the country's populace and leaders seek security far beyond that enjoyed by most states and peoples.[21] Moreover, their means of attaining this security renders the normalization of Israeli relations with the Arab world elusive.

Arabs have seen Israel as a Western creation, a quasi colony carved out of the Arab world to expiate Western guilt over treatment of the Jews.[22] The precarious nature of Israel's economy even with the large-scale infusion of funds it has received and the dependence on the West for the advanced technology Israel has used to develop and to establish military superiority—these Arab perceptions reinforce the conclusion that Israel is alien to the Middle East. Yet, Israelis fervently reject dependence on any country in principle and are clearly discomfitted at the degree to which they have had to look to the United States for assistance since 1970. That Israel has been able to depend on the United States to the extent it has is partially a function of the important political role of the American Jewish community, but even the strength of this community and the general sympathy Israel has enjoyed among the American populace[23] do not guarantee continued U.S. support at previous levels, as Israel's leaders recognize. The key to the continuity of the Arab-Israeli conflict has been the Palestinian issue, but the operational factor that gave that issue meaning was the solidarity of the Arab coalition against Israel. On numerous occasions Israeli leaders tried to break up this coalition by dividing it or by taking one of the principal confrontation states out of the coalition. Not until 1975[24] did they achieve even a partial victory in removing a confrontation state. The Camp David agreements and later accords have resulted in an interim separate peace with Egypt.[25] No Arab coalition lacking Egypt poses a credible conventional threat of unacceptable loss to Israel. The severing of Egypt's military tie to the Arab coalition against Israel is the greatest short-term political victory Israel has ever won. If Egyptian-Israeli relations can be normalized and Egypt kept outside the Arab coalition, Israel may be able to avoid compromises on the Golan and West Bank, which could prove destabilizing over the long term. Israeli elites understand that this is the American perception, and therefore expect to encounter substantial U.S. pressure to make compromises on the West Bank autonomy issue.

The removal of Egypt from the Arab coalition is critical because no Arab alliance without Egypt poses a credible conventional threat to Israel. It can be argued that nuclearization of the conflict could alter this reality over the long term. Countries like Iraq, which is on the verge of nuclear power for civilian purposes, may be induced for a variety of reasons to develop a nuclear military capability. Such a capability is not yet developed, however, and the Iraqis are unlikely to be able to effectively deliver nuclear warheads or explosives to Israel for some time into the future, well after they have a nuclear weapons inventory. (The platforms exist, but Israeli policy and resources can and will neutralize Iraqi nuclear capable aircraft.) Moreover, the Arab-Israeli conflict has been a convenience for Iraq to date. We do not believe Baghdad will want to assume the mantle of *real* military leadership against Israel. Thus nuclearization will probably *not* alter the strategic essentials of the conflict,[26] especially since Israel already possesses nuclear weapons and the ability to deliver them.[27]

Israel's leaders have watched the Jordanian alliance with Syria and have participated in the dissolution of Lebanon, aware that Jordan and Lebanon long appeared the most likely Arab states to normalize their relations with Israel. (And indeed a *modus vivendi* was established with each.) There remains the hope that these two weak Arab countries will eventually follow Egypt in reaching a peace with the Jewish State, but meanwhile they continue to treat Israel as an outsider at the official level.

In order to further promote Israeli security, Israel's leaders have viewed the establishment of a Palestinian state in Jordan or the West Bank as unacceptable. The West Bank is believed to be too close with inadequate natural barriers to protect Israel proper. Jordan was under the dominion of what was long the most tractable Arab government from the Israeli perspective. Thus, Israel was prepared to intervene in 1970 to protect Hussein's throne against the Palestinians. Since 1973 the resolution of the Palestinian question has been accepted by most governments as the *sine qua non* of regional settlement.[28] Consequently, many Israelis have had second thoughts about the Hashemite regime in Jordan,[29] coming to the conclusion that a Palestinian state established there would permit Israel to retain the West Bank while providing an adequate resolution to the Palestinian issue for the purposes and intents of the United States, a number of Arab governments, and, depending upon the process through which the change evolves, for several (perhaps most) major Palestinian groups as well. The reluctance of King Hussein to support the Camp David accords and the vigor with which he associated Jordan with the Baghdad countries vowing opposition to Camp David have only served to fuel the change in Israeli attitudes toward Jordan.

Only in 1979 with the Likud in power did a substantial segment of Israeli public opinion seem to shift toward greater accommodation in the West Bank. To a degree such a shift probably entailed Sephardic (Oriental Jewish) frustration at the sums the Begin government, for whose election the long downtrodden Sephardim were largely responsible, being spent for new settlements in the West Bank. Another important factor, however, was the shift of a number of Alignment leaders at the end of the decade to views much closer to those of moderate Arab elites. Opposition positions and the opinion trends suggest a growing realization that a nonsovereign Palestinian polity linked to Jordan may be the most appropriate and safest resolution to this long-simmering issue.[30]

Currently, Israel's northern border is protected through the occupation of the Syrian Golan Heights on the east and the emergence of a Christian-dominated autonomous zone (claiming independence) under Israeli protection in southern Lebanon. The eastern front is secured by the added strategic depth resulting from the continued occupation of the West Bank (Judea and Samaria). Security in the south is enhanced by the occupation of the Gaza Strip and most of the Sinai Peninsula as well as nonbelligerency provisions of agreements with Egypt.

As we have indicated, the dilemma facing Israel is the short-term security conferred by territorial occupation against the longer-term security that might result from a general peace. This dilemma suggests that Syria, in particular, will not acquiesce in the perpetual occupation of the Golan. Yet, another approach must be found to confront Israel on this issue, since a coalition sans Egypt will not likely attack.

SYRIA

The foreign relations of Syria continue to be dominated externally by the exigencies of the conflict with Israel, occupier of the Golan Heights, but are more increasingly reflective of the domestic confessional problems addressed in the previous chapter. Hafez Assad has long been convinced that Israel will never willingly return the Golan Heights to Syrian control even if conditions to maintain Israeli security are established,[31] that the only possible approach to secure the return of the Golan lies in posing a constant and credible strategic threat to Israel as a lever for bargaining purposes.[32] This approach suffered an initial setback in the Sinai II accords and a capital loss at Camp David. With Egypt, the Arab coalition is a credible threat—not to defeat Israel, but to inflict heavy casualties. Without Egypt, no Arab coalition is a credible threat.[33]

To compensate for the loss of Egypt, Syria must enlist the support of other Arab regimes—Iraq, principally, Jordan, Libya, Saudi Arabia, and so forth. Thus to the extent Israel is the principal external factor, Syria's leaders must try to put together a coalition of desperation, submerging existing conflicts with the countries that may assist this coalition directly or indirectly. At the same time, Syrian leaders recognize they cannot afford to present Israel with any actions or situations Israeli leaders might see as an immediate threat—or might choose to use as a pretext. Syrian behavior in Lebanon[34] suggests that the Assad government believes Israel will respond on the basis of specific Arab-Israeli interactions rather than on the basis of other (e.g., third-country) considerations. Such a belief, if inaccurate, may lead to a series of actions threatening peace.[35]

Syria entered the internal conflict in Lebanon for a variety of reasons treated at length elsewhere.[36] Briefly, Assad sought to control the Lebanon front, including the Palestinians, in order to enhance Syrian bargaining power vis-à-vis Israel; to establish stability and control in a neighboring country with uniquely deep, historical ties to Syria; and to prevent sectarian partition which might have extremely adverse ramifications in religiously divided Syria.[37] Underestimating the strength and capabilities of both sides, Syrian forces were never able to achieve their strategic military objectives.[38] The war has tied down the Syrian army, sapped its morale, and eroded its discipline.[39] In the process Syrian forces have made enemies on all sides. The army and society have been divided by the conflict and by Assad's policies related to it.[40]

Between 1973 and 1976, Syria became the most important Arab country in the Levant and arguably the most critical Arab state of all. Yet, even as Lebanon provided an arena for Syria to flex its muscles, it also provided a stage on which Syrian weaknesses were displayed and, under the concentrated heat of the drama, intensified. By 1978, Syrian leaders had shown they were master neither of Lebanon nor of Syria itself.[41]

Hafez Assad and his foreign policy advisors must decide options in a straitened environment. Virtually all factions in Lebanon distrust the Syrians, and Syrian forces attempting a rapid withdrawal could easily be harrassed.[42] The readiness of the Syrian army is significantly less than in October 1973, due to its deployment in Lebanon. Some Syrian leaders are known to believe their Israeli counterparts would appreciate the opportunity to fight Syria under these conditions.[43]

Relations with Egypt have been difficult since the end of the October War, as each country negotiated separately under Kissinger's step-by-step formula,[44] raising the insecurity of the other. Since Sadat's initiative of late 1977, Egypt and Syria have been at odds with each other over the Egyptian approach to Israel. Yet, as Assad knows, Syria *needs* Egypt to create a credible threat. If Egyptian policy changed, Egypt—and Sadat—would be welcomed back to the Arab fold, especially by Syria.

Syria's 'Alawi leadership does not trust the Iraqi elite either. The historic patterns of regional rivalry to control Syria have sown a nationalist distrust of the Iraqis, exacerbated now by ideological disputes between rival branches of the Ba'th and by confessional differences. Ideological conflicts between Iraqi and Syrian wings of the Ba'th have been treated sufficiently elsewhere.[45] We feel that while this conflict has some meaning within the party structures it is marginal to the dispute that flared between them from 1974 to 1978, and reemerged in 1979, because the Ba'th is relatively peripheral to foreign policy decision-making on key issues (especially in Syria); it is a legitimizing agent rather than a participant in the decision process.[46] The dispute reflects a competition for subregional leadership, and Syria won from 1974 to 1978. After 1978, however, the situation changed.

Only with Jordan was Assad able to maintain consistently good relations from their rapprochement in 1975 until 1979.[47] Jordan's military power is of little consequence in the arms-heavy Middle East, but Jordan's position—Syria's link with Saudi Arabia, and bordering Israel and Iraq as well—was critical. Recognizing the IDF preferred to bypass the heavy fortifications in the Golan, the leaders of both countries viewed an Israeli attack on Syria through Jordan as a very real possibility should hostilities recommence, and military cooperation evolved from 1973 to 1978 to address such an Israeli strategy.[48] Moreover, King Hussein was a very useful channel in dealing with Saudi Arabia and the United States. As a Sunni leader claiming direct descent from Mohammed, Hussein was also a conveniently acceptable ally for Syria's 'Alawi leaders. Movement by Hussein toward a separate peace with Israel would be a serious strategic defeat for Syria.

Saudi Arabia plays a major role in Syrian foreign policy, a far more important role than most observers recognize. Syria's role as a revolutionary/radical/progressive state put Damascus at odds with Riyadh for some time. Even today, Syrian leaders are aware that the Saudis do not fully trust Syria and are relieved to have monarchic Jordan between the two countries.[49] Since the emergence of Hafez Assad as the undisputed leader of Syria, the relations of the two countries have been close and cooperative, but the conservative Saudi leadership still retains reservations about Syria as a whole. Syrian behavior toward Saudi Arabia reflects three considerations— Saudi financial support, regional influence, and religious leadership. Financial transfers to Syria have been considerable for some time and have been especially important in defraying the costs of the expensive Syrian military operation in Lebanon.[50] The ability of the Syrian government to pursue a guns (arms procurement)-and-butter (development) program[51] was a function of Saudi subvention. Of somewhat less consequence is Saudi regional leadership. Rather than a constraint, Syria looks upon Saudi Arabia as a resource in this context. That is, it is important to win Saudi concurrence in specified policy areas because such concurrence will affect the policies of other Arab states, particularly the peripheral states of the Arabian

Peninsula. Moreover, on some issues, Saudi policy itself constitutes a virtual issue outcome. Finally, Saudi Arabia's special role as the religious leader of the Islamic world has a special meaning in Syria. The 'Alawi leaders there have seen in Saudi Arabia a serious threat, for the latter can use Islam to mobilize subversive movements to oust the 'Alawis. The Muslim Brotherhood (*Ikhwan muslimin*) has, for example, long been a potent force in some areas of Syria (especially Homs and Hama), and the *Ikhwan* is closely tied to Saudi Arabia. In this respect Saudi power may grow now when Sunni consciousness and activism are waxing.[52]

Syria's relations with the superpowers have always been ambivalent. One of the first Arab states to secure arms from the USSR, Syria has remained generally closer to Moscow than to the West in political ideology and military affairs. However, like most Arabs, Syrians do not generally like the Russians,[53] find Western philosophy and religion more akin to their own cultural dispositions, and believe Western technology superior to its Soviet counterpart.[54] The Syrian government has used Lebanon and, recently, Jordan as windows to the West.

Neither Hafez Assad nor his brother, Rifaat, trusts the USSR. Both are, in fact, anti-Soviet in view, notwithstanding rhetoric to the contrary.[55] Both the Assad brothers are determined to maintain freedom of maneuver with regard to the Soviets. However, the salience of the Arab-Israeli conflict, the belief that Israel will not negotiate on the Golan issue, and the conclusion that military strength is required continue to force the Assad government to cooperate with the Soviet Union.[56] Syrian leaders are willing to compromise on some policy differences with Moscow on peripheral issues, especially questions outside the Middle East, but manifest independence on salient Middle East matters. For example, Soviet objections (including the embargo of arms transfers) did not deter Syria from intervening against the Palestinians in Lebanon in June 1976.[57] Assad and his chief advisors see little alternative to continued dependence on the Soviet Union for the present and foreseeable future.

Although Syrian-U.S. *relations* are fragile and tentative, there is in Syria a substantial reservoir of good feelings toward the American people. Modern Syrian history has not been characterized by shared policy perspectives with the United States,[58] and American intrigues in Syria in the early years of its independence have not yet been totally forgotten.[59] More important than this clouded past is the U.S. role as the principal external supporter of Israel, Syria's primary enemy and the occupier of Syrian territory. Recent events have shown that Americans can negotiate comfortably with Assad,[60] but that conflicts between Syrian interests and U.S. policy preclude greatly expanded or improved ties. Nevertheless, cooperation and communication on matters of importance to both countries have been evident in recent years (e.g., in Lebanon), and the Assads continue to feel more comfortable in dealing with the United States than in dealing with the USSR.

IRAQ

The foreign and defense policies of Iraq are subject to several external forces, some of which are related to one or more of Iraq's major domestic interest groups. Currently, a number of nations and transnational forces are exerting either direct or indirect influences affecting Iraq's policy formulation. Nations whose locations, ideologies, capabilities, policies, or actions are having the greatest effect on Iraqi foreign and defense policies are: the Soviet Union, Iran, and Syria. Transnational forces especially affecting Iraq's policy-makers are Pan-Arabism, Islam, and the Palestinian cause.

Iraqi relations with the superpowers have changed markedly over the past several years as Iraq has sought to broaden its resources for development and lessen its military dependence on the Soviet Union, and has become apprehensive about Soviet goals in the Middle East. In general, the trend since 1975 has shown increasing commercial relations with the West and declining economic cooperation with the Soviet Union and Eastern Europe, concomitant with a pronounced political distance between Iraq and the Soviet Union. Iraqi leaders seek to maintain cooperative ties with the Soviets but are apprehensive about Soviet regional aspirations. Coups and, later, open Soviet intervention in Afghanistan confirmed fears among some party leaders that the Soviets are willing to intervene directly in the affairs of regional countries. The Iraqi Communist Party (ICP) purge over the past year has been partially in response to perceived threats from the Soviet Union. Ba'th leaders also suspected the ICP was secretly planning a take-over based upon strictly prohibited ICP activity within the Iraqi army.[61]

The revolution in Iran has also concerned the Iraqi leadership, which has feared the new government in Iran as a source of agitation among Iraq's Shi'a majority. Iraq's sensitivities to the Shi'a problem thus overlap significantly with its new conflict with Iran. Under the shah the conflict between Iran and Iraq was principally a power struggle for leadership in the Gulf and for mutual security. It also took on territorial and to some extent ideological manifestations. The new conflict has added a far-reaching social dimension, though it retains its territorial, security, and leadership aspects.[62] Relations between Iran and Iraq became strained as Ayatollah Khomeini remembered his expulsion from Najaf in 1978, as Iranian leaders became apprehensive about Iraqi agitation among Iranian Kurds, and as increasing border firefights indicated Baghdad's determination to keep the border issue at the forefront.[63]

Iranian appeals to Iraqi Shi'as, Iraqi demands for the abrogation of that part of the 1975 Iran-Iraq treaty altering the Shatt al-'Arab boundaries, and small skirmishes along the border all contributed to the dangerous friction between the two countries. Despite the relative docility of the Iraqi Shi'as since the revolution in Iran, their potential for disruption should not be underestimated. As we have noted, Shi'a Arabs form Iraq's largest ethnoreligious group, and are, in fact, a majority in the country. Furthermore, Iraq is the historical center for Shi'ism, and a number of places in Iraq are worldwide Shi'a pilgrimage sites. It is no wonder the Shi'as pose the greatest internal threat to the tenure of the Ba'th regime in the long run.

The humiliation of the circumstances surrounding the 1975 treaty were never forgotten in Baghdad. Despite the list of Iranian provocations Iraqi leaders are quick to provide, it is difficult to escape the conclusion that Saddam Hussein saw the disarray in Iran as an opportunity to recover the Shatt, to solidify Iraq's leadership in the Gulf, and to put to rest any remaining doubts about Iraqi power in the Middle East. The 1980 war—which to some extent both realized and subverted these aims—can be seen as the continuation of Arab-Persian conflict more than a thousand years old. It is undeniably, however, also an Iran-Iraq problem.

If Iran were Iraq's only regional rival, Saddam would be far less concerned about the Iranian revolution. However, Iraq's northwestern border is also hostile. Iraq and Syria have been at odds for years, particularly after 1975, with only a brief detente in late 1978 and early 1979.[64] Again, the subjects of the dispute have varied over time. At base, there is between Baghdad and Damascus a continuing struggle for leadership in the Arab East. While Syria was the dominant power for most of the 1970s, increased internal unrest there and the growth of Iraqi economic and military power began to exert themselves toward a redistribution of leadership by 1979.

In addition to conflict between Iran and Iraq, on the one hand, and Syria and Iraq, on the other, the growing though still unpublicized linkage between Iran and Syria concerns Saddam's government. It should be noted that Syria's minority regime is first and foremost a government of 'Alawis,[65] a small religious sect most closely related to (and in fact a break-away from) Shi'ism.[66] Thus to Baghdad, both Iran and Syria are ruled by Shi'a regimes that seek the replacement of the Iraqi government by a (Shi'a?) leadership more disposed to compromising with their own interests. Moreover, the Iran-Syria connection is not merely a figment of Iraqi paranoia. The 'Alawi regime in Syria is one of the few governments able to develop a cooperative relationship with Iran's rulers since the establishment of the Islamic republic in Iran, and one of the very few to refrain from any criticism of the seizure of the U.S. embassy by Iranian students in November 1979. Contacts between the two governments have been numerous,[67] especially since the reopening of the conflictive schism between Iraq and Syria.[68] Thus although fear has abated somewhat, the Ba'th has not let down its guard vis-à-vis Iraqi Shi'as. The Shi'a clergy is closely watched for signs of opposition to the regime.

Transnational forces are also affecting Iraqi foreign policy. Currently, what has been called the Islamic Revival is affecting, in some measure, Iraqi decision-making. As we have indicated, the Ba'th regime is wary of Shi'a agitation under the shadow of the Iranian Islamic Revolution. However, Iraq has also tried to exploit the Islamic cause in its attempts to unify Arab opposition to the Egyptian-Israeli peace treaty.[69]

The reasons for and scope and potential of the Islamic resurgence in the Middle East all require close scrutiny. However, although detailed information on the Islamic revival has not been collected or analyzed, there is no question that the Ba'th leadership of Iraq has reason to fear Islamic-inspired disruption. Recent demonstrations in Tehran calling for a Shi'a overthrow of the Ba'th regime, the arrest of Ayatollah Mohammed Baqr Sadr (a Shi'a religious leader) in Najaf by Iraqi authorities, and a war of words in the press between the two countries have led to charges in the official Iraqi newspaper *al-Ba'th* that the Iranian regime is inciting Iraqi Shi'as to revolt. The threat of Iranian-inspired disruption has important ramifications on Gulf stability. If either regime decides it can wield enough influence within the other country to maintain a successful or resource-consuming revolt, the threat of war is real.[70] At least as long as Khomeini is in power, Iran will be the least flexible of the two sides in reaching a solution for peaceful coexistence.

Ba'th ideology is Pan-Arabist in nature.[71] Despite the failure of Pan-Arabism to unite the Arab world and the highly skeptical view toward Pan-Arabist ideals and movements held by Westerners in general as well as by many Arabs, the cultural identity shared by Arabs has enabled the Ba'th to exploit this tool whose emotional power is substantial throughout the Arab world. The Ba'th is somewhat constrained by Pan-Arabism in that actions must be justified on their integrative force. To the extent actions divide the Arab world, they require alternative justifications that are more immediately compelling.

The Palestinian cause has also been used by the Iraqi regime to achieve Arab leadership. Despite its historical support of the most radical Palestinian positions, and its sometimes violent disputes with moderate al-Fatah, Iraq has recently placed itself in the vanguard of support for the PLO as a result of the Egyptian-Israeli treaty. Iraq's size, potential power, geographical location, ideological base, and economic strength make it a natural leader of Arab support for the Palestinians when the latter are forced into a radical stand. This position vis-à-vis the PLO assists the Baghdad regime in its regional power struggles and is conducive to internal popularity. Pending the results of the Egyptian-Israeli peace negotiations, and the effect they will have on the Palestinians, Iraq will remain a leader in the Arab world as far as support for the Palestinians is concerned. However, majority moderate Palestinian views have generally diverged from the positions of Iraq since the mid to late 1960s. For this reason,

Iraq's "house" Palestinian commando group, the Arab Liberation Front, and various individual leaders and groups at odds with the more moderate Fatah policies have been used to maintain the appearance of Iraqi support for the Palestinian cause. Iraq's location and interests permit relatively little influence over the Palestinian movement as a whole except, as we have indicated, when external developments have temporarily unified the Palestinians.[72]

SAUDI ARABIA

Saudi leaders perceive themselves as increasingly vulnerable to both tangible and intangible threats from a variety of sources. They are eminently aware that modern technology, internal and regional politics, and their own policies ended their insulation from the eastern Mediterranean Arab-Israeli conflict. Meanwhile, the Arabian/Persian Gulf front also looms larger, as the arms inventories of several littoral nations grow. In addition, the explosive dynamism of social change poses questions of unknown magnitude in the short and long term.[73]

Until about 1973, Saudi Arabia was insulated from the Arab-Israeli confrontation and from the confrontation states themselves, except Jordan. When Nasser's Egypt and Saudi Arabia clashed over regional hegemony, Pan-Arabism, and local control, the battles were conducted largely in Yemen (1962–67), and Egypt was forced to send an expeditionary force to that country. Even today, Egypt would be unable to attack vulnerable Saudi targets without a staging point on the peninsula.[74] This applies even more fully to Syria.[75] Traditionally, Saudi Arabia has been of no military interest to Israel. As it became the financial backbone of the Arab coalition against Israel[76] and with an arsenal of rapidly growing sophistication,[77] Saudi Arabia evolved into a party to the Arab-Israeli conflict.[78] Moreover, Israeli verbal threats and military capabilities make it impossible even now to rule out an Israeli attack on the kingdom. While Saudi force deployments have been designed to reassure Israel that no offensive military operations against the Zionist state will be launched from Saudi territory, and although prime Saudi targets are generally outside the unrefueled combat radius of IAF aircraft, Israel by 1979 was the least improbable external threat to Saudi Arabia.[79]

Until the overthrow of the monarchy, Iran loomed largest in Saudi defense planning. Strangely, relations with the shah were usually correct, if at times cool. Yet, Iran's claims of Gulf policeman status and its seizure of the small Gulf islands of Abu Musa and the Tunbs concerned Saudi elites. Defense planners could not overlook the inclusion in Iran's vast and rapidly growing military inventory of the largest hydrofoil/air-cushion vehicle fleet in the world, wondering what these acquisitions were designed to accomplish if not to transport large numbers of troops quickly across the Gulf. From young to old, members of the Saudi elite came to the conclusion that Iran's leaders were thinking of capturing the nearby Saudi oil fields at some point in the future, since Iran's oil was projected to run out perhaps before the turn of the century.[80] Despite the political conservatism of the shah, Saudis did not feel comfortable during his tenure.

Contemporary Iran poses a different and threefold threat. The first and most immediate problem confronting the kingdom is that of instability in the Gulf. The chaos in Iran opens the door to the influx of subversives and *agents provocateurs,* encourages revolutionary groups and individuals, and takes place when SAVAK no longer surveils threats to Gulf stability. Previously, the Saudis could have taken comfort in SAVAK's cautious policing of dissidents (though they chose not to focus on the security spin-offs of the shah's omnipresence). Moreover, Iran took an active role in policing the Gulf, even sending troops to Oman, and if Iran's power projection in the subregion made the Saudis uneasy, the absence of that power makes them more so.[81] A second threat derives from the possibility of a leftist or otherwise anti-Saudi government in Iran that could pose a military or subversive challenge to Riyadh. The Iranian revolution has already raised the spectre of an antimonarchic movement in the Gulf; internal events in Iran may easily carry the change another step. Saudi Arabia would then be bounded on the east (Iran), north (Iraq), and south (People's Democratic Republic of Yemen) by hostily regimes. The third type of threat arising from Iran that is feared by Saudi Arabia is, ironically, the mantle of Islamic resurgence. The religious tone of the revolution in Iran has a uniquely Shi'a cast befitting this largest Shi'a nation. Resurgent Shi'ism has been felt in Iraq and may appeal as well to the half-million Shi'as in Saudi Arabia's Eastern Province.

Iraq has been an intermittent rival of Saudi Arabia since 1958, having largely underwritten revolutionary activities in the southern Arabian Peninsula for some time. The Saudi leadership recalls with revulsion the sanguinary overthrow of the Hashemite monarchy, and Iraq's later efforts to prove its revolutionary fervor and close relations with the USSR have not improved Saudi perceptions of the Baghdad regime. However, the greater pragmatism demonstrated by the Ba'th leaders in Iraq since 1973 and the growth in their economic interaction with the West, as well as their more limited support for revolutionary movements in the Arabian Peninsula/Gulf area, have encouraged some Saudi decision-makers to proceed with increased cooperation, to the point of supporting Iraq rather openly against Iran in the 1980 war between the two countries. (Of course, Iran had by then become the greater "revolutionary" threat in terms of the Saudi situation.) This cooperation began secretly in 1979 following an Iraqi initiative to improve its regional relations in 1978. By 1979 a virtual secret alliance existed between Iraq, Jordan, and Saudi Arabia. Although this entente eluded many Western observers because of the traditional rivalry between Iraq and Saudi Arabia, the relationship is in fact a continuation of Saudi policy in supporting Iraq or Syria against the other. Iraqi-Saudi cooperation is tactical from the Saudi viewpoint—though no less real for all that—and Saudis can be expected to monitor the relationship carefully for any signs that the friendship is overaged.

Egypt, whose Pan-Arab, socialist leadership in the Arab world was directed against Saudi Arabia in the mid-1960s, is no longer a regional leader. Whether relations with Sadat's Egypt are cooperative or conflictive, Saudi leaders feel confident Cairo no longer represents a threat to Saudi Arabia or its regional role.

Similarly, Syria, recently a Middle East leader (1973–77), for some time has not posed a political threat to Saudi Arabia. Like Egypt, Syria has received substantial economic and military assistance from Saudi Arabia. Moreover, neither Egypt nor Syria could attack Saudi oil fields, the only likely target of military attack by these countries. Egypt has committed itself to a cause of domestic attention, and Syria faces critical internal problems we have described in the previous chapter.

Saudi Arabia's leadership, though far from monolithic, is concerned principally with Arabian Peninsula security, secondarily with Persian Gulf stability, and then with subregional developments in the

Eastern Mediterranean and Arabian Peninsula areas.[82] Islam has played a prominent role in Saudi foreign policy, but religion has infused the consciousness of Saudi leaders to such an extent that it is integrated into strategic and tactical planning.[83]

For most of the last twenty years, Saudi Arabia has perceived an Arabian Peninsula security threat from the Yemens. From 1962 to 1967 the threat was felt to come from the Yemen Arab Republic (YAR); since 1971 the threat has arisen from the People's Democratic Republic of Yemen (PDRY). Neither of these countries has the military power to wage war against and defeat its larger neighbor; both are located such that Saudi fears are easily aroused. The PDRY has supported, with periodic seriousness, an insurgent movement in Oman that has endured for about a decade. It is precisely this type of behavior that raises Saudi anxiety. The stability of the Gulf is an important concern of Saudi leaders, partly because the country has a long coast on the Gulf and partly because the major Saudi oil fields are all very near the Gulf.

Beyond the peninsula and the Gulf, Saudi elites look to the Horn of Africa and Indian Ocean as areas relevant to their own security. Thus Riyadh took an active role in persuading Somali leaders to end their country's close relationship with the Soviet Union and in the process expel the Soviets from facilities then in use in Somalia. Similarly, Saudi Arabia has been concerned over Soviet and Cuban activities in Ethiopia and over the increase in Soviet naval activity in the Indian Ocean.[84]

It is widely believed that Saudi Arabia has never dealt with the USSR. In fact, however, Saudi-Soviet relations were at one time both active and cooperative.[85] King Faisal greatly distrusted Moscow, and saw in communism a threat to Saudi values as well as to the regime. Although his successors at the helm of the country share this view, few hold attitudes as rigid or extreme as Faisal. Before the Soviet intervention in Afghanistan in December 1979, many were prepared to treat the Soviet Union in a more relaxed manner if such a tactic had been likely to reduce anti-Saudi movements or propaganda and to improve political leverage. However, neither the royal family nor other key individuals is likely to feel comfortable about *trusting* the Soviet Union, about hosting a large number of Soviet or other communist nationals, or about sending Saudi subjects to school in communist countries. Saudi-Soviet relations cannot develop very far in the near or intermediate time.

It is to the West, and particularly to the United States, that Riyadh has looked for protection and cooperation. Saudi leaders felt they had a "special relationship" with the United States, different of course from the unique American-Israeli tie, but "special" (and in their view more equitable and more firmly founded in the U.S. interest) nevertheless. When the spectre of an oil shortage first loomed on the horizon, Saudis proposed a partnership with the United States that would ensure adequate petroleum for the United States in return for Saudi investment in that country. The suggestion was unacceptable to U.S. officials, one of a series of political jolts in the relationship since 1972.

U.S. officials and Saudi leaders shared similar misperceptions during the late 1970s. Each believed it had gone more than half way in the relationship of the two countries. Many officials in both governments believed the other country needed their country more than they needed the other; or that in the long run the other government would have no option to supporting their country and its policies. The error (on both sides) was in mistaking shared interests for "favors" and as a result in placing too high a price on cooperation. The brighter side of the picture, especially visible since January 1980, is that the United States and Saudi Arabia do continue to share a number of interests and perspectives as a result of which their relationship should remain cooperative on balance.[86]

Having become a more active participant in regional politics, Saudi elites are finding visibility suggests vulnerability. Instability in the Gulf; growing instability in the Levant; a separate peace between Egypt and Israel that has pushed Saudi Arabia and Jordan into cooperation with Iraq and PDRY, as well as other erstwhile enemies still suspect; and several confrontations with the United States—these developments trouble Saudi leaders and increase the value of Western and American friendship.

JORDAN

The principal external factor exerting influence on Jordanian foreign policy is the Arab-Israeli conflict. Although Jordan's role in this dispute has been less aggressive and more reluctant than that of Egypt and Syria over the last two decades, this reticence did not protect the kingdom from participating in the June 1967 war as a result of which all the territory of Jordan west of the Jordan River— an area generally known as the West Bank[87]—including the city of Jerusalem came under Israeli occupation. By 1967, Jordan and its king had little interest in actually annihilating Israel. Indeed, Jordanian elites were the most realistic of any of the Arab leadership groups.[88] The motives of the kingdom in participating in the war had much more to do with inter-Arab relations than with Arab-Israeli affairs.

After the war of 1967, the king recognized Israel was by far the most powerful state in the area and determined not to wage war on that country again. Meanwhile, the focal point of Jordanian foreign policy was the recovery of the occupied territories, and the focal point of domestic concern was reconstruction of the economy, the society, and, particularly, the government.[89] That Jordan should attempt to secure the return of the West Bank was not disputed inside the kingdom in 1967. Yet, the West Bank is a very populous territory whose inhabitants are by definition Palestinian. Annexed by Jordan after the 1948 Arab-Israeli war, the residents of the territory never identified with the Hashemites or considered themselves Jordanian. Heavily discriminated against under Amman's rule, they do not wish to see a return of Jordanian government; however, they *would* prefer Jordanian to Israeli rule.[90]

Since the 1973 war, in which Jordan only took a defensive role in Syria, negotiations[91] progressed to an extent that Jordanian elites began for the first time to seriously consider the possibility of the return of the West Bank to Jordanian control. Faced with this change, they began to feel after substantial study that the West Bank's return would adversely affect Jordan, that is, Jordanian control of the country. A relatively clear split emerged between the king, on the one hand, and most of the rest of the elite (including most of the king's family), on the other. Hussein favors the return of the West Bank to Jordanian real or nominal control, though not under arrangements that serve as a barely disguised continuation of Israeli control. Demographic realities and resulting political problems have persuaded East Bankers that Jordan is better off, or at least that Jordanians are better off, without the West Bank.[92]

Even as positions within Jordan began to crystallize, many key observers in the Arab world and beyond were concluding that the

Palestinian issue was indeed at the heart of the Middle East problem and that perhaps the most promising approach to that issue involved a Jordanian role in the West Bank.[93] The conclusion of the Rabat Conference[94] of 1974 was in effect rescinded, and increasingly even the PLO recognized that an Arab Palestinian homeland might best be assured in some sort of Jordanian context.[95]

Thus the principal external consideration for Jordan is a general settlement of the Arab-Israeli conflict which must almost certainly directly affect Jordan. The king is not in a position to negotiate with Israel—he cannot concede East Jerusalem or much if anything of the West Bank, if he expects to maintain support.[96] Relations with Saudi Arabia are good, and Jordan's weakness contributes to Jordanian-Saudi cooperation.[97] Saudi subsidies to Jordan have been very generous in recent years. Jordanian-Lebanese relations have deteriorated, and the two neighbors no longer interact as much as they once did.[98]

It is with Syria that King Hussein constructed Jordan's closest regional alliance the last several years. The two countries undertook extensive cooperation in military and political fields, as well as economic conditions, some of which continues. Syria's rival, Iraq, not close to Jordan since the overthrow of the Hashemite monarchy in Iraq in 1958, has also been suspect in Jordan's eyes. When Iraq threatened Syria during the latter's intervention in the Lebanese conflict, Jordan let it be known in Iraq that Jordanian forces would be quite willing to assist Syria against an Iraqi invasion on the east.[99]

Jordan's most important "friend" outside the region over the last two decades has certainly been the United States. Hussein's personal inclination is very sympathetic to the United States, and Jordan's king was long the only Arab leader arousing popular American sympathy in this country. Despite inevitable disagreements and misunderstandings, the leaders of Jordan and those of the United States believed they held similar views of the desirable directions for the Middle East. Jordan's potentially key role in and support of a general Middle East settlement; the reluctance of East Bankers to favor a Palestinian state; the conservative economic, social, and political philosophy of Jordan's leaders; their distrust of the Soviet Union and frequent and open support of and praise for the United States; and Jordan's willingness to support the security of the sheikhdoms of the Persian Gulf actively through military aid in the form of training and the secondment of officers—each of these considerations has helped maintain good relations between the United States and Jordan.[100]

Perhaps Jordan's basic foreign relations constraint is its economic and military weakness in a heavily armed region. These weaknesses reduce Jordan's influence and increase its vulnerability. Given Jordan's military limitations, for example, the king needs a potent ally, a role Syria assumed after 1973 and one the United States has partially filled in the past. Specifically, too, Jordan's leaders have been concerned to prevent outside forces from mobilizing and supporting the country's Palestinian majority in an anti-Hashemite uprising.[101]

OTHER STATES
Libya

As stated in Chapter 1, domestic considerations do not usually play a role in Libya's foreign policy decision-making. That is, the Libyan regime is seldom hindered by domestic interest groups in its pursuit of foreign policy objectives. Of course, Libyan actions are limited by the relatively meager military capabilities of the state.[102] Countries influencing Libya's defense and foreign policies are Egypt, the superpowers, Israel, and the Palestinians.

The most significant regional actor directly influencing Libyan policy-making is Egypt. Qaddafi is highly concerned about the possibility of an Egyptian invasion of Libya with tacit U.S. and possibly even Arab world approval. Egypt continues to experience extreme economic and social problems based upon its high population, limited resource base, and other structural difficulties such as crippling bureaucracy, inadequate housing, and ominous income distribution patterns. Libya's small population and army—and Libya's large oil deposits—must appear attractive to Egyptian leaders, attractive like a "power vacuum." Furthermore, with the present world oil situation threatening recessions in Japan and Western Europe, Anwar Sadat could claim that by invading Libya he would be acting in the interests of the Middle East and the West, as well as of Egypt.[103] Libya's fear of Egypt has caused Qaddafi to moderate his radical stances in practice, attempt to cement relations with other Arab states, and rely heavily on the Soviet Union for arms for defense.

Despite the facts that U.S. business interests in Libya are on the rise,[104] and that Libya supplies 10 percent of American oil imports, Libyan-U.S. relations are dwarfed by Libya's relations with the Soviet Union. Muammar Qaddafi, the unofficial chief of state, would like to improve his relations with the United States in principle. However, past Libyan actions (especially vis-à-vis Palestinian terrorists[105] and U.S. nationals) prevent the United States from normalizing relations with Libya. Libya has drawn much closer to the Soviet Union during Qaddafi's rule and has purchased $12 billion of modern Soviet military hardware[106] largely to defend itself against Egypt. The Soviets are also participating in a number of development projects and are trying to reveal a low profile within the country in an effort to avoid a repetition in Libya of Egypt's expulsion of thousands of Soviet technicians in 1972.[107]

Like other Arab countries, Libya has used the Palestinian cause to advance its own interests in the Middle East. By financing and siding with the most radical elements of the PLO, Libya has attempted to be a leader of the radical Arab states. However, Libya's extremist views have caused embarrassment for leaders of other *soi-disant* "radical" Arab states, especially Syria and Iraq.[108] Thus Libya's policies toward the Palestinians, Pakistan, Oman, Sudan, Tunisia, and the former Spanish Sahara have served to isolate Libya from virtually all major Arab states.

The most significant regional actor directly influencing Libyan policy-making is Egypt. Qaddafi is highly concerned about the possibility of an Egyptian invasion of Libya with tacit U.S. and possibly even Arab world approval. Egypt is currently experiencing increased economic problems due to its growing isolation from the Arab world. Furthermore, the present world oil situation is threatening recessions in Japan and Western Europe. Thus Anwar Sadat could claim that by invading Libya he would be acting in the interests of the Middle East and the West, as well as of Egypt. Libya's fear of Egypt has caused Qaddafi to moderate his radical stances in practice, attempt to cement relations with other Arab states, and rely heavily on the Soviet Union for arms for defense.

Algeria

Algeria has very few external pressures on its foreign policy-making. The most significant external constraint comes from Algeria's main regional rival, Morocco. The nature of the competition between these two countries is over dominance of the Maghreb, although it has manifested itself in a variety of ways—ideological and territorial disputes and border warfare, for example. While Algeria has supported the Steadfastness Front opposing the Camp David peace process in general and has backed the Palestinians in particular, this position is due to Algeria's desire to keep a hand in Arab affairs and to a certain extent assert itself against Morocco.

Kuwait

Kuwait's foreign policy is strongly affected by external factors, principally its fear of Iraq, Iran, Saudi Arabia, and the Palestinians. In its attempt to prevent itself from being swallowed up by either Iraq or Saudi Arabia, Kuwait has worked diligently to establish smooth relations with both countries and has bought the support of the Arab world for its independence. Kuwait's support of the Palestinian cause, in turn, is largely due to its desire to placate its two much larger neighbors and the Kuwaiti Palestinians who perform vital functions in the country. Kuwait's break in relations with Egypt is an example of Kuwaiti concern over foreign pressure. Kuwait has supported the Sadat regime since Sadat assumed control in order to help prevent a radical government from coming into power. However, due to Kuwait's concerns over its more immediate neighbors, it has joined the majority of Arab countries that oppose the Camp David framework for peace.

Kuwait is also trying to build ties to Saudi Arabia and Iraq in order to receive support against the new Iranian regime. The Iranian threat has served in part to unite these three Arab countries since they all have reasons to suspect the Khomeini government.

THE PALESTINE LIBERATION ORGANIZATION (PLO)

The international relations of the PLO have been a major factor in the political evolution of the Middle East since 1967. Before the June War the Palestinian *issue* commanded rhetorical allegiance and attention from all the Arab states, but the Palestinian people, lacking an institutional channel through which to focus their power, exerted relatively little influence on the course of Middle East events. The magnitude of the Israeli victory in 1967 allowed the still-infant PLO to exercise substantial strength, including virtual territorial dominion within parts of Syria, Jordan, and (to a lesser extent) Egypt. The influx of additional refugees into Lebanon brought about a similar situation there, despite the fact that Lebanon was not a party to the war.

We have examined the dynamics of the PLO relationship with Arab states elsewhere.[109] Essentially, it is important to note that as each government reconstructed its political, economic, and military power following the June War, it was forced to overcome the temporal power of the Palestinian movement. In Egypt, there was little contest, except in the realm of debate. In Syria, resistance was quickly overcome by the new regime (of Hafez Assad) that assumed power in 1970, although Palestinians allied themselves with Assad's opponents to try to block Syrian assertion of its control over activities on Syrian territory. The confrontation in Jordan was predictably bloodier for two reasons. First, the government was weaker, giving the PLO reason to contest Jordanian power with the hope of victory. Second, Jordan was one of the last two Palestinian sanctuaries, one of only two remaining countries from which operations into Israel could be mounted directly without government approval. The PLO was unwilling to give up such a sanctuary without a fight, especially since it was aware of the presence of a near majority of Palestinians in Jordan. The final state in which the PLO was able to operate with impunity (except from Israel) was Lebanon. Palestinian autonomy within Lebanon led to serious clashes in 1969, 1971, and 1973, and it has played a major role in Palestinian motivation during the Lebanese civil war.[110]

The PLO has learned from several experiences that no Arab state can be regarded as a dependable ally; each will "betray" the PLO if state or regime interests require. Nevertheless, circumstances have dictated that the PLO ally itself with one or more regional governments. By itself, the PLO has little power against established governments, except in Lebanon. Its power has been substantially enhanced at critical junctures by timely alliances. With relatively little to offer Arab governments, the PLO recognizes that these alliances are bound to be temporary, that both the organization and the Palestinian people are being exploited by the Arab regimes.

PLO foreign relations are influenced by Saudi and Gulf financial contributions; Syrian military and political contributions; Lebanese weakness; Egyptian strength; and tactical considerations regarding these and other Arab states. Saudi Arabia's financial support has been extremely important to the PLO, but the number of Palestinians in Saudi Arabia and elsewhere in the Arab Gulf states provides unstated leverage for the movement. The important positions of many of the Gulf Palestinians are exceeded in significance by their alleged and presumed ability to create substantial dislocation. Some have even suggested the possibility of a Palestinian coup or take-over in Kuwait, where Palestinians comprise 40 percent of the expatriate population and 20 percent of the total population. We believe the willingness of Palestinians to create problems in the Gulf has been greatly exaggerated, particularly in Kuwait and Saudi Arabia. Saudi Arabia will continue to be attentive to the Palestinian issue and the PLO, but much of the reason is the determination of Saudi Arabia to maintain some influence over the PLO and some weight in the Arab world. (Saudi Arabia continues to be the single most important external influence on Fatah, the largest PLO group, and much of the senior leadership of Fatah is close to the Saudis.)

Syrian strength vis-à-vis the PLO has lain in the fact that Syrian forces staff both much of the Palestinian Liberation Army (PLA) and Saiqa; that Syrian confrontation with Israel is the most deep-seated of all the front-line states; and that the Syrian relationship to Palestine has deep historical roots that are transnational in nature.[111] Damascus is the least likely Arab (front-line) regime to reach a settlement with Israel that does not address the Palestinian problem. Yet, PLO-Syrian relations have vacillated. As the power behind Saiqa, Syria and the PLO have rarely been public enemies, but Fatah and Saiqa have not infrequently competed for position within the PLO, meaning Fatah and *Syria* have competed. Moreover, Syria has not allowed Palestinian raids on Israel from Syrian territory without the permission of the local Syrian army commander. The extreme expression of Syrian determination to control the Palestinian "card" in the Middle East was Syrian intervention in the Lebanese conflict, where, however, Syria was never able to defeat the Palestinian forces completely.

Unlike Syria, Lebanon until recently has been weaker as a unit than the Palestinian forces, largely because of the 300,000 Palestinian refugees there.[112] Posing a challenge to the confessional political balance in Lebanon,[113] the Palestinians eventually were able to rally important leftist and Muslim Lebanese support for the PLO. Without outside backing and lacking a consensus, the Lebanese Army had neither the political nor the military solidarity to confront the Palestinians. The result was substantial freedom of PLO action in Lebanon which became the last PLO base of operations. Despite the Cairo and Melkart accords which purported to delineate Palestinian rights and obligations in Lebanon, Palestinians there continued to operate as a "state within a state." Eventually, the power vacuum in Lebanon was to draw in Israel as well as Syria and was to lead to a proliferation of armed forces and quasi-autonomous polities. Lebanon continues to be the principal host to PLO forces,[114] although Israeli-supported Christian militias, Israeli forces, and international troops do limit Palestinian movements and action.

The PLO was evicted from Jordan as a result of the 1970 civil war. Since 1970, numerous attempts at reconciliation have been made, but the PLO has viewed the Hashemites with unremitting opprobrium. Not until the Egyptian-Israeli negotiations matured did the PLO relent. Since 1978, however, a rapprochement has begun. Nevertheless, it is unlikely that the army or the leading Jordanian families will tolerate the restoration of a full PLO role if this means large-scale PLO forces or a return to the situation existing before September 1970.

The Palestinian issue was never as crucial to Egypt as to the Levantine states. Nasser discovered the Palestine issue's volatility in the mid-1950s and exploited it increasingly later on. There are relatively few Palestinians in Egypt, and the emergence or nonemergence of a Palestinian state would affect Egypt far less than other Arab countries in the eastern Mediterranean. Thus Egypt is the freest major Arab country with respect to the Palestine, the only front-line state without a Palestinian problem or population. This invulnerability was of great concern to the PLO. Since Sinai II, the PLO has generally been at odds with Egypt, but has little leverage vis-à-vis Egyptian leaders. Lacking a presence, the PLO can resort only to isolated violence (assassination, sabotage, terrorism) but must act in recognition that it does not wish to alienate the Egyptian people and it does not wish Egypt to take reprisals against the many Palestinian students there.

Iraq and Libya are often associated with the PLO but are, in fact, largely peripheral to its needs. By themselves, Iraq and Libya are too far both from Israel and from the bulk of the Palestinian people to serve as bases of operations. Each country has been used by the PLO in tactical alliances and, more commonly, by PLO factions generally out of sympathy with the dominant PLO groups. Thus before and after the fall of Tel Zaatar, many ALF and PFLP supporters travelled to Iraq and Libya, respectively. Both countries have supported the PLO, but their importance is a function of PLO relations with the front-line states. They serve as sanctuaries for PLO leaders, and sometimes as arms caches. In the role of arms *suppliers* Iraq and Libya have provided important materiel to the PLO, but rarely has either sent enough alone to account for PLO victories.

In this chapter we have seen that despite the constant influence of domestic considerations on foreign policy in all states of the Middle East, external and regional factors have also played an important role. Indeed in the more homogeneous countries (like Egypt, Jordan, and Saudi Arabia) that are less subject to the power of disintegrative forces, foreign policy decision-making tends to emphasize the "merits" of the cases, that is, tends to address issues in terms of the tactical and strategic objectives of national level foreign policy. We have also seen that the role of the smaller countries and of the Palestinians is a function of the strength, policy, and will of the key Arab governments. Under certain circumstances the PLO, for example, has played a pivotal role in the region, while at other times the same organization has found itself isolated and impotent. This range of power is usually explained by strengths and weaknesses at the national level of existing Arab states. All Arab peoples identify with the Palestinian *issue,* but support for the *Palestinians* is much more limited and dependent upon the nature of their operations, the cost of those operations, and the power of the central governments.

3

Emerging Alignments

T HE PERIOD IMMEDIATELY FOLLOWING A WAR is generally a time of transition, and this fact is particularly true when the conflict itself is inconclusive.[1] After October 1973 all the major parties to the Arab-Israeli conflict were subject to new political pressures as a result of which alignments changed significantly over the remainder of the decade. It is not all clear that the transition period has ended yet, although some of the outlines of a new regional alignment subsystem are emerging.

The most important single change has been the breakdown of the Arab coalition against Israel. For almost thirty years, despite incessant inter-Arab rivalries, animosities, and even wars, no Arab government broke ranks on the Arab-Israeli issue. True, there were secret meetings of Arab and Israeli elites, but that they were held in secret is itself revealing: no Arab government was willing publicly to accept, recognize, and interact officially with Israel.[2]

In 1975, Egypt and Israel signed the second disengagement agreement for the Sinai. Provisions of this accord purported to temporarily remove Egypt from the military confrontation with Israel.[3] The PLO, Syrian leaders, and some other Arab governments indicated concern ranging from fear to outrage. A little more than two years later Anwar Sadat visited Israel, initiating a process that culminated in the Camp David agreements and, in March 1979, the Egyptian-Israeli peace treaty.[4] This process will have a profound impact on the international relations of the Middle East, because Sadat is determined to move forward with the development of improved Egyptian-Israeli relations.

One of the remarkable and noteworthy concomitants of Egypt's policy initiative vis-à-vis Israel has been the inability of the rest of the Arab world to develop a coordinated, coherent, and effective response. There is every reason to believe that a meaningful alternative to Sadat's policy, an alternative that united all or most of the Arab world behind an action plan that set out something more positive than the traditional response—"no," the only common denominator of the Arabs toward proposals regarding the Arab-Israeli conflict—would have attracted Egyptian support.[5] But no constructive response to the Sadat initiative emerged. After Camp David the Arab world met at Baghdad to develop a response, and was still unable to agree on a meaningful plan.[6] This Egyptian initiative and its denouement, then, constitute the first element of the foundation of a new alignment system.

The second basis is instability in several key countries, instability arising from minority unrest, renewed challenges to governmental legitimacy, and related disintegrative forces. This problem has already significantly affected Iran and Lebanon, has begun to affect Syria, and may reach Jordan, Iraq, and some of the Gulf states over the next five years.[7]

A third and final element in the regional alignments will certainly be the oil wealth of the Gulf states, particularly Saudi Arabia. On the one hand this financial strength will drive Saudi Arabia to pursue a political role commensurate with the country's economic power, as the kingdom has done the last few years. On the other, the Saudis will continue to react defensively in their foreign policy and will seek to avoid the emergence of countries or blocs with substantial military potential.[8]

THE LEVANT

From 1973, and particularly from 1975, to 1979, the single cohesive alliance in the Middle East was the Jordanian-Syrian entente. Much the result of the personal determination of the two leaders to cooperate, the relationship was vehemently opposed by important groups in both countries at its inception.[9] Later generally accepted in Jordan[10] and Syria, the alliance served both governments well. It dissolved in 1979, however, when Jordan entered an alliance with Iraq. Only the façade of Jordanian-Syrian cooperation lasted into 1980.

The 'Alawi-Sunni conflict in Syria will in the end unseat Hafez Assad and may result in the creation of an 'Alawi state along the

Mediterranean littoral. It has already weakened the Jordan-Syrian entente, as Jordan seeks a stronger partner and protector. The Assad regime, beset by rising levels of domestic violence against 'Alawis[11] (and occasionally against Soviet advisors and interests as well[12]), has begun to react in a manner that will only hasten Syria's regional isolation and increase domestic unrest. The Syrian government has also chosen to depend more heavily upon the Soviet Union than in the past, but this approach is unlikely to compensate for the decline in its regional relationships.

The 1978–79 Syrian-Iraqi rapprochement was foredoomed to failure. Neither Saddam Hussein, Iraq's strongman vice-president (now president) nor Hafez Assad, Syria's president, trusted the other or the elites surrounding the other. Both saw the rapprochement as a timely development dictated by other considerations. For Syria, the deteriorating domestic sectarian situation and the Camp David accords provided the impetus to tone down the rhetoric and hostility on the east and to enlist the support of a country that—on paper— appears to be a powerful military ally. For Iraq, too, domestic problems were increasing. Even before Ayatollah Khomeini returned in triumph to Iran a new restiveness and consciousness among Iraqi Shi'as was evident. The instability in Iran which became pronounced in late 1978 and only heightened after the deposition of the shah was an added concern. In addition to these two factors, Iraqi-Soviet relations were encountering troubled times by late 1978. In the face of these diverse problems, and challenged by the Camp David agreements, Iraqi leaders saw tactical advantages to improving relations with Syria. Neither country's leaders ever seriously considered a political union; neither was prepared to go very far to accommodate the other on salient issues; both sought to maximize the public visibility and dimensions of the rapprochement to derive as much political mileage as possible in the *other* domains. The Syrian 'Alawi government later supported fellow Shi'a Iran openly in the 1980 Iran-Iraq war, but nevertheless (for financial reasons) allowed Iraqi oil to pass through Syria.

A concurrent change in relations in the Levant involved Jordan. Since 1975, Hafez Assad had tried to bring about a reconciliation of the PLO and Jordan, the two having parted company following the 1970 Jordanian civil war ("Black September") during which the PLO was evicted from the territory of the Hashemite Kingdom.

Part of Assad's eastern front strategy,[13] such a reconciliation also interested King Hussein to the extent it might serve to further reduce his isolation and legitimize a more active regional role for Jordan.[14] However, despite several Jordanian attempts to explore a reconciliation, the PLO hierarchy was not able to overcome internal opposition to the change.

Finally, in the face of the Camp David accords and an impending peace treaty between Egypt and Israel, and after Jordan had taken a strong stand against Sadat's approach to an Egyptian separate peace with Israel, PLO interest in restoring and need to improve relations with Jordan permitted explorations of the possibility.[15] Within the PLO there remain many who recall the battles of 1970 too vividly to support any alliance with the Hashemite monarchy. Within Jordan there likewise remain many who recall the same battles, and the political conditions anterior to them, with the same reaction.[16]

Having reached the contested decision to cooperate with Jordan, the PLO will move to reestablish itself as firmly as possible in the country. Given the number of Palestinians in Jordan, PLO leaders recognize they have much to gain and little to lose at this point. They will for some time attempt to prevent conspiracy with the Palestinians in Jordan or involvement in anti-Hashemite activities, although it is unlikely that such behavior can be totally curbed in view of PLO diversity.

For their part, the leading Jordanian tribes and families have been quite concerned about the rapprochement with the PLO, for they are determined not to permit a return to the situation that existed prior to September 1970. They will keep a close eye on developments and will counsel the king against any real PLO freedom of action within Jordan. Because Hussein shares their suspicion of the PLO, he can be expected to direct a thorough surveillance of PLO activities by his very competent intelligence service and to carefully circumscribe PLO interactions with Palestinians. Ironically, even Jordan's majority Palestinian community is concerned at the return of the PLO, for they fear PLO presence may force them to choose sides or play a "Palestinian" role which in time could subject them to expulsion or at least greater Jordanian suspicion. Should the PLO become active in Jordan, the pressures on the Palestinian population will be intense and conflicting; most preferred the previous environment.

A third Levantine relationship of note has been the link between Lebanon and Syria. These two states share a long tradition of transnational linkages, and in fact have never exchanged ambassadors because their relationship was felt to be too close to be so expressed. For some time, the political distance was, however, far greater than the social distance. The Assad years in Syria have seen a generally greater degree of political cooperation between the two, but anti-Syrian feelings are almost universal in Lebanon today after more than three years of Syrian occupation. Since late 1975 or, arguably, mid-1976, the government of Lebanon has been largely a protectorate of Syria, and the latter has alienated all sectors of Lebanese opinion. However, as Syria's attention and power in Lebanon were diverted because of Syria's internal problems and the consequent need to bring about a lasting settlement in Lebanon, the power of the Christians was solidified over part of the south (which "seceded" to form "Free Lebanon," a virtual Israeli protectorate) and certain parts of the north (East Beirut, Mt. Lebanon). Meanwhile, it appears that Christian-Shi'a cooperation grew in 1979 so that the Sunnis were increasingly extruded from power by Christian-Shi'a-Druze agreement.

Several alternative futures are possible for Lebanon. The prevailing expectation appears to be that Lebanon will devolve toward a loose, confederal system, probably with almost complete autonomy for the Christian areas of Ashrafiyeh and Mt. Lebanon, the Shi'a areas of Bekaa and southern Lebanon, the Druze in the Shuf, and Sunni enclaves in Beirut, Sidon, and Tripoli. Such a possibility might not affect the Palestinians significantly in theory, although their influence in the whole of Lebanon will certainly have been drastically reduced from 1975. An alternative outlook for Lebanon includes greater unity and centralization of the country under Christian, especially Maronite, leadership. This prospect is dependent upon the nascent cooperation between Christian, Shi'a, and to a lesser extent Druze elements at the expense of the Sunnis. If Lebanon in its traditional boundaries remains on the map of the Middle East under these conditions, it may mean the eviction of large numbers of Muslim Palestinians from the south of Lebanon. The reasons Sunnis do not figure prominently in Lebanon's immediate political future are: the Sunnis lack of an effective leader; Lebanese Sunnis are now substantially less numerous than Shi'as; and Sunnis do not have extensive geographical regions of predominance. Their majority areas are largely confined to West Beirut, Sidon, and Tripoli.

Another possibility that can no longer be discounted is the emergence of 'Alawi, Christian, and Druze states in northern and western Syria and Lebanon. If such a situation eventuated, the international relations of the Middle East would be fundamentally changed. Christian and Druze polities, and possibly even the 'Alawi state, would come under the protection of Israel, and Syria would cease to be a major Middle East power. Some of the less populous and militarily weaker states such as Jordan and Saudi Arabia would both be relieved by Syria's impotence, even though these are Assad's two principal external supporters. If existing states fragment along sectarian lines, Israeli relations with the Christian littoral state, certainly, and probably with the 'Alawi littoral state will be cooperative and, in the former case, close. It is difficult to overestimate the importance of such a development, since under these circumstances Israel will have broken its isolation on the north and northeast as well as on the south. Moreover, the Jordanian government has been the easiest with which to effect a *modus vivendi,* so that in effect Israel will have a *cordon sanitaire* of buffer states between itself and the rejectionists and irreconcilables.[17] The diplomatic, economic, and social isolation of Israel in the Middle East will be at an end, and the moral basis of the Israeli state legitimized.[18]

ISRAEL

Although it is certainly true that a second Israeli breakthrough would signal the end of effective Arab isolation of Israel, the critical Israeli tie will continue to be that with Egypt, the largest and most important country in the Arab world. Cooperation with small Arab states may be viewed as ephemeral and without significance; cooperation with Egypt can be seen as short lived but is nevertheless by itself of capital importance.

From the Egyptian perspective, the relationship with Israel is becoming a fundamental element of foreign—and domestic—policy. Opponents and potential opponents of Egypt's move toward Israel are being bypassed by Sadat's appointments, and it is clear Sadat is endeavoring to ensure that the new approach to relations with Israel will be continued even after his death or political demise. By no means is the relationship with Israel expected to replace the Sudan as a preoccupation; good relations with the Sudan remain a *sine qua non* of Egyptian foreign policy. Yet, Sadat insists on the development of relations with Israel and will continue to do so—at least until all occupied Egyptian territory is returned to Egyptian control.

It is important to recognize that even in defiance of the Arab world Sadat still does not expcet to push Egyptian-Israeli relations beyond the government-to-government level except in such areas as tourism. There remains deep and widespread resistance in Egypt to "forced normalization," and various anti-Sadat groups would not hesitate to exploit this resistance. Should the Israeli isolation to the north and northeast be broken, feelings against social normalization could be expected to erode more quickly.

Sadat's vision that Egypt and Israel could break the psychological barriers to Arab-Israeli peace rested upon the concept that ultimately Israeli public opinion would favor security (a general peace agreement) over territorial aggrandizement, i.e., the annexation of territories occupied by Israel after the 1967 war. Such a choice offered in Sadat's view a reasonable possibility that the agreement would later be endorsed by Jordan and Syria, since it would offer the best chance for both governments to recover the territories. The later Israeli action of annexing Jerusalem, whose status had remained legally ambiguous from 1967 to 1980, seriously undermined the potential of the Camp David accords. Further Israeli consideration of the annexation of the Golan Heights—an action apparently more and more accepted in Israel—would virtually end any hope that the Camp David peace process might be accepted by other Arab states.

Whether Egypt will pursue the relationship with Israel as single-mindedly after Israeli evacuation of all Egyptian territory is problematical. Indeed, one can assume Sadat believes no more in the inevitability and perpetuity of Israeli friendship than he does in the applicability of those characteristics with respect to Arab states. Presently, the cooperation is intimately connected to Sadat's objectives vis-à-vis the United States, as well, since that country must directly or indirectly fill much of the financial and political vacuum created by the Arab reaction to Sadat's initiative. Israel is less central to mid-term Egyptian foreign policy than the United States is, for the economic (both commercial and financial) input Israel can be expected to make to the Egyptian economy and, indeed, the maximum level of bilateral cooperation between the two countries must both be realistically assessed as very limited,[19] while the role of the United States, by contrast, could be significantly greater.

Neither does the new Arab opening represent great economic opportunities for Israel. Israel's exports duplicate Egypt's in non-high-technology areas, and most Egyptians prefer to import industrial and other sophisticated goods from Western Europe or the United States. Israel continues to aspire to a position as regional *entrepot* and as an exporter of industrial goods to Arab countries.[20]

An effective cooperative relationship must ultimately involve a certain level of trust, and trust has been noticeably absent on both sides of the Arab-Israeli problem for many years. Yet, it cannot be doubted that Egyptian behavior is beginning to lay some of the foundation of trust prerequisite to effective cooperation. If both governments continue to abide by the Camp David accords and their peace treaty, a substantial degree of mutual trust and agreed mutual expectations can conceivably emerge within only a few years. Sadat or his successors may easily coordinate several policy areas with Israeli leaders.

For both countries—immediately for Egypt, eventually for Israel—a major benefit of the current detente and developing cooperation lies in the potential for reducing budgetary outlays on defense.[21] Although the Israeli economy devotes a higher proportion of financial expenditures to defense,[22] Egypt is at least as adversely affected because of the limits on its skilled manpower reserves and because of the far greater needs of its larger population and its lower level of socioeconomic development.

IRAN

Shi'a Iran's interactions with other regional states has always been affected by the country's non-Arab character, affected far more than, for example, Sunni Pakistan's links to the Arab world. We have already discussed the demise of Iranian-Iraqi detente in the aftermath of the shah's deposition. It should be noted that other Gulf Arabs reflect Iraqi attitudes that extend so far as to envisage another

"Israel" in the form of "Zionist" Shi'ism in the Gulf. The vague resurrection of the claim to Bahrain,[23] the retention of the imperial annexations (Abu Musa and the Tunbs),[24] and the peripatetics of Shi'a Mullahs throughout the Gulf—all these developments have an ominous appearance in Baghdad and other Arab Gulf capitals.[25] Thus in spite of early signs that the Islamic Republic might improve Iran's ties to the Arab world through greater support of the PLO and opposition to Israel, in fact republican Iran has excited greater Arab concern than imperial Iran did. This was most evident during the Iran-Iraq war of 1980, when virtually all Arab states (except Syria and distant Libya) supported Iraq politically.

By contrast with the Arab world, Pakistan continues to enjoy cooperative relations with Iran. The two countries share several important security problems, including large Baluchi minorities believed by both to be exploited by Soviet subversive designs.

IRAQ

Iraq sits in a critical position. Closely linked throughout this century to the Levant and Palestine, Iraq is not strictly speaking a Levantine state. Nor is Iraq an Arabian peninsular country, but history and its location on the Gulf have also conspired to involve Iraq in peninsular affairs. Iraq *is* a Persian Gulf state and has taken an active role in security and other political issues of the Gulf. As a result of its historical role, then, Iraq is at the crossroads of the Gulf and the Levant and is one of only two regional countries actively involved in both theaters[26] (the other being Saudi Arabia[27]). For some years, and to a degree since the coup of 1958, Iraq has been "odd man out" in the Middle East. Relations with Jordan have never been characterized by warmth or substantive cooperation since that time; those with Saudi Arabia and the other Gulf states, including Iran, have generally been hostile to barely neutral; and ties with Syria have vacillated greatly between sometime cooperation and usual hostility. The only neighboring country with which Iaaq has enjoyed relatively consistent good relations is Turkey.

Since the early 1970s Iraq has led an uncharacteristically pragmatic course,[28] but like Syria under Assad it has continued to clothe its behavior in revolutionary rhetoric. As we have indicated, cooperative bilateral relations with its neighbors until now have not been a concomitant of Iraq's new moderation, and Iraq continued to be rather isolated in the Arab world. Perhaps the most startling example of this pragmatic but isolated course was Iraq's material assistance to the Lebanese Christians at a time when not one other Arab state provided them support.[29] Concurrent with the recent change in Iraq's leadership (to which we adverted in Chapter 1) have been the indications of new relations with its neighbors.

The recent moves by new President Saddam Hussein to consolidate his power have had a lasting impact on Iraqi-Syrian relations, as we have indicated. It is interesting to note, however, that Saddam Hussein has never been greatly in favor of union with Syria while he is in favor of increasing cooperation with Saudi Arabia and is a close friend of Crown Prince Fahd. Saddam Hussein's newly concentrated power has enabled him to turn Iraq away from Syria. At the same time, Iraq may continue to warm up to moderate nations such as Saudi Arabia. Saddam is known to hold attitudes sympathetic to the West in terms of business transactions, and Iraq's political orientation may shift more toward the West now that Hussein appears to be in full control.

The sharply increased moderate stance of Iraq is due to a variety of factors. That Iraqi oil, and resulting petroleum revenues, are a major consideration is clear. Iraqi elites recognize that they are in the midst of a critical period in their country's development. Although concerned about a number of political issues and threats, they are determined to bring about substantial development of Iraq. To accomplish this objective Iraqis seek to produce and sell large quantities of oil in order to use the revenue to import infrastructural development and advanced technology, and to create for Iraq a diversified, balanced, and dynamic economy. Yet, these goals can be accomplished only in political stability. Iraqi leaders know that the major petroleum markets (and hard currencies) are in the West along with the technology they seek.

The problems between Iraq and the Soviet Union are not only short-term economic conflicts. Iraqi leaders see few benefits to reliance on the Soviet Union. Distrusting the Russians, they have the luxury of choice now, since they are courted by Western Europe, and, given that luxury they will move toward the West and resist Soviet blandishments—unless, and except to the extent that, real, major, and immediate conflicts should place a high priority on short-term military readiness (e.g., the Soviet supply of spare parts for the 1980 war). Iraq's anti-Western image has always been a misleading façade. Most of Iraq's leading technocrats have been educated and trained in the West, many of them in the United States. A brief and limited experiment in trade with the Soviet Union proved unsatisfactory to those in charge of Iraq's development planning. Since 1973, trade with and technology transfer from the West have increased enormously,[30] while trade with the Soviet Union has plummeted to less than 10 percent of Iraq's foreign commerce.[31] Moreover, Iraq has attempted to attract some few Arab Americans to interact with Iraqi intellectuals and technocrats, although Baghdad remains loath—perhaps wisely—to entertain large numbers of Westerners on a long-term basis.[32]

It must be clear that the most pressing Iraqi interests are involved in the Persian Gulf and regions immediately contiguous to Iraq; relatively little is at stake in the Arab-Israeli realm, or in Palestine/Israel itself. The Arab-Israeli issue has been a vehicle, one of the few available vehicles, by which Iraq has attempted to assert regional influence, even if only as a constraint.[33] Yet, Iraqi decision-makers are eminently aware of the marginal nature of their own role in regard to the Arab-Israeli conflict, and, faced with what are to them more immediate and far-reaching challenges, Iraq's leaders will continue to place the highest priority on Iran and Syria. Iraqi initiatives should be viewed in this context.

Iraqi ties with Iran had achieved an acceptable level of neutrality after the 1975 treaty between the two countries. Both governments made sincere efforts to live up to the spirit and letter of the agreements, and the result was a clear-cut reduction in hostility and a marked increase in parallel thinking concerning Gulf security. The ouster of the shah reversed this process: both governments began acting provocatively toward each other, each interfering in the most sensitive internal affairs of the other. Ultimately, Saddam Hussein initiated hostilities against a weakened Iran. On the one hand, the war was merely the continuation of a conflict more than a millennium in age—the Arab-Persian conflict traditionally fought in the same general vicinity. On the other hand, the conflict was a war between today's Iran and Iraq, and poses significant implications for the subregional future. It will have something of a unifying impact on Iran, although probably not enough to overcome the centrifugation we have already discussed. It will provide a theme for Iranian revenge, just as the 1975 humiliation did to Saddam Hussein. Thus whereas the two countries could have continued their uneasy cooperation in the stability of Iran's dominance under the shah, a future of continued conflict is now virtually assured.

With Jordan and Saudi Arabia, Iraq's leaders will continue the present course of cooperation which has been aided by the shared (but different) oppositions to the Camp David and subsequent accords, profound concern over the nature of the Iranian revolution, and mutual interdependence. Visits between the leaders are more frequent, and many of the issues previously separating them have faded. All three countries' leaders are concerned about instability in the Gulf, all are aligned against Syria (though for different reasons), and all face some important internal problems themselves. When the Iraqis are at loggerheads with the extraregional friends—viz., the USSR—they wish the support or at least neutrality of their other neighbors. Moreover, Saddam believes Iraq has a regional role to play, and further that this role need not be as the radical, the outcast, of the Middle East. The broad support Iraq received from the Arab world in its war against Iran in 1980 is evidence of the effectiveness of Iraq's bold new strategy in the region.

King Hussein is deeply concerned at events in Syria. Instability in Syria would face Jordan with a number of proximate and significant questions. It has mortally weakened a one-time foe that had become his closest ally. While Syria was strong from 1973 to 1977 or 1978, the king pursued his cooperative schemes in a variety of areas and even, when necessary, redeployed his army to confront Iraq in order to strengthen Assad's hand in Lebanon.[34] Since then, the king has looked to Iraq as Jordan's protector and closest ally in the region. As Syrian power dissolved, Jordan established a *modus vivendi* and then a covert but intimate relationship with Iraq based on a far firmer foundation than opposition to the Camp David accords. The two governments share some behaviorally similar values, especially in the Gulf area, and King Hussein consciously exerted an effort to keep his Syrian alliance from alienating Iraq any further. The Iran-Iraq war provided the forum for public disclosure of the new Jordanian policy.

For Jordan, Iraq represents an important political option. Of its many donors, Jordan has found Baghdad the most dependable in following through with financial aid once promised. In addition to its munificence, however, Iraq represents a protector which relatively weak Jordan needs, as Syria's internal problems grow. Moreover, befriending Iraq assists Jordan to resist Saudi pressures. Finally, Jordan's Gulf mission, peripheral to Assad, is seen by the Iraqis to be of substantial political value. Iraq's leaders would like to present an alternative to Saudi hegemony on the Arab side of the Gulf, but Iraq's political past and contemporary rhetoric hamper its efforts and destroy its credibility among the traditional rulers of the Gulf.[35] By contrast, King Hussein has played an active and well-accepted role in the Gulf among these same rulers. The recent development of improved relations between Iraq and Jordan is an expression of both an increased mutuality of interests and an Iraqi desire to pull Jordan out of its close relationship with Syria. We have described the concordance of Amman's activities and Baghdad's interests in the Gulf and on the Arabian Peninsula. A further consideration is Saddam's perception that Jordan and its king constitute one of the best channels to the United States. Increasingly, Iraqi leaders recognize the importance and potential of interests shared with the United States. Thus Jordan represents both a window to the West (especially the United States) and a window on the Gulf.

Toward Saudi Arabia, by contrast, Iraq's leaders have made strong overtures of detente after years of hostility. They are, for example, playing a heavily Islamic theme. They have sought to maintain Saudi opposition to Camp David through suasion; *threats* have come not from the traditional enemy, Iraq, but, instead, from the traditional friend, the United States. Saudi elites continue to focus on their immediate area, and both the instability in Iran and Iraq's current problems with the Soviet Union give impetus to their new interest in Iraq, an interest already whetted and mediated by Jordan. Discussions between the two countries on security and police cooperation are only the most visible signs of their rapprochement.[36]

Thus both Jordan and Saudi Arabia are far along in their rapprochements with Iraq. Since both are intimately familiar with Iraq's political tides in recent times, it is unlikely either will swim too far. Jordan will of course try to secure financial benefits. Iraq's behavior vis-à-vis the PLO and Jordanian internal affairs has been a gauge of the speed and breadth of cooperation for Amman, and initial reactions to Iraq's role in this regard have been very positive. Yet, sensitive areas will be pursued only with great caution during the next five years, while general development strategy, political affairs affecting the region, and such military considerations as terminological differences will be addressed and partially coordinated. Hussein is likely to provide the same quality of support to Iraq now as was previously given to Syria—and that has already been evidenced with the king's strong backing during the Gulf war of 1980, when Jordan offered to send military personnel and whatever else Iraq might need. (In the event, Jordan and Saudi Arabia both served as rear area sites for the deployment of Iraqi aircraft, and Jordan also provided a safe channel for the shipment of supplies to Iraq.)

SAUDI ARABIA

Saudi alignments are in the process of change reflecting changing patterns of internal and international power. All of the three principal Arab confrontation states were recipients of Saudi financial largesse and political support until 1978.[37] Egypt's "separate peace" with Israel and Syria's vicissitudes have given Riyadh pause. We do not believe the Saudis will continue to isolate and punish Sadat privately as much as they will castigate him publicly.[38] Yet, certainly for the immediate present, Egypt can hardly be viewed as a Saudi ally.

Saudi attitudes toward Syria have been related to Syrian strength. While a Jordan-Syria alignment was barely acceptable, a Syrian-controlled bloc of Syria, Jordan, and Lebanon discomfitted Saudi leaders and caused[39] the shift toward improvement of relations with Iraq. Syria's inability to dominate Lebanon, though disappointing to the Saudis in terms of Lebanon, has been a reassurance, too. Syria's domestic problems raise some serious questions[40] in Saudi Arabia, but Muslim Brotherhood activity in Syria, which is symbolic of the troubles there, is also subject to some Saudi influence.[41] Hafez Assad distinguished himself as a canny leader on the Middle East scene with the ability to deal *strategically,* rather than tactically as recent Syrian leaders had done. However, the 'Alawi position had become so perilous by 1980 that Assad was sacrificing the strategic for the tactical. And the strategic cost appears to be first and foremost the alignment with Saudi Arabia.

The Jordanian-Saudi relationship has been very cooperative the last few years, and few allow the memories (and feelings) of house rivalries to surface frequently or meaningfully. Questions about Jordan's future are almost as important to conservative and insecure Saudi leaders as they are to the Jordanians, and those who assume that an assassination or coup in favor of a Palestinian government would necessarily convey control of the whole of Jordan to such a government do not understand the transnational linkages of many of the leading tribes and families of the interior with Saudi Arabia.[42]

Domestic Saudi events and the Soviet intervention in Afghanistan in 1979 will have a pronounced effect on Saudi foreign policy over the next five years. On the one hand, both events have reinforced leadership paranoia, elite suspicion of the Soviet Union, and determination to assist other countries in opposing the growth of Soviet influence in the Middle East, the Gulf, South Asia, the Horn of Africa, the Indian Ocean, and especially the Arabian Peninsula. On the other hand, Saudi leaders are much less confident of internal security than before and are therefore likely to put greater emphasis on national security issues than they have in the past.

To address the Soviet challenge Saudi Arabia will use its religious credentials in an attempt to mobilize the region's peoples and their consciousness. The Saudis will provide additional support to conservative, anti-Soviet regimes like that of Pakistan. (Clearly, Egypt presents a major policy dilemma to the Saudis.) Surprisingly, but commendably, Saudi leaders have already begun to try to open their political system more with new institutions resembling a constitution.

An immediate Saudi concern will be the Yemen Arab Republic, long under strong Saudi influence. Notwithstanding major interdependencies (approximately one million Yemeni laborers are in Saudi Arabia), the Saudis have neglected Yemen too long. There exists a growing Yemeni resentment that is beginning to reflect itself in Yemeni foreign policy, which has moved away from that of Saudi Arabia. It can be expected that the Saudis will exert substantial effort to reestablish Saudi influence in Yemen.

Major changes, then, can be expected in Middle East political alignments over the next five years. The principal factors underlying these changes will be the disintegration of the Arab coalition against Israel and the centrifugal forces at work within Iran, Syria, and Lebanon. While Israel will certainly not become an active partner in regional politics during this period, its relationship with its neighbors will change markedly, especially if Syria disintegrates into two or more states.

In the Gulf subregion the continued fractionation of Iran will affect alignments and foreign policies, combined as it will be with the forces of social change that must come to the area. It is unlikely but not at all impossible that several of the Gulf's traditional governments will be overthrown in the next five years. However, it is likely that diverse social pressures resulting from the influx of foreign nationals and ideas will affect these governments. Addressing the destabilizing influences of regional upheaval and domestic social change will be extremely difficult for the smaller Gulf states, especially those new to international politics such as the United Arab Emirates, Qatar, and Oman.

4

Regional Leadership Changes

Emerging and Declining National Powers

T HE MAJOR POWERS IN THE MIDDLE EAST have been Egypt, Iran, Israel, and Saudi Arabia, although the elements of national power were mixed quite differently for these countries. Israel's strength has been military power and political stability; Iran's, perceived military power, political confidence, financial resources, and economic growth; Saudi Arabia's, financial power; and Egypt's, political power derived from a past role as Arab leader. As Egypt's reputation wavered, Syria moved into position as a major power in the Levant, largely on the basis of political stability and situational military power.

In the 1980s, however, new leadership trends will become clear. In the wake of the Camp David accords and developments in the Gulf changes are already evident. Egypt's *regional role* seems destined for a temporary decline and later resurgence, although the domestic political strength of the Egyptian government may well increase. No longer will Iran or Syria be paramount regional powers. Israel and Saudi Arabia will continue to be major factors in regional developments, although their political styles may change. Iraq is destined to play a more important regional role, particularly in the Gulf. This chapter discusses these trends and their underlying causes.

EGYPT

Egypt continues and will continue to struggle with overwhelming demographic pressures—a problem some Egyptians feel is of catastrophic magnitude. These and resulting social and economic problems dwarf the political and military threats Egypt may encounter, though perhaps not the perception of such problems. The attempt to confront these problems does not constitute a withdrawal from the Arab world and the Middle East region, although because of the reaction to Sadat's Israel policy many seem to see such a withdrawal. The isolation of Egypt has the effect of diminishing the country's political power. Undoubtedly, Egyptian influence is far less than it was at the height of Nasser's pan-Arabist appeal. Moreover, the Sadat initiative and Camp David agreement have placed Egypt outside the mainstream of Arab political thinking. Egypt is strong enough and has sufficient cultural autonomy to withstand the social and political pressure associated with this isolation for a long time, but not forever. It is not the peace initiative that will hurt Sadat, even though it could be used by an opponent as a platform; rather, Sadat's true enemy is the economic hurdles Egypt must overcome.

We feel that Egypt's regional influence would normally continue to decline. However, the changes in the region are many, and we feel that the disintegration of Syria, major political changes in Lebanon, the subregional power vacuum, and Sadat's decisive approach to leadership will allow Egypt to retain greater influence than might otherwise be expected. Moreover, the disintegration in Syria and Lebanon as well as Jordan's dilemma on the West Bank issue suggest Egypt may not long be alone in coming to peace terms with Israel.

Anwar Sadat will continue to press ahead with Egypt's newfound partner at the government level, at least until all Egyptian territory is freed of Israeli occupation. At this level, then, Egypt will be less active in Arab councils than in the past, both willingly and as a result of the isolation the Arab world has imposed. Whether or not the projected disintegration of Syria takes place and that of Lebanon is completed, Egypt will emerge stronger if some of its basic economic problems are addressed and resolved.

If Cairo's influence in the Eastern Mediterranean and at the Arab world level is at a nadir, its position vis-à-vis the Indian Ocean–Red Sea–Gulf area and in terms of the United States and Israel is quite the opposite. By creating a hero image for himself in the United States, Sadat is the first Arab leader whose views carry substantial weight in American public opinion. Sadat has already begun to reap the benefits of this prestige by acquiring weapons systems few would have believed the U.S. Congress would permit any Arab state to procure. Similarly, by providing Israel a vested interest in the continuation of his administration and policies, Egypt has even gathered some indirect influence over Israeli attitudes and behaviors and has reinforced the accommodationist bloc in Israel.

Quite apart from the Arab-Israeli theatre, Egypt's staunch anti-Soviet position, outspoken support for the United States, and traditional African and Arab leadership role have put Egypt in the forefront of those concerned with regional stability and the role of military force in supporting stability. Sadat has taken an active and personal interest in the security of the Nile countries and of the Red Sea and Indian Ocean. Although Nasser's Yemen adventure[1] has not been forgotten in Saudi Arabia, Saudi elites look with favor on Sadat's anti-communism and zealous opposition to Soviet influence. It would not be at all surprising to see greater Egyptian-Saudi security cooperation in the future, possibly with the United States, notwithstanding Sadat's policy toward Israel.

During the next five years Egypt will retain its Western orientation, and Sadat will continue to maintain control over the various groups supporting and opposing his policies. Relations with the Soviet Union will not improve greatly during this period if Sadat continues to serve as president. If he is replaced, willingly or otherwise, Egyptian-Soviet relations will probably improve but only fitfully and not significantly by the end of the five years.

Relative to Israel, Egypt's military strength has declined since 1973. Although many systems are likely to be replaced over the next few years, Israel will retain a large margin of military superiority over Egypt. To the extent Sadat looks elsewhere for a threat, however, the decline in Egypt's strength is unimportant, because Egypt will retain a decisive edge over any proximate state (other than Israel) in conventional military power.[2]

Internally, the Sadat regime is stronger than many of its detractors realize, in part because of Egyptian political culture and in large part, too, because of the determination, courage, and foresight of Anwar Sadat. However, while Egypt can afford to be more independent of Arab currents than any other Arab state, even Egypt cannot remain isolated from the Arab world indefinitely. If Sadat loses power, it will be over domestic problems, but isolation in the Arab world will play an important part in his political demise. There are indications Sadat is aware of the urgency of this problem, and even stronger evidences that Saudi Arabia, for one, is seeking a covert rapprochement. As Egypt's president realizes, attraction of additional Arab support for the peace process (not necessarily the specific provisions of the Camp David accords) is vital to both the settlement and to Anwar Sadat.

IRAN

Since the popular revolution that resulted in the deposition of the shah, central government authority in Iran has steadily declined. The reason for this decline has been discussed in Chapter 1, and the results by now are clear. When the shah left Iran he took with him the only common denominator of Iran's integrity and nationalism and the closest approximation of legitimacy Iran has had or will have for some years to come. Not until the revolution consumes even more of its own will stability ensue. Meanwhile, Iran has lost its role as premier power in the Gulf for the foreseeable future.

The centrifugal forces loosed by the end of the shah's reign have manifested themselves along ideological, religious, ethnic, and regional dimensions. Of these the most widely noticed has been the Kurdish demand for autonomy. Moreover, because the Kurds are also found in Iraq, Syria, and Turkey, and because of the history of Kurdish secession movements in each of these countries, the international aspects of the Kurdish problem have also received some attention by foreign observers (and have been exploited by local authorities).

Kurdish nationalism is a time-honored Middle East problem. While each of the countries with Kurds has used this minority to create problems for one or more of the others, Middle East governments have usually refrained from support or have actually opposed secession when the threats to other governments became serious.[3] They do not seek a center of Kurdish nationalism with whom to compete for the loyalties of their own Kurds. Iraqi and Turkish elites, whatever they may think of Khomeini, have enough Kurdish problems already without promoting the existence of a Kurdish state to exacerbate them. Thus Iraqi support to Iran's Kurds may stop well short of the actuality of secession. And the Iraqis realize Tehran could be so weakened that the emergence of a Kurdish state might become inevitable.

By itself, the Kurdish struggle can go no further than autonomy. The central government in Tehran should be able to generate enough power to deal with a civil war in Kurdistan, even if it achieves no more than a stalemate, as Iraq accomplished, at best, with its own Kurdish insurgency in the 1960s. But Iran is ill prepared to deal with more than one insurgency, whether secessionist in nature or based on political opposition. Given the several minorities manifesting particularist attitudes, and the depth of their perceived social alienation, concurrent challenges of political violence could yet overwhelm Iran.

The intervening variable is Iraq, specifically the Iraqi invasion of Iran launched in September of 1980. On the one hand this invasion has clearly increased the level of *national* unity in Iran, Iranian nationalism. On the other hand, the inability of the once-powerful Iranian armed forces to defeat Iraq, or even to prevent the take-over of oil-rich Khuzistan, and the resulting social and economic hardships that clearly derived from Iran's virtually complete international isolation, have weakened the appeal and hold on power of the clerics. It is too early to say what effect these developments will have on Khomeini's personal following, but they only hasten the end of the clerical power base.

There can be no doubt of the depth of religious feeling in Iran, nor of the antipathy toward the shah. If the United States has received its share of the latter, this is hardly surprising in view of the common perception that the United States installed and protected the shah over the years. Unable to deal with the shah, the Iranian people took out their frustration on the United States. It is difficult to see how any government in Iran during the next few years can easily return to an acceptably cooperative relationship with the United States. (Of course, it is even more difficult to see why the United States government would seek to return to such a relationship if it means alienating Iraq.)

The momentum of anti-U.S. and Iranian nationalist behavior led to Iran's isolation and to pressures antipathetic to many of the interest groups extant in Iran as a result of the process of modernization. The result—even before the war with Iraq—was further degra-

dation of national unity, organization, and direction with the result
that the central government now confronts multiple centers of power,
each concerned about its own problems, with little muscle and less
legitimacy. The euphoric unanimity behind Ayatollah Khomeini has
dissipated, so that other figures and groups have returned to positions
of greater regional or sectoral popularity. Indeed, as a result of the
war, even the Iranian armed forces can no longer be discounted as
an alternative power base.

The Soviet intervention in Afghanistan and the Iraqi invasion
added ominous notes to the Iranian cacophony. While many Iranians
remain convinced the United States is Iran's greatest enemy, others
note the difference between Washington's response to the collapse
of the monarchy and to the hostage crisis, on the one hand, and
Moscow's response to the imminent collapse of the Hafizullah Amin
regime in Kabul, on the other. It is true that there is a body of
opinion in Iran that sees the Soviet action in Afghanistan as a more
direct and fundamental threat to Iran's integrity and therefore supports
the idea of supplying and in other ways assisting Afghan insurgents.
However, it is also true that to many in Iran, including Khomeini,
minority issues and questions of military threat are less significant
than the central challenge of articulating and implementing a truly
Islamic state and less significant than the theological issues this
challenge raises. That Khomeini and the Islamic Republican clerics
could remain obdurate concerning the American diplomatic hostages
at a time when, under attack, Iran desperately needed international
support, military spare parts, ammunition, and so forth amply demonstrates the degree to which this group is removed from the realities
of politics—and survival.

What is clear from all this is that Iran's role in the Middle
East has changed. From a regional power, Iran has become a regional
trouble-spot, and although much of the political violence resulting
from its weakness can be largely confined to the area currently
within the national borders of Iran, the political concerns and interests of many countries are involved, suggesting that the Persian Gulf
will be less stable and more tense than in the past, even after the
conclusion of the Iran-Iraq war. Iran will of course try to return to
the production and marketing of oil—assuming control of Khuzistan
(Arabistan) reverts to Tehran through negotiation, which is anything
but assured—but the country's leaders are likely to discover, as Iraq

did earlier, that optimum production of oil and investment of oil revenues do not seem to go hand in hand with political instability. Economically, as well as socially, politically, and militarily, Iran's strength has declined and will continue to want until political order, coherence, and direction are restored. Such a development is not in sight. At the same time, if the country is able to remain unified at all, the size of its population ordains a substantial role for Iran in the affairs of the subregion once its political house is in order.

If Iran's strength has eroded, it is not only the centrifugation within the country that may lead to regional turmoil. Among the forces unleashed in the anti-imperial revolution (for it was more anti-imperial in spirit than any other singly definable motif) in Iran was that of Shi'a consciousness. Islamic fundamentalism is clearly affecting the Middle East profoundly; this is a cyclical phenomenon that was already in evidence before the events in Tehran. Shi'a awareness, however, should it continue to grow, may deeply and significantly alter the course of Gulf developments. Unquestionably, the governments throughout the Gulf are very narrowly and anachronistically based. More clearly still, the large Shi'a communities within those city-states, and even in Iraq, have been discriminated against or ignored in the past. Just the threat of rising Shi'a consciousness has already begun to exert a powerful influence on official behavior, and it remains to be seen to what extent or in what direction this element of potential instability may shape the region.

ISRAEL

Despite continuing and growing economic difficulties, social problems, and the increase in military prowess of the Arab world, Israel is and will remain the single most powerful country in the Middle East, from a military standpoint. Manpower figures concern some Israeli military planners for the 1980s, but at least to this time Israel's technological acquisitions have more than offset hostile manpower improvements. Because of the deterioration of the Arab coalition confronting Israel and in view of the internal disorders and their likely aftermath in Syria, practical Israeli military superiority over "the Arabs" will increase during the next five years. Israel's political influence in the region is limited to the immediate bordering states—

Egypt, Jordan, Lebanon, and Syria—and Saudi Arabia. During the next five years Israel will further escape the isolation that has lasted so long, however. Lebanon or the Christian Mediterranean state that succeeds it will maintain and expand the open relationship the Lebanese Christians already maintain with Israel. If an 'Alawi state emerges farther north along the coast, that state too may maintain cooperative relations with Israel, though less close than the Christian Lebanese. Eventually, Jordan may also be attracted to this grouping, but despite all of these changes Israel's influence on political developments will continue to be largely confined to its immediately surrounding governments.

Israelis have long sought to play economic and political roles commensurate with their military power in the region. Perhaps as a reaction to wars from 1948 to 1973, Israeli elites have dreamed of a time when their country might "lead" the Middle East. Even now it is likely that many Israeli politicians and citizens see Israel as a Middle East "leader." However, it is clear that Arab countries distinguish between dealing with Israel, on the one hand, and accepting Israel, on the other. Egyptians believe Israel must go *through Egypt* to deal with the Arab world. Certainly, Israel is not going to be an acknowledged leader of the Arab world. Probably, Israelis should look to Iran's example under the shah—a regional power, but never fully accepted as a legitimate actor in *Arab* politics.

In some respects Israel will be weaker than at present. Social divisions between Israeli Jews may continue to increase, especially if the uniting factor of the Arab threat is reduced. The future of the Israeli Arabs, too, will continue to be problematical, as demographic factors make them an ever-larger component of Israel.[4] However, the social distance and alienation between Arab and Jew may diminish, if the Arab-Israeli confrontation abates to some extent as a result of the developments we have projected. If it does not, the Arab-Jewish relationship in Israel, already strained, will become even worse.

The Israeli economy is not likely to soon prosper from the new Arab ties. Meanwhile, it is becoming more and more dependent on American financial and military subvention. If Israel's leaders decide they can afford to reduce defense outlay in the face of a clearly diminishing threat, they can at least somewhat ameliorate a part of the country's economic burdens. It is not yet clear that the Israeli elite would be prepared to take this step.

Some Israeli groups reached the conclusion, particularly in the aftermath of the Egyptian-Israeli peace treaty which required the abandonment of the Israeli settlements in the Sinai, that preemptive political action was the best policy as regards other occupied territories. While such action was supported by diverse groups for quite different reasons, the implications of the movement are significant. In 1980 Jerusalem was formally annexed to Israel. Although this action aroused the ire of the whole Muslim world, the impact on settlement was limited, since no one Arab state had clear title to Jerusalem, and since the importance of Jerusalem to the Islamic community might still be assured through special provisions arrived at during peace negotiations. (At least so many thought.) However, following the successful attempt to persuade the Knesset to annex Jerusalem, additional bills were advanced to follow the same course with respect to the Golan Heights. If the Golan Heights should be annexed to Israel, how can Syria even entertain the idea of a peaceful settlement? How can Egypt pretend for long that its separate peace is in fact a viable track toward a general peace? How can the United States argue to the Arab states that its policy is in fact progressing toward an acceptable settlement? The new approach in Israeli politics, which takes full advantage of the difficult political climate for those who appear too "soft" on the Arab issue, may raise insuperable obstacles to settlement and therefore to the continuity of Egyptian-Israeli peace.

SYRIA

Syria's power and role in the Middle East are on the decline. As we have indicated, communal tensions are seriously affecting the ability of the central government to maintain public safety, in both Sunni and 'Alawi areas. The continuing murder of 'Alawis even in Damascus is a token of the deep feelings harbored by Syria's Sunni majority against the 'Alawis. Consequently, the active and once forward-looking foreign policy of Syria is of necessity falling victim to the necessity to protect the security of the regime. The role, level, and activities, and even the presence, of the Syrian Arab Deterrent Forces (ADF) units in Lebanon will be determined by domestic events in Syria.

The Syrian armed forces are still substantial in size and capabilities by third world or Middle East standards. Although they have no sustained offensive capabilities against Israel—less even than in 1973—and only marginal offensive capabilities against Iraq, they constitute a formidable static defense against the former and an overwhelming defense against the latter, but only as long as the regime holds together. Substantial numbers of Syrian army personnel—approximately 30,000—have been deployed continuously to Lebanon for over three years, greatly reducing the overall capabilities, and subverting the morale and discipline, of the army.

Borders—even those arbitrarily delineated by the colonial suzerain—have been viewed as sacrosanct in the decolonization and postcolonial periods.[5] With few exceptions (e.g., Bangladesh), boundaries have been stable irrespective of the disorder within or across them. Thus it is almost inconceivable to envisage major changes in Middle East borders. We suggest, however, that there exists a strong possibility that the Middle East regional system may soon go through fundamental changes in the Levant.

The small 'Alawi minority cannot forever dominate and control as large a state as Syria when the majority Sunnis are opposed to 'Alawi domination.[6] As the Sunnis begin to work more effectively to bring about the paralysis of 'Alawi control, Assad will be forced to choose between losing the battle to control Syria and undertaking the establishment of a separate 'Alawi state. The reasons such an 'Alawi state is possible and may be successful despite the Zeitgeist that weighs heavily against redefining polities are several:

• Their geographical concentration in the Latakia and Tartus areas, where they are the majority, gives 'Alawis an easily and clearly delimited area.[7]

• 'Alawi control of the armed forces, especially the Syrian Army, means that military equipment and personnel to defend the nascent state's integrity should not be lacking, while the Syrian armed forces without the 'Alawis will be disorganized at first and vulnerable to sabotage.

• Israeli support for the new state may be available if Assad is prepared to take the route of some of the Lebanese Christians.

The new state will be readily accessible to sources of foreign support since it will be adjacent to Christian-dominated Lebanon (see below) and has two major harbors at Latakia and Tartus.

• Moreover, the withdrawal of the Syrian Army from Lebanon,

a necessary end or precursor of 'Alawi separatism, may well result in the establishment of a Christian state running from the Syrian border to either the Litani River or the present border with Israel. The leaders of such a state may join cause[8] with the new "Alaouites,"[9] especially in view of the Phalange-Syrian rapprochement, and 'Alawi control of and interest in the Beka'a and northern Lebanon.[10]

A less likely but still possible additional development that might assist the secession of an 'Alawi state would be the creation of a Druze state.[11] The Druzes are a large and important minority in eastern Lebanon and Syria.[12] Like the 'Alawis they tend to be geographically concentrated, and they too have been prominent in the Syrian Army. Although there is a greater tradition of particularism and secessionism among the Druzes than among the 'Alawis, this difference is more than offset by the current respective positions in the control of the military. It would be far more difficult for the Druzes to defend a separate state than for the 'Alawis. Only a virtual state of anarchy in Syria would offer sufficient protection (unless Israel provided support), and Jordan and Iraq, as well as other states, might well step in before the Syrian situation deteriorated to that extent.

The result of these possibilities[13] is the clear decline of Syria's role and power in the Middle East. A major question is the political future of Syria if or, as we believe, when the 'Alawis secede. Leadership patterns have been greatly altered by sectarian and regional conflicts within Syria, as well as by Ba'th party behavior. One cannot exclude the possibility of a Jordanian or even an Iraqi role, particularly if a vacuum of leadership begins to appear more like anarchy, if a civil war breaks out, or if Djebel Druze moves toward a secessionist posture. An opposition political leadership has only begun to take form (in Amman and Paris), and if it does not have time to unify Saudi views and power (through the Muslim Brotherhood) may also have substantial influence on the emergence of indigenous leaders. A Syria partitioned by Iraq and Jordan cannot be wholly discounted.

SAUDI ARABIA

During the next five years Saudi Arabia will retain an extremely important role in the Middle East and in the world economy. Confronting social problems at home and complex and threatening situations in its foreign relations, the Saudi monarchy will nevertheless remain stable and will continue to exercise great influence as a result of its commercial and financial position.

Social change fed by wealth and by the influx of foreign ideas and foreign nationals will be the monarchy's largest single challenge. Attenuated by the location of the oil fields vis-à-vis the country's small population, the strength of Wahhabism and cultural confidence (or arrogance), the societal stresses of modernization versus traditionalism, of Bedouin values versus those concomitant with an industrial society—these strains will certainly present problems for Saudi Arabia. We believe, however, that the Saudis are far better equipped to deal with them than was Iran. Monarchy has not undermined its roots in the peninsula as it did in Iran; the people are far more homogeneous and the government more open; and that government has a much smaller population to work with. This is not to say the modernization problem may not be destablizing; it is only to say that we believe the monarchy will be able to manage it for the next five years.

The seizure of the Grand Mosque in Mecca in December 1979 by approximately 300 dissidents probably represents a much higher and more widespread level of dissent than the government is prepared to acknowledge. The tribal affiliations of some of the dissidents[14] have raised important danger signals that Saudi leaders are too sensitive to ignore. The result of the Mosque episode will certainly be greater attentiveness to internal security and a less complacent attitude about the loyalty of the Saudi population to the royal government. However, the Afghan invasion, by reinforcing existing Saudi fears of Soviet imperialism, will of necessity divert at least a part of the new security concerns to the external threat.

Another problem Saudi Arabia may face in terms of effectively exercising the power it derives from its financial resources is the quality and unity of its leadership. Too many observers insist on judging the effectiveness of Saudi leadership on the basis of coup potential, on the one extreme, or the existence of differing views on the other. Saudi government has never been as centralized or insulated as most Arab governments are or most observers believe. While it is true that the king has in two periods—King 'Abd al-Aziz ibn-Sa'ud and King Faisal ibn 'Abd al-Aziz—been in virtually complete control, the royal family has still been important since the death of King 'Abd al-Aziz. In Chapter 1 we discussed the decision-making process, and the importance of consensus is clear. The processes of give-and-take and of family participation continue to be a strong binding force in the kingdom. That the royal family has its dissidents cannot be gainsaid; but the government is probably as stable as any in the region, certainly including the democracies. Indeed, it is the ability to air dissenting views within the family and tribes that are the hallmarks of Saudi administration. The proliferation of armed forces and of important princes is a primitive system of checks and balances, and in many ways the administrative form is, like the Bedouin tradition from whence it came, a sort of representative government. Whether this highly personalized system can adapt to the greater velocity of interest articulation characteristic of modernization remains to be seen. But it should survive the next five years.

No contemporary Saudi figure has taken the mantle of leadership left by the death of Faisal ibn 'Abd al-Aziz. Crown Prince Fahd was believed likely to be the dominant figure in intra-Saudi councils, but foreign policy leadership has been divided among the king and several of the senior princes. It is very possible that a more clear-cut leadership pattern will emerge over the next five years, but it is at least equally possible that no single personality will dominate, and highly unlikely that any one of the princes will be as dominant as the late King Faisal was. The result of this divided leadership may well be contradictory behavior and indecision. Saudi Arabia will not act as firmly or predictably as it did during Faisal's last years. Consequently, the country's regional power may be diluted through reactive rather than active policy, especially if the Saudi decision elite does not coordinate its policies with another influential country— Iraq, Egypt, or the United States.

Finally, Saudi power may be diluted through the adoption of a "tout-azimuth" foreign policy. Concerning themselves with the Gulf, the Peninsula, the Indian Ocean, the Eastern Mediterranean, and the Horn of Africa, Saudi elites may find their resources are spread far too thin. Even Saudi Arabia has not sufficient disposable wealth after development investment to buy off all interested parties and eliminate all threats in so broad an arena. To be sure, the priority remains firmly on the Arabian Peninsula, but the disturbing tendency to react in each direction to events that may pose a threat could easily reduce the limited credibility Riyadh now maintains.[15] The move to improve relations with Iraq shows, however, that Saudi leaders are aware of this problem. Their priorities remain the Peninsula and then the Gulf. If they retain cooperative ties with the West, the concerted efforts of the kingdom and the United States should keep Saudi Arabia in a position of leadership in spite of the weaknesses we have cited.

IRAQ

Iraq has long been the sleeping giant of the Middle East. Its population, resource base, location, and history are all conducive to regional leadership. Yet, since independence and particularly since the establishment of the republic in 1958, aspirations have been thwarted by political problems. Principal among these problems have been national unity and political stability.

For years, the secessionist impulse of the Kurds forced Iraq to allocate substantial sums to fight the Pesh Merga which, under Mulla Mustafa Barzani's leadership, nevertheless was able to maintain control of much of Kurdistan. The Kurdish insurgency alternated with political instability or destabilizing conflicts with outside powers to sap Iraqi resources. Thus whenever it appeared that Iraq might move forward to assume greater regional leadership, one of these debilitating forces reappeared to keep Iraq out of the leadership role. A historian, observing the systematic recurrence of such phenomena, would be loath to project a brighter future.

Yet, Iraq's strengths are often camouflaged by its historical weaknesses. Iraqi oil resources are extensive, thought now to be second in the area only to those of Saudi Arabia. Traditional rivals Iran and Syria are weak and constitute no real threat to Iraq. Baghdad's isolation has been broken, and Iraq has become a leader in the Arab world in the opposition to the Khomeini regime and its policies, to the Camp David agreements, and to Soviet influence. Although Iraq retains a highly xenophobic perspective—which, incidentally, may protect the country against destabilizingly rapid social change—the degree has been modulated, and Iraq's ties with the West are growing rapidly. This movement away from reliance on Soviet and Eastern technology and weapons is based largely on Iraqi perceptions of Western and Japanese technological superiority, but also partly on Iraq's desire to lessen the need for Soviet presence in the country. Utilization of Western capabilities does not suggest that Iraqi leaders will follow U.S. policy in the Middle East to any large extent; nor does it mean that Iraq has ceased regarding the Soviet Union as a potentially valuable friend. The Ba'th regime's primary objective is maintaining its hold on power; the Ba'th is more than willing to take advantage of whatever benefits either the West, including the United States, or the Soviet Union can provide.

Ironically, Iraq's desire for stability in the Gulf area is directly related to the decision to proceed with an invasion of Iran in 1980. Iraqi apprehensions about the Islamic revolution in Iran impelled Iraq toward a rapprochement with one of its principal long-time rivals, Saudi Arabia. Once the entente of status-quo powers, Iraq, Jordan, and Saudi Arabia, was established, the groundwork was laid to undermine what was seen as the greatest threat to Gulf stability, Iran and its revolutionary regime. This concern with stability has also led to cooperation with Saudi Arabia to keep oil prices from rising too steeply and thus crippling Western economies.[16]

Apart from the Kurds, whose potential for disruption has been significantly reduced as a result of Iraqi resettlement and other policies, the major problems still facing Iraq are the relatively narrow base of leadership and the politicization of the army. Those who compared the Syrian and Iraqi power bases must have come away with the realization that until communal alienation reached an unacceptable level Syria's leadership was inherently more stable. Assassination cannot be excluded in any political system, but short of assassination a coup in Syria had become almost impossible by the time of the October War.[17] Communal tensions are now rapidly reaching unacceptable levels there, and we do not expect the current government to be able to maintain control for more than a year— probably less. Still, Assad has reached the position where virtually all 'Alawis could be trusted, a much broader power structure than exists in Iraq where even those closest to Saddam Hussein may participate in a conspiracy to oust him.

Despite its narrow power base, the Ba'th regime has governed Iraq for over a decade now, and has constructed institutionalized channels of information and decision-making. Infrastructural concentration in past economic development is beginning to pay dividends, and Iraq's economy may be—barring new political crises—at a real take-off point.

The growth of the Iraqi armed forces has been an effective symbol of Iraq's increased power. Iraq's military was long reputed to be the most ill-trained and -disciplined troops of any major Arab army, was known for abysmal gunnery and nonexistent leadership, and had little experience in the conduct and management of modern military operations. (The Iraqi participation in the October War was in a support role after all, and was carefully limited by the Syrians. Most of the Iraqi military experience derived from the counter-insurgency operations against the Kurds inside Iraq, a very different type of military situation.) Politicization of the military and the basic skills and experience levels of armed forces personnel place a ceiling on the performance level to which Iraqi armed forces may aspire. Certainly, their effectiveness in the war with Iran disappointed many observers who had erroneously concluded that Iraq was the new Arab military giant. It is important to remember that new equipment—which Iraq had—is not very important absent highly skilled manpower to use the equipment optimally.

All the above notwithstanding, Iraq's military capabilities can be expected to increase significantly. Iraqi leaders should learn much from the 1980 hostilities. For the first time, they will have a firm and clear grasp on the greatest problem areas they face. This set of "lessons learned" should stand them in good stead to improve the quality of Iraqi armed forces, even if it will not change the underlying limitations we have already noted. In addition, the deterioration of Iran and Syria, Iraq's enemies, constitutes a growth in Iraqi power by default, since power is relative.

Iraq is changing. If the separatist tendencies of the Kurdish minority can be overcome and the representational concern of the Shi'a majority contained, Iraq with its substantial oil income and potential for greatly increased revenues has an opportunity to become the most important and decisive single actor in the Middle East. In the past, however, domestic considerations have always limited Iraq's role. The narrow base of the present government suggests that internal factors may continue to play a limiting role, even if reduced in effect. The armed forces remain questionable, but the overall power and influence of Iraq will increase as a function of the weaknesses of Iran and Syria.

REGIONAL POWER, REGIONAL POLITICS, AND REGIONAL SUBSYSTEMS

Over the next five years, two Persian Gulf states will emerge as the most influential Middle Eastern countries. Israel will remain the most powerful country in the region, and even after manpower ceilings are attained in the early 1980s Israel will completely dominate the military equation in the Eastern Mediterranean/Levant arena. However, Israel's political influence will continue to be limited to its immediate area. Similarly, as a result of Sadat's (presumably temporary) departure from the Arab world, Egypt's political paramountcy in that community will continue to be restricted unless Israel's isolation is shattered elsewhere beyond the Sinai or Sadat moves away from Israel. (As long as the focus of Egyptian policy is the United States, changes in the approach to Israel can only be attempted with the greatest caution.) The Levant will be fundamentally altered by the communal separatism already in evidence there. A Christian (or Christian/Shi'a-dominated) state in Lebanon is probable, and an 'Alawi state along the Mediterranean littoral of what is now Syria may also eventuate. Indeed, even a Druze state is not altogether unlikely in Djebel Druze and the Shuf area of Lebanon. These areas will not be responsive to Iraqi power but will probably entertain some form of association with Israel.

The result of the changes we are summarizing is the strong possibility of a shift in the locus of regional power to the Gulf. Of course, to the extent the changes may lead to a settlement of the Arab-Israeli conflict we must anticipate less shift in the subregional military power balance, but perhaps an accelerated shift in the political power balance. On its face, this proposition seems self-contradictory: With less conflict, and with greater concentration on cooperation and on the productive employment of national resources, the political and economic power of the Eastern Mediterranean region should increase even in the face of (and perhaps assisted by) the decline of certain of its states. The apparent contradiction is explained by the *perceptual* base of political power.[18]

Power is influence. Essentially, national power is the ability to influence other states to behave in certain ways (though these reactions may be contrary to one's desires). Thus the degree to which nation B is persuaded to respond *because of* nation A is a measure of A's power, whether B's responsive behavior is cooperative with (supportive of) or conflictive with (subversive of) A's objectives. What has kept the Eastern Mediterranean at the forefront of world attention and led to that area's being treated as the core of the Middle East is the high conflict level there with the great potential for a superpower confrontation resulting from the outbreak of hostilities. In fact, the resources of the Middle East that are of greatest importance to the rest of the world, and at least arguably of greatest importance to the Middle East itself, today lie in the Gulf subregion, not the Eastern Mediterranean. To the extent the Arab-Israeli conflict abates, to the extent it begins to appear similar in structure and properties[19] to other third world conflicts, its salience will diminish. This diminution in salience means it will exert less and less *influence* over other states' policies relative to other policy problems.

Today, and for the next decade, the petroleum of the Gulf states—particularly Saudi Arabia and Iraq—will be critical to the economies of the West, vital to Western defense planning and operations, and central to the international monetary system. Conflicts among Gulf states—between Iran and Iraq, Iran and Saudi Arabia, and possibly again between Iraq and other Arab states, for example—loom large as threats to the stability of the flow of precious mineral resources from the Gulf. A less commonly considered problem, however, may become even more threatening: disintegration of the polities in the Gulf subregion. Political disintegration is a process already well under way, as we have seen, in Iran, Lebanon, and Syria. Spread of the disease to Iraq, Saudi Arabia, and the Gulf's city-states is a real, and ominous, possibility.

5

U.S. Policy in the Emerging Middle East

S INCE WORLD WAR II American Middle East policies have been driven by two conflicting approaches—on the one hand, to view the region in terms of the strategic U.S. competition with the Soviet Union; on the other, to deal with the Middle East on its own terms and for its own sake. This ambivalence in American policy has weakened both interests and is particularly lamentable at a time when direct U.S. interests in the Middle East have become vital.

Notwithstanding the manifest importance of the Middle East, including the Arab-Persian Gulf, to the United States, this country has attempted to interact with that region for several years without the benefit of a general strategy or a regional policy designed to optimize the realization of American interests. An area as complex and as characterized by conflict as the Middle East necessarily poses critical problems of choice at times. Without a general strategy, policy is inconsistent and policies are often incompatible.

We have criticized the step-by-step method to a Middle East settlement favored by former Secretary of State Kissinger. Such an approach undermines the long-term prospects of settlement by misconstruing the integral nature of Middle East problems and needlessly increasing the costs of even small steps toward a peace. Yet, despite our dissent from the policy, the period from 1973 to 1976 did see progress, and progress *in the context* of a general strategic understanding of the Middle East and its relationship to the United States. Indisputably, this period laid the foundation for Anwar Sadat's own initiative.

Since the Sadat initiative, however, American policy has been to "muddle through." Camp David can only become a triumph for peace, for American policy, and for American "full partnership" if it is followed by a strategy to bring about autonomy on the West

Bank, to arrest renascent Israeli expansionist legislation, to clarify the purposive ambiguities of Camp David, and to attract Jordanian and Saudi participation rather than secure it through a possibly evanescent perception of Soviet threat. Indeed, the local concept of a Soviet threat is misunderstood by many American policy-makers. While specific events may heighten the sense of danger from Soviet behavior or "communism" for brief periods, failure to resolve the Palestinian problem is seen by even the most conservative Arab governments as the greater danger.[1]

As the 1980s begin, the United States is confronted with a complex and dangerous situation in the Middle East. Specifically:

• The Soviet intervention in Afghanistan places USSR troops close to the oil fields of the Arab-Persian Gulf and raises the spectre of Soviet control over these vital resources.

• An Islamic resurgence with a substantial anti-American caste[2] is sweeping across the Muslim world.

• Egyptian-Israeli talks on Palestinian autonomy are stalemated, East Jerusalem has been formally annexed, and Golan annexation is threatened—mooting the hope for additional support for and participation in the Camp David peace process and leaving no clear solution to the Palestinian problem.

• Increasing instability in several key countries suggests a possible return to the days of frequent regime changes.

• American credibility is more suspect than ever before, and these new challenges to the United States further erode the image of the United States as a dependable ally.

FACTORS OF CHANGE

Over the last three decades U.S. policy has often placed this country in opposition to the governments and peoples of the Middle East. We believe a combination of factors has provided the United States a unique opportunity to act in its own interest and in accordance with political trends and will in the Middle East. These factors are: Soviet intervention in Afghanistan; the Islamic resurgence; the failure of the opposition to the Camp David peace process; and the end of America's "Vietnam syndrome."

Opposition to the Soviet intervention in Afghanistan is virtually unanimous in the Middle East.[3] Whether based upon concern about Soviet intentions toward their own regimes or political or religious principle, all Middle East governments, justifiedly or otherwise, sense that this is an important and sinister new development for their region. (It is not necessarily true, we hasten to add, that this sense is widely shared among the populace of these countries.) None alone, however, has the resources to respond appropriately—to reinforce the political independence and territorial integrity of the regional states. For this counterpoise to a perceived Soviet threat they *must* look to the United States. For those who have long opposed Soviet influence—e.g., Sadat's Egypt, Israel, Jordan, Saudi Arabia—the Soviet action in Afghanistan provides an opportunity publicly to express solidarity with the United States and alarm about Soviet intentions. For others, the Soviet behavior has been a useful reminder of basic differences between the superpowers in their treatment of third world states and peoples.

The growth of Islamic fervor has been noted by Western observers principally because of the religious tone of the Iranian revolution.[4] In fact, however, an Islamic resurgence has been under way for some time across most of the Muslim world.[5] It was observable at least a year before the Iran events in places like Jordan, Egypt, and Syria.[6] While this renascent Islamic consciousness has appeared to manifest an anti-American hue, in large part because of Iran, in fact Muslims generally feel far more antipathetic to communism and more socially uncomfortable with Russians and the Soviet Union.[7] (In Islam, Christians are seen to believe in the same God as Muslims, after all, and Jesus is also a prophet in Islam.) Moreover, American restraint in its confrontation with a Muslim country (e.g., Iran) can be contrasted with the bloody Soviet hand in Afghanistan.

A third factor in creating important new opportunities for the United States is the failure of opposition to the Camp David accords.[8] To date, Egypt has demonstrated independence from the Arab world rather than dependence on Arab support. The development of Egyptian-Israeli relations has proceeded inexorably toward full normalization,[9] and the Arab "front-line" states that do have an interest in the outcome—Jordan and Syria—recognize their bargaining position has deteriorated and may continue to deteriorate, rather than improve.

Finally, and also of capital importance, Middle East elites

were eminently aware of America's Vietnam syndrome, which precluded virtually any activist role involving intelligence or military operations in the third world.[10] U.S. reactions to the Iran crisis, which concerned many regional leaders as they seemed to go too far and threaten a response that might have forced them all to condemn U.S. action, and to Soviet intervention in Afghanistan confirm their conclusion that the United States may be newly prepared to take an active role in the Middle East, including the Gulf, once again.

PRIORITIES AND A STRATEGY FOR THE 1980s

There should be no question that the principal U.S. *regional* interest in the Middle East is the oil of the Gulf/Arabian Peninsula area. This oil is important to the United States and essential to the vitality of NATO and Japan. However, the United States also has a *global* interest that goes beyond any tangible resources associated with the Middle East. This global interest is the credibility of the United States as a superpower, both as opponent and as ally. Other important interests include:

- avoidance of a conflict with the Soviet Union;
- denial of significant Soviet influence over the Middle East;
- security of U.S. strategic assets;
- security of friendly powers; and
- maintenance of U.S. freedom of action.

American objectives are intended to support these interests. Policies are the practical steps by which a country seeks to optimize the realization of its objectives. That is, one country's interests are sometimes mutually antagonistic. So, too, are objectives. It is left to national policies to structure and orchestrate behavior in such a way that objectives are *optimally* realized, with some balance between competing goals.

The Arab-Israeli Sector

It has long been felt that the Arab-Israeli conflict is the single most destructive element in terms of the achievement of American goals in the Middle East. It threatens access to and availability of oil; it undermines U.S credibility by suggesting America acquiesces in the occupation of the territory of countries long closely associated with the United States and by continually raising questions about American constancy in support of Israel when Washington undertakes to resolve the conflict; it suggests bias against, or at least apathy toward Jews (in Israeli eyes) or Muslims (in Arab eyes) or Arabs (in Christian and other Arab eyes); it both threatens a confrontation with and facilitates regional penetration by the Soviet Union; and it undermines the security of U.S. strategic assets and cooperative relations with the countries of the Middle East. Americans who know the Middle East understand that Arab peoples cannot and will not "just accept" the situation. Neither should Israelis be expected or encouraged to live in a hostile environment, surrounded by enemies and perpetually in the shadows of another war.

We have identified some fundamental changes taking place in the Middle East, and these changes may materially improve security and long-term stability as well as the tractability of the Arab-Israeli problem, even if they assume short-term instability and low-level conflict. Whether or not these changes eventuate, the United States has become a "full partner" in the peace process and has important reasons to take an active role in achieving what we think is a practical and feasible settlement.

Contrary to widespread belief, the general outline of a settlement is clear. It has been articulated in bits and pieces throughout the voluminous literature of the conflict, but is best summarized in a 1975 Brookings Institution report:

Security. All parties to the settlement commit themselves to respect the sovereignty and territorial integrity of the others and to refrain from the threat or use of force against them.

Stages. Withdrawal to agreed boundaries and the establishment of peaceful relations carried out in stages over a period of years, each stage being undertaken only when the agreed provisions of the previous stage have been faithfully implemented.

Peaceful relations. The Arab parties undertake not only to end such hostile actions against Israel as armed incursions, blockades, boycotts, and propaganda attacks, but also to give evidence of progress toward the development of normal international and regional political and economic relations.

Boundaries. Israel undertakes to withdraw by agreed stages to the June 5, 1967 lines with only [presumably minor] modifications as are mutually accepted. Boundaries will probably need to be safeguarded by demilitarized zones supervised by UN forces.

Palestine. There should be provision for Palestinian self-determination, subject to Palestinian acceptance of the sovereignty and integrity of Israel within agreed boundaries. This might take the form either of an independent Palestine state accepting the obligations and commitments of the peace agreements or of a Palestine entity voluntarily federated with Jordan but exercising extensive political autonomy.

Jerusalem. . . . [As a minimum]
—there should be unimpeded access to all of the holy places and each should be under the custodianship of its own faith;
—there should be no barriers dividing the city which would prevent free circulation throughout it; and
—each national group within the city should, if it so desires, have substantial political autonomy within the area where it predominates.

Guarantees. It would be desirable that the UN Security Council endorse the peace agreements and take . . . other actions to support them . . . . In addition, there may well be need for unilateral or multilateral guarantees to some or all of the parties, substantial economic aid, and military assistance pending the adoption of agreed arms control measures.[11]

It is probably fair to note that although Palestinian self-determination continues to be a necessary ingredient in a settlement, the scope of self-determination is less clear. Most governments in the Middle East would be more comfortable with a Palestinian entity linked to Jordan, "but exercising extensive political autonomy," than with a sovereign Palestinian state. Similarly, even before annexation of Jerusalem in 1980 the significant changes Israel was making in the demographic composition and layout of Jerusalem were having an undeniable effect on the nature of the agreements that were feasible for that city.

That the general substance of a settlement is apparent has not facilitated its achievement or even the articulation of a framework that is accepted by all the parties. In this respect, the Camp David "framework agreements" and the subsequent treaty between Egypt and Israel constitute a *process* that may (or, of course, may not) attract the participation of Jordan and Saudi Arabia. What is important about these agreements is less their specific provisions than their ability, as a coherent vehicle, to maintain *progress* toward a general settlement. If Jordan and Saudi Arabia could be attracted to join in the peace process at the *cost* of the Camp David accords—that is, with the agreement by *all* parties that some new framework was more appropriate—they will have served their purpose admirably. (Annexation of the Golan Heights by Israel, however, may inter both the agreements *and* the process and will certainly grievously damage American *bona fides* in the region.)

The United States has undertaken the burden of "full partnership" on its own. While U.S. credibility may have been limited with respect to the conflict earlier, the two are now directly and extensively associated. We believe it is imperative for the United States to propel the talks and to assist both sides in making the sacrifices required for a viable compromise. By "assist" we mean the United States must establish incentives and disincentives to support a settlement that will be acceptable to Egypt, Israel, Jordan, Saudi Arabia, and the Palestinians.[12]

It is our belief that a full peace settlement between Israel, on the one hand, and Egypt, Jordan, Saudi Arabia, and the Palestinians, on the other, can be negotiated along the lines indicated above, *and can be "sold"* to those five publics. Will there be opposition? Yes, of course. But if the governments place themselves solidly behind the agreements and orchestrate the presentation of benefits properly, they will receive an adequate degree of public support. A consistent problem in this conflict's history has been the prejudice of negotiation outcome support as a result of public opinion manipulation during the negotiation. We believe, however, that a full settlement is inherently more defensible than partial or interim agreements.

A common belief on this side of the Atlantic has been that the U.S. administration runs grave political risks in becoming overly associated with the peace process. We believe the American people will support an even-handed approach to Middle East conflict resolution. Various interest groups on both sides (pro-Israeli, pro-Arab, commercial groups) will object, citing injury to parochial interests and describing how these interests are really America's. In fact, however, the American public as a whole is much more prepared today to listen to and to understand the merits of the case than it was even five years ago. For the truth is that a settlement must be balanced to be viable, and a general settlement is far more important to the *long-term* interests, far more basic to the security, of the Arab-Israeli core countries than the maximum satisfaction of countless conflicting "needs" articulated by each of the parties to the point of continued stalemate. More important, perhaps, such a settlement has more tangible and obvious benefits to U.S. interests, including those of the public, than ever before. As a once-senior U.S. policy-maker has written: "The president must be prepared to devote considerable time and energy to building domestic support in Congress and in public opinion for his Middle East policy. It is here that the quality of leadership will be tested."[13]

Changes in Syria and Lebanon; the inability of the opponents of the Camp David accords to punish Egypt; and the formidable hurdles that lie in the path to a general settlement—these are important considerations the awareness of which is critical to the evolution of the region and some of which may ease a number of the greatest problems inherent in the Arab-Israeli conflict as we know it today. But they should not and must not be allowed to shackle U.S. efforts or be advanced as reasons to slow American attempts to actively assist the parties in reaching a settlement. Moreover, other developments (e.g., the possible annexation of the Golan by Israel) work to exacerbate Arab-Israeli tension.

Promotion of Democratic/Human Rights

The American government's much-maligned human rights policy has been more misunderstood at home than abroad. It is not, and should not be touted as, the most critical or salient aspect of U.S. foreign relations on the day-to-day level. Yet, the "policy" touches the core of the most attractive elements of the American image abroad. Moreover, it represents the genuine preferences of most Americans in public life as well as out of it. The issue is not to be the fulcrum for economic assistance or political support. Rather, human rights and the access to some means of political expression are valuable and meaningful goals of political development sought nominally or actually by virtually all peoples and groups.

It is unrealistic, presumptuous, and unreasonable for the

United States to dictate the speed or direction of political development in, say, the countries of the Gulf. Yet, it is reasonable, feasible—and expected—for U.S. representatives to *encourage* and *promote,* perhaps privately at times, wider participation in government and tolerance of voices of dissent. Even those who disagree with these views will understand the intent behind them. There are trends toward allowing some primitive forms of participation in some of the most traditional regimes of the region. These trends should be supported.

The American Presence

We believe there have been serious American misperceptions of the concept of "presence" in the Middle East. In spite of differences in culture, both a public and a private presence are desirable and effective. However, this is hardly to say that the nature and amplitude of the presence do not bear monitoring.

People-to-people contact is important, and, the legend of *The Ugly American* notwithstanding, personal interaction over time with Americans more often than not is positive—it demonstrates, as Americans demonstrate, the pluralism, spontaneity, and openness of the American way of life. At the same time, a surfeit of Americans easily becomes a *threat,* alien influence rather than foreign visitors, and this problem is particularly pronounced in traditional societies. Too great an influx of American nationals can be both psychologically counterproductive and, as in Iran, politically destabilizing.

A public American presence is also both desirable and dangerous. On the one hand, countries like Saudi Arabia would feel more secure if an American military presence were established on a more continuous basis. Ship visits, and even the permanent stationing of a naval task force or fleet, though useful, do not convey the same level of commitment as ground forces.[14] At the same time, such a presence deployed in one or more of the regional countries can once again easily become involved in the domestic political unrest that may be common over the years ahead or may at least find itself accused of supporting an unpopular government—an accusation that could reduce the legitimacy of both the government and the U.S. presence. Moreover, large numbers of American forces, like private citizens, can become an alien and unwanted element.

How should U.S. policy steer a course between the Scylla of

an insufficient presence and Charybdis of a superfluous one? Recognizing that ours is a free society in which the government has less directive control than suasive influence, U.S. policy should not encourage a large civilian presence in Middle East countries in which commercial exchange is extensive or growing. Such a visible presence by a people with vastly different values and little real interest in respecting the traditions and mores of the host country may be an important causal factor in potential instability in fragile societies already challenged by numerous and varied aspects of social change. To the extent military, naval, or air personnel are deployed to Middle East countries they should be stationed outside populated areas as much as possible.

A U.S. military presence in the Middle East is desirable, but physical presence of combat forces on the Arabian Peninsula probably is not. Instead, we believe the United States should, in support of the government of Egypt, establish one or two Egyptian training installations in the Sinai near the Israeli border. American equipment should be forward-positioned at these Egyptian installations, and they should if possible be regional facilities at which the training of military personnel from several countries is accomplished. (They may also serve a quasi-peacekeeping function between Egypt and Israel.)

Many of the countries of the region seek stability but oppose the physical presence of either the United States or the Soviet Union. This is a reasonable and responsible view to which the United States should be sensitive. The presence of a sizeable or permanent naval presence in the Gulf, for example, may reassure some of the smaller countries on the Arabian Peninsula but runs counter to Iranian and Iraqi views, perceived interests, and policies. It is our belief that U.S. interests do not demand a strong U.S. naval *presence in* the Gulf so much as a *capability* that is close enough to be *credible*.

New Alignments, New Leaders, and New Policies

It is apparent that the changes we project in this book will greatly alter the nature of both Middle East politics and the pattern of U.S. relations with the region. We have pointed to the importance of the Arab-Israeli problem, but today it is the Gulf dimensions of that conflict which threaten U.S. interests more than the immediate Levantine effects. The reawakening consciousness of ethnic, religious, and tribal groups poses major challenges to many Middle Eastern regimes and certainly suggests new perspectives with which even most American regional experts and policy-makers are emotionally ill-equipped to deal.

The erosion of the Jordanian-Syrian entente and of Syrian power generally raises new questions about the Palestinians as well as about Syria's future leadership and integrity. In the event of 'Alawi secession or civil war, Iraqi intervention is a distinct possibility, and a possibility that also raises the spectre of Israeli counteraction. How should the United States react to these far-reaching possibilities?

Syria's growing weakness means greater freedom of the Palestinians to establish a *modus vivendi* with Israel. While PLO freedom of action has been restricted in its last territorial sanctuary (in Lebanon), its rapprochement with Jordan has opened new vistas of potential future cooperation regarding the establishment of a Palestinian West Bank polity linked in some way to Jordan. Syria would not have permitted the PLO to accept such an option without Israeli withdrawal from the occupied Golan Heights. It is no longer clear that Syria could stop the PLO from pursuing this option. The United States should continue to encourage the PLO to indicate the latter's willingness to accept Israel, and should encourage Israel, for its part, to be less rigid with regard to the PLO issue.

The growing cooperation between Iraq and Jordan and between Iraq and Saudi Arabia are illustrative of the "pragmatization" of Iraqi policy. We believe that in spite of several major conflicts of interest and perspective, the United States and Iraq share a number of important values. Americans are often less flexible than Arabs; we fail to remember that just as we have no eternal allies "we have no perpetual enemies. Our interests . . . it is our duty to follow."[15] Recognizing the duality of Iraqi policy,[16] the United States should endeavor to maintain and enrich the existing dialog with Iraqi leaders; should look to Iraq for an important role in Gulf leadership; and should support the quiet side of Iraqi diplomacy with U.S. friends in the Middle East. American policy-makers and planners should also begin to give serious thought to the effects and impact on U.S. regional interests and objectives of nuclear proliferation in the Middle East, for it is likely that Iraq will move in the direction of a nuclear military capability.

The earlier chapters of this book have adverted to many other emerging challenges to American policy, and the purpose of this chapter is not so much to respond to those challenges as to call attention to some of the more important ones again, to suggest some possible approaches to a few, and to provoke the reader into a search for his or her own answers—and questions.

APPENDIX A

Camp David Agreements

Text of Agreements Signed September 17, 1978[*]

A FRAMEWORK FOR PEACE IN THE MIDDLE EAST
AGREED AT CAMP DAVID

Muhammad Anwar al-Sadat, President of the Arab Republic of Egypt, and Menachem Begin, Prime Minister of Israel, met with Jimmy Carter, President of the United States of America, at Camp David from September 5 to September 17, 1978, and have agreed on the following framework for peace in the Middle East. They invite other parties to the Arab-Israeli conflict to adhere to it.

Preamble

The search for peace in the Middle East must be guided by the following:

—The agreed basis for a peaceful settlement of the conflict between Israel and its neighbors is United Nations Security Council Resolution 242, in all its parts.[†]

—After four wars during thirty years, despite intensive human efforts, the Middle East, which is the cradle of civilization and the birthplace of three great religions, does not yet enjoy the blessings of peace. The people of the Middle East yearn for peace so that the vast human and natural resources of the region can be turned to the pursuits of peace and so that this area can become a model for coexistence and cooperation among nations.

—The historic initiative of President Sadat in visiting Jerusalem and the reception accorded to him by the Parliament, government and people of Israel, and the reciprocal visit of Prime Minister Begin to Ismailia, the peace proposals made by both leaders, as well as the warm reception of these missions by the peoples of both countries, have created an unprecedented

*The Camp David Summit, September 1978, Department of State Publication 8954, Near East and South Asian Series 88 (Washington, D.C.: USGPO, 1978).
†The texts of Resolutions 242 and 338 are annexed to this document.

opportunity for peace which must not be lost if this generation and future generations are to be spared the tragedies of war.

—The provisions of the Charter of the United Nations and the other accepted norms of international law and legitimacy now provide accepted standards for the conduct of relations among all states.

—To achieve a relationship of peace, in the spirit of Article 2 of the United Nations Charter, future negotiations between Israel and any neighbor prepared to negotiate peace and security with it, are necessary for the purpose of carrying out all the provisions and principles of Resolutions 242 and 338.

—Peace requires respect for the sovereignty, territorial integrity and political independence of every state in the area and their right to live in peace within secure and recognized boundaries free from threats or acts of force. Progress toward that goal can accelerate movement toward a new era of reconciliation in the Middle East marked by cooperation in promoting economic development, in maintaining stability, and in assuring security.

—Security is enhanced by a relationship of peace and by cooperation between nations which enjoy normal relations. In addition, under the terms of peace treaties, the parties can, on the basis of reciprocity, agree to special security arrangements such as demilitarized zones, limited armaments areas, early warning stations, the presence of international forces, liaison, agreed measures for monitoring, and other arrangements that they agree are useful.

Framework

Taking these factors into account, the parties are determined to reach a just, comprehensive, and durable settlement of the Middle East conflict through the conclusion of peace treaties based on Security Council Resolutions 242 and 338 in all their parts. Their purpose is to achieve peace and good neighborly relations. They recognize that, for peace to endure, it must involve all those who have been most deeply affected by the conflict. They therefore agree that this framework as appropriate is intended by them to constitute a basis for peace not only between Egypt and Israel, but also between Israel and each of its other neighbors which is prepared to negotiate peace with Israel on this basis. With that objective in mind, they have agreed to proceed as follows:

A. *West Bank and Gaza*

1. Egypt, Israel, Jordan and the representatives of the Palestinian people should participate in negotiations on the resolution of the Palestinian problem in all its aspects. To achieve that objective, negotiations relating to the West Bank and Gaza should proceed in three stages:

(a) Egypt and Israel agree that, in order to ensure a peaceful and orderly transfer of authority, and taking into account the security concerns of all the parties, there should be transitional arrangements for the West Bank and Gaza for a period not exceeding five years. In order to provide full autonomy to the inhabitants, under these arrangements the Israeli military government and its civilian administration will be withdrawn as soon as a self-governing authority has been freely elected by the inhabitants of these areas to replace the existing military government. To negotiate the details of a transitional arrangement, the Government of Jordan will be invited to join the negotiations on the basis of this framework. These new arrangements should give due consideration both to the principle of self-government by the inhabitants of these terrorities and to the legitimate security concerns of the parties involved.

(b) Egypt, Israel, and Jordan will agree on the modalities for establishing the elected self-governing authority in the West Bank and Gaza. The delegations of Egypt and Jordan may include Palestinians from the West Bank and Gaza or other Palestinians as mutually agreed. The parties will negotiate an agreement which will define the powers and responsibilities of the self-governing authority to be exercised in the West Bank and Gaza. A withdrawal of Israeli armed forces will take place and there will be a rede-ployment of the remaining Israeli forces into specified security locations. The agreement will also include arrangements for assuring internal and external security and public order. A strong local police force will be estab-lished, which may include Jordanian citizens. In addition, Israeli and Jor-danian forces will participate in joint patrols and in the manning of control posts to assure the security of the borders.

(c) When the self-governing authority (administrative council) in the West Bank and Gaza is established and inaugurated, the transitional period of five years will begin. As soon as possible, but not later than the third year after the beginning of the transitional period, negotiations will take place to determine the final status of the West Bank and Gaza and its relationship with its neighbors, and to conclude a peace treaty between Israel and Jordan by the end of the transitional period. These negotiations will be conducted among Egypt, Israel, Jordan, and the elected representatives of the inhabitants of the West Bank and Gaza. Two separate but related com-mittees will be convened, one committee, consisting of representatives of the four parties which will negotiate and agree on the final status of the West Bank and Gaza, and its relationship with its neighbors, and the second committee, consisting of representatives of Israel and representatives of Jordan to be joined by the elected representatives of the inhabitants of the West Bank and Gaza, to negotiate the peace treaty between Israel and Jordan, taking into account the agreement reached on the final status of the West Bank and Gaza. The negotiations shall be based on all the provisions and principles of UN Security Council Resolution 242. The negotiations will resolve, among other matters, the location of the boundaries and the nature of the security arrangements. The solution from the negotiations must also recognize the legitimate rights of the Palestinian people and their just requirements. In this way, the Palestinians will participate in the determination of their own future through:

1) The negotiations among Egypt, Israel, Jordan and the representatives of the inhabitants of the West Bank and Gaza to agree on the final status of the West Bank and Gaza and other outstanding issues by the end of the transitional period.

2) Submitting their agreement to a vote by the elected representatives of the inhabitants of the West Bank and Gaza.

3) Providing for the elected representatives of the inhabitants of the West Bank and Gaza to decide how they shall govern themselves consistent with the provisions of their agreement.

4) Participating as stated above in the work of the committee negotiating the peace treaty between Israel and Jordan.

2. All necessary measures will be taken and provisions made to assure the security of Israel and its neighbors during the transitional period and beyond. To assist in providing such security, a strong local police force will be constituted by the self-governing authority. It will be composed of inhabitants of the West Bank and Gaza. The police will maintain continuing liaison on internal security matters with the designated Israeli, Jordanian, and Egyptian officers.

3. During the transitional period, representatives of Egypt, Israel, Jordan, and the self-governing authority will constitute a continuing committee to decide by agreement on the modalities of admission of persons displaced from the West Bank and Gaza in 1967, together with necessary measures to prevent disruption and disorder. Other matters of common concern may also be dealt with by this committee.

4. Egypt and Israel will work with each other and with other interested parties to establish agreed procedures for a prompt, just and permanent implementation of the resolution of the refugee problem.

B. *Egypt-Israel*

1. Egypt and Israel undertake not to resort to the threat or the use of force to settle disputes. Any disputes shall be settled by peaceful means in accordance with the provisions of Article 33 of the Charter of the United Nations.

2. In order to achieve peace between them, the parties agree to negotiate in good faith with a goal of concluding within three months from the

signing of this Framework a peace treaty between them, while inviting the other parties to the conflict to proceed simultaneously to negotiate and conclude similar peace treaties with a view to achieving a comprehensive peace in the area. The Framework for the Conclusion of a Peace Treaty between Egypt and Israel will govern the peace negotiations between them. The parties will agree on the modalities and the timetable for the implementation of their obligations under the treaty.

C. *Associated Principles*

1. Egypt and Israel state that the principles and provisions described below should apply to peace treaties between Israel and each of its neighbors—Egypt, Jordan, Syria and Lebanon.

2. Signatories shall establish among themselves relationships normal to states at peace with one another. To this end, they should undertake to abide by all the provisions of the Charter of the United Nations. Steps to be taken in this respect include:

(a) full recognition;

(b) abolishing economic boycotts;

(c) guaranteeing that under their jurisdiction the citizens of the other parties shall enjoy the protection of the due process of law.

3. Signatories should explore possibilities for economic development in the context of final peace treaties, with the objective of contributing to the atmosphere of peace, cooperation and friendship which is their common goal.

4. Claims Commissions may be established for the mutual settlement of all financial claims.

5. The United States shall be invited to participate in the talks on matters related to the modalities of the implementation of the agreements and working out the timetable for the carrying out of the obligations of the parties.

6. The United Nations Security Council shall be requested to endorse the peace treaties and ensure that their provisions shall not be violated. The permanent members of the Security Council shall be requested to underwrite the peace treaties and ensure respect for their provisions. They shall also be requested to conform their policies and actions with the undertakings contained in this Framework.

For the Government of the   For the Government
Arab Republic of Egypt: of Israel:

A. SADAT   M. BEGIN

Witnessed by:

JIMMY CARTER

Jimmy Carter, President
of the United States of America

ANNEX

**Text of United Nations Security Council
Resolution 242 of November 22, 1967**

Adopted unanimously at the 1382nd meeting

The Security Council,

Expressing its continuing concern with the grave situation in the Middle East,

Emphasizing the inadmissibility of the acquisition of territory by war and the need to work for a just and lasting peace in which every State in the area can live in security,

Emphasizing further that all Member States in their acceptance of the Charter of the United Nations have undertaken a commitment to act in accordance with Article 2 of the Charter,

1. *Affirms* that the fulfilment of Charter principles requires the establishment of a just and lasting peace in the Middle East which should include the application of both the following principles:

(i) Withdrawal of Israeli armed forces from territories occupied in the recent conflict;

(ii) Termination of all claims or states of belligerency and respect for and acknowledgement of the sovereignty, territorial integrity and political independence of every State in the area and their right to live in peace within secure and recognized boundaries free from threats or acts of force;

2. *Affirms further* the necessity

(a) For guaranteeing freedom of navigation through international waterways in the area;

(b) For achieving a just settlement of the refugee problem;

(c) For guaranteeing the territorial inviolability and political independence of every State in the area, through measures including the establishment of demilitarized zones;

3. *Requests* the Secretary-General to designate a Special Repre-

sentative to proceed to the Middle East to establish and maintain contacts with the States concerned in order to promote agreement and assist efforts to achieve a peaceful and accepted settlement in accordance with the provisions and principles of this resolution.

4. *Requests* the Secretary-General to report to the Security Council on the progress of the efforts of the Special Representative as soon as possible.

Text of United Nations Security Council Resolution 338

Adopted by the Security Council at its 1747th meeting, on 21/22 October 1973

The Security Council

1. *Calls upon* all parties to the present fighting to cease all firing and terminate all military activity immediately, no later than 12 hours after the moment of the adoption of this decision, in the positions they now occupy;

2. *Calls upon* the parties concerned to start immediately after the cease-fire the implementation of Security Council Resolution 242 (1967) in all of its parts;

3. *Decides* that, immediately and concurrently with the cease-fire, negotiations start between the parties concerned under appropriate auspices aimed at establishing a just and durable peace in the Middle East.

FRAMEWORK FOR THE CONCLUSION OF A PEACE TREATY BETWEEN EGYPT AND ISRAEL

In order to achieve peace between them, Israel and Egypt agree to negotiate in good faith with a goal of concluding within three months of the signing of this framework a peace treaty between them.

It is agreed that:

The site of the negotiations will be under a United Nations flag at a location or locations to be mutually agreed.

All of the principles of U.N. Resolution 242 will apply in this resolution of the dispute between Israel and Egypt.

Unless otherwise mutually agreed, terms of the peace treaty will be implemented between two and three years after the peace treaty is signed.

The following matters are agreed between the parties:

(a) the full exercise of Egyptian sovereignty up to the internationally recognized border between Egypt and mandated Palestine;

(b) the withdrawal of Israeli armed forces from the Sinai;

(c) the use of airfields left by the Israelis near El Arish, Rafah, Ras en Naqb, and Sharm el Sheikh for civilian purposes only, including possible commercial use by all nations;

(d) the right of free passage by ships of Israel through the Gulf of Suez and the Suez Canal on the basis of the Constantinople Convention of 1888 applying to all nations; the Strait of Tiran and the Gulf of Aqaba are international waterways to be open to all nations for unimpeded and nonsuspendable freedom of navigation and overflight;

(e) the construction of a highway between the Sinai and Jordan near Elat with guaranteed free and peaceful passage by Egypt and Jordan; and

(f) the stationing of military forces listed below.

Stationing of Forces

A. No more than one division (mechanized or infantry) of Egyptian armed forces will be stationed within an area lying approximately 50 kilometers (km) east of the Gulf of Suez and the Suez Canal.

B. Only United Nations forces and civil police equipped with light weapons to perform normal police functions will be stationed within an area lying west of the international border and the Gulf of Aqaba, varying in width from 20 km to 40 km.

C. In the area within 3 km east of the international border there will be Israeli limited military forces not to exceed four infantry battalions and United Nations observers.

D. Border patrol units, not to exceed three battalions, will supplement the civil police in maintaining order in the area not included above.

The exact demarcation of the above areas will be as decided during the peace negotiations.

Early warning stations may exist to insure compliance with the terms of the agreement.

United Nations forces will be stationed: (a) in part of the area in the Sinai lying within about 20 km of the Mediterranean Sea and adjacent to the international border, and (b) in the Sharm el Sheikh area to ensure freedom of passage through the Strait of Tiran; and these forces will not be removed unless such removal is approved by the Security Council of the United Nations with a unanimous vote of the five permanent members.

After a peace treaty is signed, and after the interim withdrawal is complete, normal relations will be established between Egypt and Israel, including: full recognition, including diplomatic, economic and cultural relations; termination of economic boycotts and barriers to the free movement of goods and people; and mutual protection of citizens by the due process of law.

Interim Withdrawal

Between the three months and nine months after the signing of the peace treaty, all Israeli forces will withdraw east of a line extending from a point east of El Arish to Ras Muhammad, the exact location of this time to be determined by mutual agreement.

For the Government of the
Arab Republic of Egypt:

For the Government
of Israel:

A. Sadat

M. Begin

Witnessed by:

Jimmy Carter

Jimmy Carter, *President*
of the United States of America

Accompanying Letters[1]

SEPTEMBER 17, 1978

DEAR MR. PRESIDENT:

I have the honor to inform you that during two weeks after my return home I will submit a motion before Israel's Parliament (the Knesset) to decide on the following question:

If during the negotiations to conclude a peace treaty between Israel and Egypt all outstanding issues are agreed upon, "are you in favor of the removal of the Israeli settlers from the northern and southern Sinai areas or are you in favor of keeping the aforementioned settlers in those areas?"

The vote, Mr. President, on this issue will be completely free from the usual Parliamentary Party discipline to the effect that although the coalition is being now supported by 70 members out of 120, every member of the Knesset, as I believe, both on the Government and the Opposition benches will be enabled to vote in accordance with his own conscience.

Sincerely yours,
(signed)
MENACHEM BEGIN

The President
Camp David
Thurmont, Maryland

---

[1]Correspondence concerning the Israeli settlements in the West Bank and Gaza was not ready when these letters were released, as had been anticipated.

SEPTEMBER 22, 1978

DEAR MR. PRESIDENT:

I transmit herewith a copy of a letter to me from Prime Minister Begin setting forth how he proposes to present the issue of the Sinai settlements to the Knesset for the latter's decision.

In this connection, I understand from your letter that Knesset approval to withdraw all Israeli settlers from Sinai according to a timetable within the period specified for the implementation of the peace treaty is a prerequisite to any negotiations on a peace treaty between Egypt and Israel.

Sincerely,
(signed)
JIMMY CARTER

Enclosure:
Letter from Prime Minister Begin (Letter at Tab A)

His Excellency
ANWAR AL-SADAT
President of the Arab
Republic of Egypt
Cairo

SEPTEMBER 17, 1978

DEAR MR. PRESIDENT:

In connection with the "Framework for a Settlement in Sinai" to be signed tonight, I would like to reaffirm the position of the Arab Republic of Egypt with respect to the settlements:

1. All Israeli settlers must be withdrawn from Sinai according to a timetable within the period specified for the implementation of the peace treaty.

2. Agreement by the Israeli Government and its constitutional institutions to this basic principle is therefore a prerequisite to starting peace negotiations for concluding a peace treaty.

3. If Israel fails to meet this commitment, the "Framework" shall be void and invalid.

Sincerely,
(signed)
MOHAMED ANWAR EL SADAT

His Excellency JIMMY CARTER
President of the United States

SEPTEMBER 22, 1978

DEAR MR. PRIME MINISTER:

I have received your letter of September 17, 1978, describing how you intend to place the question of the future of Israeli settlements in Sinai before the Knesset for its decision.

Enclosed is a copy of President Sadat's letter to me on this subject.

Sincerely,
(signed)
JIMMY CARTER

Enclosure:
Letter from President Sadat (Letter at Tab C)

His Excellency
MENACHEM BEGIN
Prime Minister of Israel

[JERUSALEM]

SEPTEMBER 17, 1978

DEAR MR. PRESIDENT,

I am writing you to reaffirm the position of the Arab Republic of Egypt with respect to Jerusalem:

1. Arab Jerusalem is an integral part of the West Bank. Legal and historical Arab rights in the City must be respected and restored.

2. Arab Jerusalem should be under Arab sovereignty.

3. The Palestinian inhabitants of Arab Jerusalem are entitled to exercise their legitimate national rights, being part of the Palestinian People in the West Bank.

4. Relevant Security Council Resolutions, particularly Resolutions 242 and 267, must be applied with regard to Jerusalem. All the measures taken by Israel to alter the status of the City are null and void and should be rescinded.

5. All peoples must have free access to the City and enjoy the free exercise of worship and the right to visit and transit to the holy places without distinction or discrimination.

6. The holy places of each faith may be placed under the administration and control of their representatives.

7. Essential functions in the City should be undivided and a joint municipal council composed of an equal number of Arab and Israeli mem-

bers can supervise the carrying out of these functions. In this way, the City shall be undivided.

Sincerely,
(signed)
MOHAMED ANWAR EL SADAT

His Excellency JIMMY CARTER
President of the United States

17 SEPTEMBER 1978

DEAR MR. PRESIDENT,

I have the honor to inform you, Mr. President, that on 28 June 1967—Israel's Parliament (The Knesset) promulgated and adopted a law to the effect: "the Government is empowered by a decree to apply the law, the jurisdiction and administration of the State to any part of Eretz Israel (land of Israel—Palestine), as stated in that decree."

On the basis of this law, the Government of Israel decreed in July 1967 that Jerusalem is one city indivisible, the Capital of the State of Israel.

Sincerely,
(signed)
MENACHEM BEGIN

The President
Camp David
Thurmont, Maryland

SEPTEMBER 22, 1978

DEAR MR. PRESIDENT:

I have received your letter of September 17, 1978, setting forth the Egyptian position on Jerusalem. I am transmitting a copy of that letter to Prime Minister Begin for his information.

The position of the United States on Jerusalem remains as stated by Ambassador Goldberg in the United Nations General Assembly on July 14, 1967,[2] and subsequently by Ambassador Yost in the United Nations Security Council on July 1, 1969.[3]

Sincerely,
(signed)
JIMMY CARTER

[2]For text, see Department of State *Bulletin* of July 31, 1967, p. 148.
[3]For text, see Department of State *Bulletin* of July 28, 1969, p. 76. Footnotes added by the Department of State.

His Excellency
   ANWAR AL-SADAT
     President of the Arab
      Republic of Egypt
       Cairo

[IMPLEMENTATION OF COMPREHENSIVE SETTLEMENT]

SEPTEMBER 17, 1978
DEAR MR. PRESIDENT:
   In connection with the "Framework for Peace in the Middle East", I am writing you this letter to inform you of the position of the Arab Republic of Egypt, with respect to the implementation of the comprehensive settlement.
   To ensure the implementation of the provisions related to the West Bank and Gaza and in order to safeguard the legitimate rights of the Palestinian people, Egypt will be prepared to assume the Arab role emanating from these provisions, following consultations with Jordan and the representatives of the Palestinian people.

Sincerely,
(signed)
MOHAMED ANWAR EL SADAT

His Excellency
   JIMMY CARTER
     President of the United States
      The White House
      Washington, DC

[DEFINITION OF TERMS]

SEPTEMBER 22, 1978
DEAR MR. PRIME MINISTER:
   I hereby acknowledge that you have informed me as follows:
   A) In each paragraph of the Agreed Framework Document the expressions "Palestinians" or "Palestinian People" are being and will be construed and understood by you as "Palestinian Arabs."
   B) In each paragraph in which the expression "West Bank" appears, it

is being, and will be, understood by the Government of Israel as Judea and
Samaria.

Sincerely,

(signed)

JIMMY CARTER

His Excellency
 MENACHEM BEGIN
  Prime Minister of Israel

[AIRBASES]

THE SECRETARY OF DEFENSE
WASHINGTON, D.C. 20301

SEPTEMBER 28, 1978

DEAR MR. MINISTER:

The U.S. understands that, in connection with carrying out the agreements reached at Camp David, Israel intends to build two military airbases at
appropriate sites in the Negev to replace the airbases at Eitam and Etzion
which will be evacuated by Israel in accordance with the peace treaty to be
concluded between Egypt and Israel. We also understand the special urgency
and priority which Israel attaches to preparing the new bases in light of its
conviction that it cannot safely leave the Sinai airbases until the new ones are
operational.

I suggest that our two governments consult on the scope and costs of
the two new airbases as well as on related forms of assistance which the
United States might appropriately provide in light of the special problems
which may be presented by carrying out such a project on an urgent basis.
The President is prepared to seek the necessary Congressional approvals for
such assistance as may be agreed upon by the U.S. side as a result of such
consultations.

(signed)

HAROLD BROWN

The Honorable
 EZER WEIZMAN
  Minister of Defense
  Government of Israel

APPENDIX B

Egyptian-Israeli Peace Treaty

The Egyptian-Israeli Peace Treaty[*]

TREATY OF PEACE BETWEEN
THE ARAB REPUBLIC OF EGYPT AND THE STATE OF ISRAEL

The Government of the Arab Republic of Egypt and the Government of the State of Israel:

Preamble

Convinced of the urgent necessity of the establishment of a just, comprehensive and lasting peace in the Middle East in accordance with Security Council Resolutions 242 and 338;

Reaffirming their adherence to the "Framework for Peace in the Middle East Agreed at Camp David," dated September 17, 1978;

Noting that the aforementioned Framework as appropriate is intended to constitute a basis for peace not only between Egypt and Israel but also between Israel and each of its other Arab neighbors which is prepared to negotiate peace with it on this basis;

Desiring to bring to an end the state of war between them and to establish a peace in which every state in the area can live in security;

Convinced that the conclusion of a Treaty of Peace between Egypt and Israel is an important step in the search for comprehensive peace in the area and for the attainment of the settlement of the Arab-Israeli conflict in all its aspects;

Inviting the other Arab parties to this dispute to join the peace process with Israel guided by and based on the principles of the aforementioned Framework;

Desiring as well to develop friendly relations and cooperation between themselves in accordance with the United Nations Charter and the

*The Egyptian-Israeli Peace Treaty, March 26, 1979, Department of State Publication 8976, Near Eastern and South Asian Series 91, Selected Documents no. 11 (Washington, D.C.: USGPO, 1979).

principles of international law governing international relations in times of peace;

Agree to the following provisions in the free exercise of their sovereignty, in order to implement the "Framework for the Conclusion of a Peace Treaty Between Egypt and Israel":

Article I

1. The state of war between the Parties will be terminated and peace will be established between them upon the exchange of instruments of ratification of this Treaty.

2. Israel will withdraw all its armed forces and civilians from the Sinai behind the international boundary between Egypt and mandated Palestine, as provided in the annexed protocol (Annex I), and Egypt will resume the exercise of its full sovereignty over the Sinai.

3. Upon completion of the interim withdrawal provided for in Annex I, the Parties will establish normal and friendly relations, in accordance with Article III (3).

Article II

The permanent boundary between Egypt and Israel is the recognized international boundary between Egypt and the former mandated territory of Palestine, as shown on the map at Annex II, without prejudice to the issue of the status of the Gaza Strip. The Parties recognize this boundary as inviolable. Each will respect the territorial integrity of the other, including their territorial waters and airspace.

Article III

1. The Parties will apply between them the provisions of the Charter of the United Nations and the principles of international law governing relations among states in times of peace. In particular:

   a. They recognize and will respect each other's sovereignty, territorial integrity and political independence;

   b. They recognize and will respect each other's right to live in peace within their secure and recognized boundaries;

   c. They will refrain from the threat or use of force, directly or indirectly, against each other and will settle all disputes between them by peaceful means.

2. Each Party undertakes to ensure that acts or threats of belligerency, hostility, or violence do not originate from and are not committed from

within its territory, or by any forces subject to its control or by any other forces stationed on its territory, against the population, citizens or property of the other Party. Each Party also undertakes to refrain from organizing, instigating, inciting, assisting or participating in acts or threats of belligerency, hostility, subversion or violence against the other Party, anywhere, and undertakes to ensure that perpetrators of such acts are brought to justice.

3. The Parties agree that the normal relationship established between them will include full recognition, diplomatic, economic and cultural relations, termination of economic boycotts and discriminatory barriers to the free movement of people and goods, and will guarantee the mutual enjoyment by citizens of the due process of law. The process by which they undertake to achieve such a relationship parallel to the implementation of other provisions of this Treaty is set out in the annexed protocol (Annex III).

Article IV

1. In order to provide maximum security for both Parties on the basis of reciprocity, agreed security arrangements will be established including limited force zones in Egyptian and Israeli territory, and United Nations forces and observers, described in detail as to nature and timing in Annex I, and other security arrangements the Parties may agree upon.

2. The Parties agree to the stationing of United Nations personnel in areas described in Annex I. The Parties agree not to request withdrawal of the United Nations personnel and that these personnel will not be removed unless such removal is approved by the Security Council of the United Nations, with the affirmative vote of the five Permanent Members, unless the Parties otherwise agree.

3. A Joint Commission will be established to facilitate the implementation of the Treaty, as provided for in Annex I.

4. The security arrangements provided for in paragraphs 1 and 2 of this Article may at the request of either party be reviewed and amended by mutual agreement of the Parties.

Article V

1. Ships of Israel, and cargoes destined for or coming from Israel, shall enjoy the right of free passage through the Suez Canal and its approaches through the Gulf of Suez and the Mediterranean Sea on the basis of the Constantinople Convention of 1888, applying to all nations. Israeli nationals, vessels and cargoes, as well as persons, vessels and cargoes destined for or coming from Israel, shall be accorded non-discriminatory treatment in all matters connected with usage of the canal.

2. The Parties consider the Strait of Tiran and the Gulf of Aqaba to be international waterways open to all nations for unimpeded and non-suspendable freedom of navigation and overflight. The Parties will respect each other's right to navigation and overflight for access to either country through the Strait of Tiran and the Gulf of Aqaba.

Article VI

1. This Treaty does not affect and shall not be interpreted as affecting in any way the rights and obligations of the Parties under the Charter of the United Nations.

2. The Parties undertake to fulfill in good faith their obligations under this Treaty, without regard to action or inaction of any other party and independently of any instrument external to this Treaty.

3. They further undertake to take all the necessary measures for the application in their relations of the provisions of the multilateral conventions to which they are parties, including the submission of appropriate notification to the Secretary General of the United Nations and other depositaries of such conventions.

4. The Parties undertake not to enter into any obligation in conflict with this Treaty.

5. Subject to Article 103 of the United Nations Charter, in the event of a conflict between the obligations of the Parties under the present Treaty and any of their other obligations, the obligations under this Treaty will be binding and implemented.

Article VII

1. Disputes arising out of the application or interpretation of this Treaty shall be resolved by negotiations.

2. Any such disputes which cannot be settled by negotiations shall be resolved by conciliation or submitted to arbitration.

Article VIII

The Parties agree to establish a claims commission for the mutual settlement of all financial claims.

Article IX

1. This Treaty shall enter into force upon exchange of instruments of ratification.

2. This Treaty supersedes the Agreement between Egypt and Israel of September, 1975.

3. All protocols, annexes, and maps attached to this Treaty shall be regarded as an integral part hereof.

4. The Treaty shall be communicated to the Secretary General of the United Nations for registration in accordance with the provisions of Article 102 of the Charter of the United Nations.

[Facsimile of signature page of Treaty as executed]

DONE at Washington, D.C. this 26th day of March, 1979, in triplicate in the English, Arabic, and Hebrew languages, each text being equally authentic. In case of any divergence of interpretation, the English text shall prevail.

حررت فى واشنطن دى . سى . فى ٢٦ مارس ١٩٧٩م ، ٢٧ ربيع الاول ١٣٩٩ هـ من ثلاث نسخ باللغات الانجليزية والعربية والعبرية وتعتبر جميعهـا متساويـة الحجيـة ، وفى حالة الخلاف حول التفسير فيكون النص الانجليزى هو الذى يعتد به .

נעשה בוושינגטון, די.סי. ביום זה כ"ז באדר לשנת תשל"ט, 26 במרץ 1979, בשלושה עותקים בשפות האנגלית, הערבית והעברית וכל נוסח אמין במידה שווה. במקרה של הבדלי פרשנות, יכריע הנוסח האנגלי .

For the Government of the
Arab Republic of Egypt:

For the Government
of Israel:

عن حكومـة
جمهورية مصـر العربيـة :

عن حكومـة
اسرائيـــل :

בשם ממשלת הרפובליקה הערבית
של מצרים :

בשם ממשלת ישראל :

Witnessed by:
شهد التوقيـع :
הועד על-ידי :

Jimmy Carter, President
of the United States of America

جيمى كارتـــر ، رئيـــــس
الولايات المتحـــدة الامريكيـة

ג'ימי קארטר, נשיא
ארצות הברית של אמריקה

Annex I

PROTOCOL CONCERNING ISRAELI
WITHDRAWAL AND SECURITY ARRANGEMENTS

Article I
Concept of Withdrawal

1. Israel will complete withdrawal of all its armed forces and civilians from the Sinai not later than three years from the date of exchange of instruments of ratification of this Treaty.

2. To ensure the mutual security of the Parties, the implementation of phased withdrawal will be accompanied by the military measures and establishment of zones set out in this Annex and in Map 1, hereinafter referred to as "the Zones."

3. The withdrawal from the Sinai will be accomplished in two phases:

a. The interim withdrawal behind the line from east of El Arish to Ras Muhammed as delineated on Map 2 within nine months from the date of exchange of instruments of ratification of this Treaty.

b. The final withdrawal from the Sinai behind the international boundary not later than three years from the date of this Treaty.

4. A Joint Commission will be formed immediately after the exchange of instruments of ratification of this Treaty in order to supervise and coordinate movements and schedules during the withdrawal, and to adjust plans and timetables as necessary within the limits established by paragraph 3, above. Details relating to the Joint Commission are set out in Article IV of the attached Appendix. The Joint Commission will be dissolved upon completion of final Israeli withdrawal from the Sinai.

Article II
Determination of Final Lines and Zones

1. In order to provide maximum security for both Parties after the final withdrawal, the lines and the Zones delineated on Map 1 are to be established and organized as follows:

128

a. Zone A

(1) Zone A is bounded on the east by line A (red line) and on the west by the Suez Canal and the east coast of the Gulf of Suez, as shown on Map 1.

(2) An Egyptian armed force of one mechanized infantry division and its military installations, and field fortifications, will be in this Zone.

(3) The main elements of that Division will consist of:

(a) Three mechanized infantry brigades.

(b) One armored brigade.

(c) Seven field artillery battalions including up to 126 artillery pieces.

(d) Seven anti-aircraft artillery battalions including individual surface-to-air missiles and up to 126 anti-aircraft guns of 37 mm and above.

(e) Up to 230 tanks.

(f) Up to 480 armored personnel vehicles of all types.

(g) Up to a total of twenty-two thousand personnel.

b. Zone B

(1) Zone B is bounded by line B (green-line) on the east and by line A (red line) on the west, as shown on Map 1.

(2) Egyptian border units of four battalions equipped with light weapons and wheeled vehicles will provide security and supplement the civil police in maintaining order in Zone B. The main elements of the four Border Battalions will consist of up to a total of four thousand personnel.

(3) Land based, short range, low power, coastal warning points of the border patrol units may be established on the coast of this Zone.

(4) There will be in Zone B field fortifications and military installations for the four border battalions.

c. Zone C

(1) Zone C is bounded by line B (green line) on the west and the International Boundary and the Gulf of Aqaba on the east, as shown on Map 1.

(2) Only United Nations forces and Egyptian civil police will be stationed in Zone C.

(3) The Egyptian civil police armed with light weapons will perform normal police functions within this Zone.

(4) The United Nations Force will be deployed within Zone C and perform its functions as defined in Article VI of this Annex.

(5) The United Nations Force will be stationed mainly in camps located within the following stationing areas shown on Map 1, and will establish its precise locations after consultations with Egypt:

(a) In that part of the area in the Sinai lying within about 20 Km. of the Mediterranean Sea and adjacent to the International Boundary.

(b) In the Sharm el Sheikh area.

d. Zone D

(1) Zone D is bounded by line D (blue line) on the east and the international boundary on the west, as shown on Map 1.

(2) In this Zone there will be an Israeli limited force of four infantry battalions, their military installations, and field fortifications, and United Nations observers.

(3) The Israeli forces in Zone D will not include tanks, artillery and antiaircraft missiles except individual surface-to-air missiles.

(4) The main elements of the four Israeli infantry battalions will consist of up to 180 armored personnel vehicles of all types and up to a total of four thousand personnel.

2. Access across the international boundary shall only be permitted through entry check points designated by each Party and under its control. Such access shall be in accordance with laws and regulations of each country.

3. Only those field fortifications, military installations, forces, and weapons specifically permitted by this Annex shall be in the Zones.

Article III
Aerial Military Regime

1. Flights of combat aircraft and reconnaisance flights of Egypt and Israel shall take place only over Zones A and D respectively.

2. Only unarmed, non-combat aircraft of Egypt and Israel will be stationed in Zones A and D, respectively.

3. Only Egyptian unarmed transport aircraft will take off and land in Zone B and up to eight such aircraft may maintained in Zone B. The Egyptian border units may be equipped with unarmed helicopters to perform their functions in Zone B.

4. The Egyptian civil police may be equipped with unarmed police helicopters to perform normal police functions in Zone C.

5. Only civilian airfields may be built in the Zones.

6. Without prejudice to the provisions of this Treaty, only those military aerial activities specifically permitted by this Annex shall be allowed in the Zones and the airspace above their territorial waters.

Article IV
Naval Regime

1. Egypt and Israel may base and operate naval vessels along the coasts of Zones A and D, respectively.

2. Egyptian coast guard boats, lightly armed, may be stationed and operate in the territorial waters of Zone B to assist the border units in performing their functions in this Zone.

3. Egyptian civil police equipped with light boats, lightly armed, shall perform normal police functions within the territorial waters of Zone C.

4. Nothing in this Annex shall be considered as derogating from the right of innocent passage of the naval vessels of either party.

5. Only civilian maritime ports and installations may be built in the Zones.

6. Without prejudice to the provisions of this Treaty, only those naval activities specifically permitted by this Annex shall be allowed in the Zones and in their territorial waters.

Article V
Early Warning Systems

Egypt and Israel may establish and operate early warning systems only in Zones A and D respectively.

Article VI
United Nations Operations

1. The Parties will request the United Nations to provide forces and observers to supervise the implementation of this Annex and employ their best efforts to prevent any violation of its terms.

2. With respect to these United Nations forces and observers, as appropriate, the Parties agree to request the following arrangements:

a. Operation of check points, reconnaisance patrols, and observation posts along the international boundary and line B, and within Zone C.

b. Periodic verification of the implementation of the provisions of this Annex will be carried out not less than twice a month unless otherwise agreed by the Parties.

c. Additional verifications within 48 hours after the receipt of a request from either Party.

d. Ensuring the freedom of navigation through the Strait of Tiran in accordance with Article V of the Treaty of Peace.

3. The arrangements described in this article for each zone will be implemented in Zones A, B, and C by the United Nations Force and in Zone D by the United Nations Observers.

4. United Nations verification teams shall be accompanied by liaison officers of the respective Party.

5. The United Nations Force and observers will report their findings to both Parties.

6. The United Nations Force and Observers operating in the Zones will enjoy freedom of movement and other facilities necessary for the performance of their tasks.

7. The United Nations Force and Observers are not empowered to authorize the crossing of the international boundary.

8. The Parties shall agree on the nations from which the United Nations Force and Observers will be drawn. They will be drawn from nations other than those which are permanent members of the United Nations Security Council.

9. The Parties agree that the United Nations should make those command arrangements that will best assure the effective implementation of its responsibilities.

Article VII
Liaison System

1. Upon dissolution of the Joint Commission, a liaison system between the Parties will be established. This liaison system is intended to provide an effective method to assess progress in the implementation of obligations under the present Annex and to resolve any problem that may arise in the course of implementation, and refer other unresolved matters to the higher military authorities of the two countries respectively for consideration. It is also intended to prevent situations resulting from errors or misinterpretation on the part of either Party.

2. An Egyptian liaison office will be established in the city of El-Arish and an Israeli liaison office will be established in the city of Beer-Sheba. Each office will be headed by an officer of the respective country, and assisted by a number of officers.

3. A direct telephone link between the two offices will be set up and also direct telephone lines with the United Nations command will be maintained by both offices.

Article VIII
Respect for War Memorials

Each Party undertakes to preserve in good condition the War Memorials erected in the memory of soldiers of the other Party, namely those erected by Israel in the Sinai and those to be erected by Egypt in Israel, and shall permit access to such monuments.

Article IX
Interim Arrangements

The withdrawal of Israeli armed forces and civilians behind the interim withdrawal line, and the conduct of the forces of the Parties and the United Nations prior to the final withdrawal, will be governed by the attached Appendix and Maps 2 and 3.

APPENDIX TO ANNEX I
ORGANIZATION OF MOVEMENTS IN THE SINAI

Article I
Principles of Withdrawal

1. The withdrawal of Israeli armed forces and civilians from the Sinai will be accomplished in two phases as described in Article I of Annex I. The description and timing of the withdrawal are included in this Appendix. The Joint Commission will develop and present to the Chief Coordinator of the United Nations forces in the Middle East the details of these phases not later than one month before the initiation of each phase of withdrawal.

2. Both Parties agree on the following principles for the sequence of military movements.

a. Notwithstanding the provisions of Article IX, paragraph 2, of this Treaty, until Israeli armed forces complete withdrawal from the current J and M Lines established by the Egyptian-Israeli Agreement of September 1975, hereinafter referred to as the 1975 Agreement, up to the interim withdrawal line, all military arrangements existing under that Agreement will remain in effect, except those military arrangements otherwise provided for in this Appendix.

b. As Israeli armed forces withdraw, United Nations forces will immediately enter the evacuated areas to establish interim and temporary buffer zones as shown on Maps 2 and 3, respectively, for the purpose of maintaining a separation of forces. United Nations forces' deployment will precede the movement of any other personnel into these areas.

c. Within a period of seven days after Israeli armed forces have evacuated any area located in Zone A, units of Egyptian armed forces shall deploy in accordance with the provisions of Article II of this Appendix.

d. Within a period of seven days after Israeli armed forces have evacuated any area located in Zones A or B, Egyptian border units shall deploy in accordance with the provisions of Article II of this Appendix, and will function in accordance with the provisions of Article II of Annex I.

e. Egyptian civil police will enter evacuated areas immediately after the United Nations forces to perform normal police functions.

f. Egyptian naval units shall deploy in the Gulf of Suez in accordance with the provisions of Article II of this Appendix.

g. Except those movements mentioned above, deployments of Egyptian armed forces and the activities covered in Annex I will be effected in the evacuated areas when Israeli armed forces have completed their withdrawal behind the interim withdrawal line.

Article II
Subphases of the Withdrawal to the Interim
Withdrawal Line

1. The withdrawal to the interim withdrawal line will be accomplished in subphases as described in this Article and as shown on Map 3. Each subphase will be completed within the indicated number of months from the date of the exchange of instruments of ratification of this Treaty.

a. First subphase: within two months, Israeli armed forces will withdraw from the area of El Arish, including the town of El Arish and its airfield, shown as Area I on Map 3.

b. Second subphase: within three months, Israeli armed forces will withdraw from the area between line M of the 1975 Agreement and line A, shown as Area II on Map 3.

c. Third subphase: within five months, Israeli armed forces will withdraw from the areas east and south of Area II, shown as Area III on Map 3.

d. Fourth subphase: within seven months, Israeli armed forces will withdraw from the area of El Tor-Ras El Kenisa, shown as Area IV on Map 3.

e. Fifth subphase: Within nine months, Israeli armed forces will withdraw from the remaining areas west of the interim withdrawal line, including the areas of Santa Katrina and the areas east of the Giddi and Mitla passes, shown as Area V on Map 3, thereby completing Israeli withdrawal behind the interim withdrawal line.

2. Egyptian forces will deploy in the areas evacuated by Israeli armed forces as follows:

a. Up to one-third of the Egyptian armed forces in the Sinai in accordance with the 1975 Agreement will deploy in the portions of Zone A lying within Area I, until the completion of interim withdrawal. Thereafter, Egyptian armed forces as described in Article II of Annex I will be deployed in Zone A up to the limits of the interim buffer zone.

b. The Egyptian naval activity in accordance with Article IV of Annex I will commence along the coasts of Areas II, III, and IV, upon completion of the second, third, and fourth subphases, respectively.

c. Of the Egyptian border units described in Article II of Annex I, upon completion of the first subphase one battalion will be deployed in Area I. A second battalion will be deployed in Area II upon completion of the second subphase. A third battalion will be deployed in Area III upon completion of the third subphase. The second and third battalions mentioned above may also be deployed in any of the subsequently evacuated areas of the southern Sinai.

3. United Nations forces in Buffer Zone I of the 1975 Agreement will redeploy to enable the deployment of Egyptian forces described above upon the completion of the first subphase, but will otherwise continue to function in accordance with the provisions of that Agreement in the remainder of that zone until the completion of interim withdrawal, as indicated in Article I of this Appendix.

4. Israeli convoys may use the roads south and east of the main road junction east of El Arish to evacuate Israeli forces and equipment up to the completion of interim withdrawal. These convoys will proceed in daylight upon four hours notice to the Egyptian liaison group and United Nations forces, will be escorted by United Nations forces, and will be in accordance with schedules coordinated by the Joint Commission. An Egyptian liaison officer will accompany convoys to assure uninterrupted movement. The Joint Commission may approve other arrangements for convoys.

Article III
United Nations Forces

1. The Parties shall request that United Nations forces be deployed as necessary to perform the functions described in this Appendix up to the time

of completion of final Israeli withdrawal. For that purpose, the Parties agree to the redeployment of the United Nations Emergency Force.

2. United Nations forces will supervise the implementation of this Appendix and will employ their best efforts to prevent any violation of its terms.

3. When United Nations forces deploy in accordance with the provisions of Articles I and II of this Appendix, they will perform the functions of verification in limited force zones in accordance with Article VI of Annex I, and will establish check points, reconnaissance patrols, and observation posts in the temporary buffer zones described in Article II above. Other functions of the United Nations forces which concern the interim buffer zone are described in Article V of this Appendix.

Article IV
Joint Commission and Liaison

1. The Joint Commission referred to in Article IV of this Treaty will function from the date of exchange of instruments of ratification of this Treaty up to the date of completion of final Israeli withdrawal from the Sinai.

2. The Joint Commission will be composed of representatives of each Party headed by senior officers. This Commission shall invite a representative of the United Nations when discussing subjects concerning the United Nations, or when either Party requests United Nations presence. Decisions of the Joint Commission will be reached by agreement of Egypt and Israel.

3. The Joint Commission will supervise the implementation of the arrangements described in Annex I and this Appendix. To this end, and by agreement of both Parties, it will:

a. coordinate military movements described in this Appendix and supervise their implementation;

b. address and seek to resolve any problem arising out of the implementation of Annex I and this Appendix, and discuss any violations reported by the United Nations Force and Observers and refer to the Governments of Egypt and Israel any unresolved problems;

c. assist the United Nations Force and Observers in the execution of their mandates, and deal with the timetables of the periodic verifications when referred to it by the Parties as provided for in Annex I and in this Appendix;

d. organize the demarcation of the international boundary and all lines and zones described in Annex I and this Appendix;

e. supervise the handing over of the main installations in the Sinai from Israel to Egypt;

f. agree on necessary arrangements for finding and returning missing bodies of Egyptian and Israeli soldiers;

g. organize the setting up and operation of entry check points along the El Arish-Ras Muhammed line in accordance with the provisions of Article 4 of Annex III;

h. conduct its operations through the use of joint liaison teams consisting of one Israeli representative and one Egyptian representative, provided from a standing Liaison Group, which will conduct activities as directed by the Joint Commission;

i. provide liaison and coordination to the United Nations command implementing provisions of the Treaty, and, through the joint liaison teams, maintain local coordination and cooperation with the United Nations Force stationed in specific areas or United Nations Observers monitoring specific areas for any assistance as needed;

j. discuss any other matters which the Parties by agreement may place before it.

4. Meetings of the Joint Commission shall be held at least once a month. In the event that either Party or the Command of the United Nations Force requests a special meeting, it will be convened within 24 hours.

5. The Joint Commission will meet in the buffer zone until the completion of the interim withdrawal and in El Arish and Beer-Sheba alternately afterwards. The first meeting will be held not later than two weeks after the entry into force of this Treaty.

Article V
Definition of the Interim Buffer Zone and Its Activities

1. An interim buffer zone, by which the United Nations Force will effect a separation of Egyptian and Israeli elements, will be established west of and adjacent to the interim withdrawal line as shown on Map 2 after implementation of Israeli withdrawal and deployment behind the interim withdrawal line. Egyptian civil police equipped with light weapons will perform normal police functions within this zone.

2. The United Nations Force will operate check points, reconnaissance patrols, and observation posts within the interim buffer zone in order to ensure compliance with the terms of this Article.

3. In accordance with arrangements agreed upon by both Parties and to be coordinated by the Joint Commission, Israeli personnel will operate military technical installations at four specific locations shown on Map 2 and designated as T1 (map central coordinate 57163940) T2 (map central coordinate 59351541), T3 (map central coordinate 59331527), and T4 (map central coordinate 61130979) under the following principles:

a. The technical installations shall be manned by technical and administrative personnel equipped with small arms required for their protection (revolvers, rifles, sub-machine guns, light machine guns, hand grenades, and ammunition), as follows:

T1–up to 150 personnel

T2 and T3–up to 350 personnel

T4–up to 200 personnel.

b. Israeli personnel will not carry weapons outside the sites, except officers who may carry personal weapons.

c. Only a third party agreed to by Egypt and Israel will enter and conduct inspections within the perimeters of technical installations in the buffer zone. The third party will conduct inspections in a random manner at least once a month. The inspections will verify the nature of the operation of the installations and the weapons and personnel therein. The third party will immediately report to the Parties any divergence from an installation's visual and electronic surveillance or communications role.

d. Supply of the installations, visits for technical and administrative purposes, and replacement of personnel and equipment situated in the sites, may occur uninterruptedly from the United Nations check points to the perimeter of the technical installations, after checking and being escorted by only the United Nations forces.

e. Israel will be permitted to introduce into its technical installations items required for the proper functioning of the installations and personnel.

f. As determined by the Joint Commission, Israel will be permitted to:

(1) Maintain in its installations fire-fighting and general maintenance equipment as well as wheeled administrative vehicles and mobile engineering equipment necessary for the maintenance of the sites. All vehicles shall be unarmed.

(2) Within the sites and in the buffer zone, maintain roads, water lines, and communications cables which serve the sites. At each of the three installation locations (T1, T2 and T3, and T4), this maintenance may be performed with up to two unarmed wheeled vehicles and by up to twelve unarmed personnel with only necessary equipment, including heavy engineering equipment if needed. This maintenance may be performed three times a week, except for special problems, and only after giving the United Nations four hours notice. The teams will be escorted by the United Nations.

g. Movement to and from the technical installations will take place only during daylight hours. Access to, and exit from, the technical installations shall be as follows:

(1) T1: through a United Nations check point, and via the road between Abu Aweigila and the intersection of the Abu Aweigila road and the Gebel Libni road (at Km. 161), as shown on Map 2.

(2) T2 and T3: through a United Nations checkpoint and via the road constructed across the buffer zone to Gebel Katrina, as shown on Map 2.

(3) T2, T3, and T4: via helicopters flying within a corridor at the times, and according to a flight profile, agreed to by the Joint Commission. The helicopters will be checked by the United Nations Force at landing sites outside the perimeter of the installations.

h. Israel will inform the United Nations Force at least one hour in advance of each intended movement to and from the installations.

i. Israel shall be entitled to evacuate sick and wounded and summon medical experts and medical teams at any time after giving immediate notice to the United Nations Force.

4. The details of the above principles and all other matters in this Article requiring coordination by the Parties will be handled by the Joint Commission.

5. These technical installations will be withdrawn when Israeli forces withdraw from the interim withdrawal line, or at a time agreed by the Parties.

Article VI
Disposition of Installations and Military Barriers

Disposition of installations and military barriers will be determined by the Parties in accordance with the following guidelines:

1. Up to three weeks before Israeli withdrawal from any area, the Joint Commission will arrange for Israeli and Egyptian liaison and technical teams to conduct a joint inspection of all appropriate installations to agree upon condition of structures and articles which will be transferred to Egyptian control and to arrange for such transfer. Israel will declare, at that time, its plans for disposition of installations and articles within the installations.

2. Israel undertakes to transfer to Egypt all agreed infrastructure, utilities, and installations intact, inter alia, airfields, roads, pumping stations, and ports. Israel will present to Egypt the information necessary for the maintenance and operation of these facilities. Egyptian technical teams will be permitted to observe and familiarize themselves with the operation of these facilities for a period of up to two weeks prior to transfer.

3. When Israel relinquishes Israeli military water points near El Arish and El Tor, Egyptian technical teams will assume control of those installa-

tions and ancillary equipment in accordance with an orderly transfer process arranged beforehand by the Joint Commission. Egypt undertakes to continue to make available at all water supply points the normal quantity of currently available water up to the time Israel withdraws behind the international boundary, unless otherwise agreed in the Joint Commission.

4. Israel will make its best effort to remove or destroy all military barriers, including obstacles and minefields, in the areas and adjacent waters from which it withdraws, according to the following concept:

a. Military barriers will be cleared first from areas near populations, roads, and major installations and utilities.

b. For those obstacles and minefields which cannot be removed or destroyed prior to Israeli withdrawal, Israel will provide detailed maps to Egypt and the United Nations through the Joint Commission not later than 15 days before entry of United Nations forces into the affected areas.

c. Egyptian military engineers will enter those areas after United Nations forces enter to conduct barrier clearance operations in accordance with Egyptian plans to be submitted prior to implementation.

Article VII
Surveillance Activities

1. Aerial surveillance activities during the withdrawal will be carried out as follows:

a. Both Parties request the United States to continue airborne surveillance flights in accordance with previous agreements until the completion of final Israeli withdrawal.

b. Flight profiles will cover the Limited Forces Zones to monitor the limitations on forces and armaments, and to determine that Israeli armed forces have withdrawn from the areas described in Article II of Annex I, Article II of this Appendix, and Maps 2 and 3, and that these forces thereafter remain behind their lines. Special inspection flights may be flown at the request of either Party or of the United Nations.

c. Only the main elements in the military organizations of each Party, as described in Annex I and in this Appendix, will be reported.

2. Both Parties request the United States operated Sinai Field Mission to continue its operations in accordance with previous agreements until completion of the Israeli withdrawal from the area east of the Giddi and Mitla Passes. Thereafter, the Mission will be terminated.

Article VIII
Exercise of Egyptian Sovereignty

Egypt will resume the exercise of its full sovereignty over evacuated parts of the Sinai upon Israeli withdrawal as provided for in Article I of this Treaty.

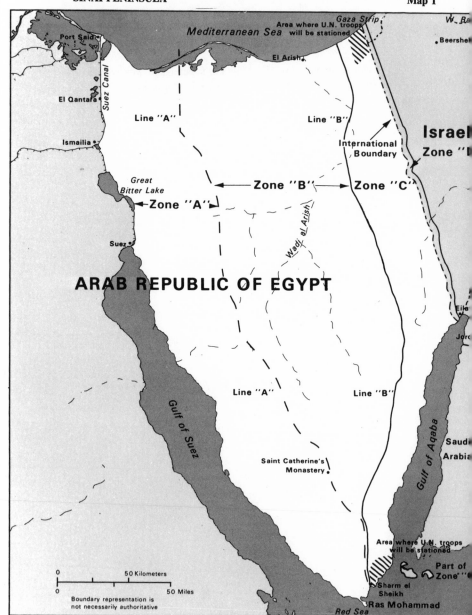

Representation of original map included in treaty.

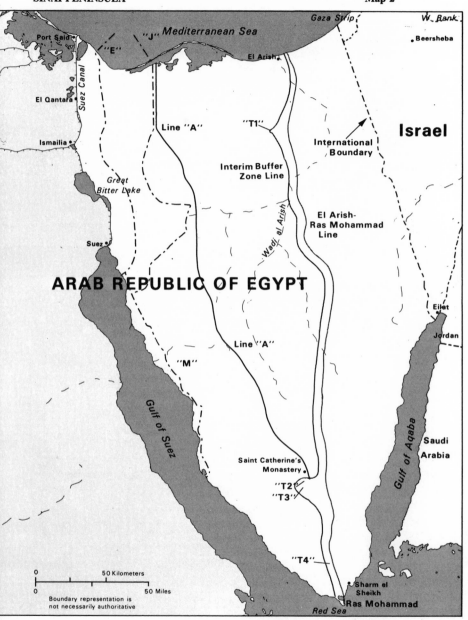

Representation of original map included in treaty.

Map 3

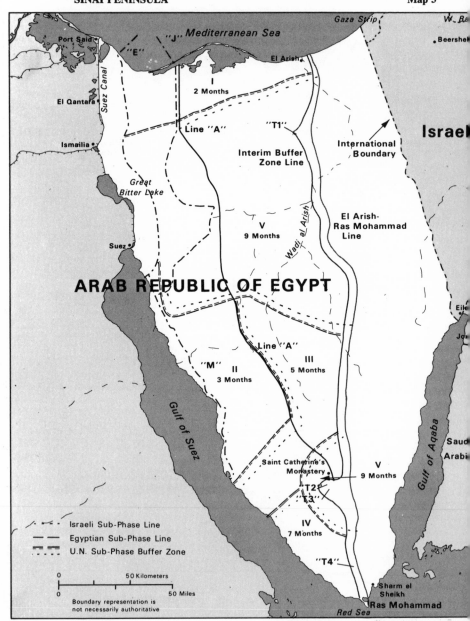

Mediterranean Sea

Gaza Strip

W. Ba

Port Said

"J"

"E"

Beershe

El Arish

El Qantara

2 Months

Suez Canal

I

Line "A"

"T1"

International
Boundary

Israel

Ismailia

Interim Buffer
Zone Line

Great
Bitter Lake

Wadi al Arish

El Arish-
Ras Mohammad
Line

V
9 Months

Suez

ARAB REPUBLIC OF EGYPT

Eile

Jo

Line "A"

"M"

II
3 Months

III
5 Months

Gulf of Suez

Saud
Arabi

Gulf of Aqaba

Saint Catherine's
Monastery

V
9 Months

T2

T3

IV
7 Months

- ·-·- Israeli Sub-Phase Line

- - - Egyptian Sub-Phase Line

---- U.N. Sub-Phase Buffer Zone

0   50 Kilometers

0   50 Miles

Boundary representation is
not necessarily authoritative

"T4"

Sharm el
Sheikh

Ras Mohammad

Red Sea

Representation of original map included in treaty.

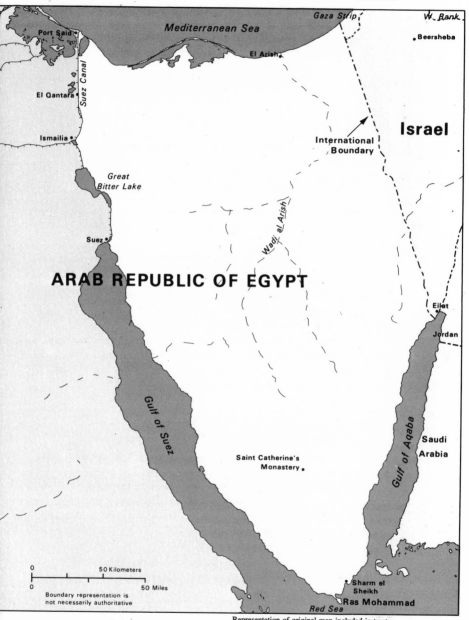

Representation of original map included in treaty.

Annex III

PROTOCOL CONCERNING RELATIONS OF THE PARTIES

Article 1
Diplomatic and Consular Relations

The Parties agree to establish diplomatic and consular relations and to exchange ambassadors upon completion of the interim withdrawal.

Article 2
Economic and Trade Relations

1. The Parties agree to remove all discriminatory barriers to normal economic relations and to terminate economic boycotts of each other upon completion of the interim withdrawal.

2. As soon as possible, and not later than six months after the completion of the interim withdrawal, the Parties will enter negotiations with a view to concluding an agreement on trade and commerce for the purpose of promoting beneficial economic relations.

Article 3
Cultural Relations

1. The Parties agree to establish normal cultural relations following completion of the interim withdrawal.

2. They agree on the desirability of cultural exchanges in all fields, and shall, as soon as possible and not later than six months after completion of the interim withdrawal, enter into negotiations with a view to concluding a cultural agreement for this purpose.

Article 4
Freedom of Movement

1. Upon completion of the interim withdrawal, each Party will permit the free movement of the nationals and vehicles of the other into and within

its territory according to the general rules applicable to nationals and vehicles of other states. Neither Party will impose discriminatory restrictions on the free movement of persons and vehicles from its territory to the territory of the other.

2. Mutual unimpeded access to places of religious and historical significance will be provided on a nondiscriminatory basis.

Article 5
Cooperation for Development and Good Neighborly Relations

1. The Parties recognize a mutuality of interest in good neighborly relations and agree to consider means to promote such relations.

2. The Parties will cooperate in promoting peace, stability and development in their region. Each agrees to consider proposals the other may wish to make to this end.

3. The Parties shall seek to foster mutual understanding and tolerance and will, accordingly, abstain from hostile propaganda against each other.

Article 6
Transportation and Telecommunications

1. The Parties recognize as applicable to each other the rights, privileges and obligations provided for by the aviation agreements to which they are both party, particularly by the Convention on International Civil Aviation, 1944 ("The Chicago Convention") and the International Air Services Transit Agreement, 1944.

2. Upon completion of the interim withdrawal any declaration of national emergency by a party under Article 89 of the Chicago Convention will not be applied to the other party on a discriminatory basis.

3. Egypt agrees that the use of airfields left by Israel near El Arish, Rafah, Ras El Nagb and Sharm El Sheikh shall be for civilian purposes only, including possible commercial use by all nations.

4. As soon as possible and not later than six months after the completion of the interim withdrawal, the Parties shall enter into negotiations for the purpose of concluding a civil aviation agreement.

5. The Parties will reopen and maintain roads and railways between their countries and will consider further road and rail links. The Parties further agree that a highway will be constructed and maintained between Egypt, Israel and Jordan near Eilat with guaranteed free and peaceful passage of persons, vehicles and goods between Egypt and Jordan, without prejudice to their sovereignty over that part of the highway which falls within their respective territory.

6. Upon completion of the interim withdrawal, normal postal, telephone, telex, data facsimile, wireless and cable communications and television relay services by cable, radio and satellite shall be established between the two Parties in accordance with all relevant international conventions and regulations.

7. Upon completion of the interim withdrawal, each Party shall grant normal access to its ports for vessels and cargoes of the other, as well as vessels and cargoes destined for or coming from the other. Such access shall be granted on the same conditions generally applicable to vessels and cargoes of other nations. Article 5 of the Treaty of Peace will be implemented upon the exchange of instruments of ratification of the aforementioned Treaty.

Article 7
Enjoyment of Human Rights

The Parties affirm their commitment to respect and observe human rights and fundamental freedoms for all, and they will promote these rights and freedoms in accordance with the United Nations Charter.

Article 8
Territorial Seas

Without prejudice to the provisions of Article 5 of the Treaty of Peace each Party recognizes the right of the vessels of the other Party to innocent passage through its territorial sea in accordance with the rules of international law.

AGREED MINUTES
TO ARTICLES I, IV, V AND VI AND ANNEXES I AND III
OF TREATY OF PEACE

Article I

Egypt's resumption of the exercise of full sovereignty over the Sinai provided for in paragraph 2 of Article I shall occur with regard to each area upon Israel's withdrawal from that area.

Article IV

It is agreed between the parties that the review provided for in Article IV(4) will be undertaken when requested by either party, commencing within three months of such a request, but that any amendment can be made only with the mutual agreement of both parties.

Article V

The second sentence of paragraph 2 of Article V shall not be construed as limiting the first sentence of that paragraph. The foregoing is not to be construed as contravening the second sentence of paragraph 2 of Article V, which reads as follows:

"The parties will respect each other's right to navigation and overflight for access to either country through the Strait of Tiran and the Gulf of Aqaba."

Article VI(2)

The provisions of Article VI shall not be construed in contradiction to the provisions of the framework for peace in the Middle East agreed at Camp David. The foregoing is not to be construed as contravening the provisions of Article VI(2) of the Treaty, which reads as follows:

"The Parties undertake to fulfill in good faith their obligations under this Treaty, without regard to action or inaction of any other party and independently of any instrument external to this Treaty."

Article VI(5)

It is agreed by the Parties that there is no assertion that this Treaty prevails over other Treaties or agreements or that other Treaties or agreements prevail over this Treaty. The foregoing is not to be construed as contravening the provisions of Article VI(5) of the Treaty, which reads as follows:

"Subject to Article 103 of the United Nations Charter, in the event of a conflict between the obligations of the Parties under the present Treaty and any of their other obligations, the obligations under this Treaty will be binding and implemented."

Annex I

Article VI, Paragraph 8, of Annex I provides as follows:

"The Parties shall agree on the nations from which the United Nations force and observers will be drawn. They will be drawn from nations other than those which are permanent members of the United Nations Security Council."

The Parties have agreed as follows:

"With respect to the provisions of paragraph 8, Article VI, of Annex I, if no agreement is reached between the Parties, they will accept or support a U.S. proposal concerning the composition of the United Nations force and observers."

Annex III

The Treaty of Peace and Annex III thereto provide for establishing normal economic relations between the Parties. In accordance therewith, it is agreed that such relations will include normal commercial sales of oil by Egypt to Israel, and that Israel shall be fully entitled to make bids for Egyptian-origin oil not needed for Egyptian domestic oil consumption, and Egypt and its oil concessionaires will entertain bids made by Israel, on the same basis and terms as apply to other bidders for such oil.

For the Government
of Israel:
M. Begin

For the Government of the
Arab Republic of Egypt:
A. Sadat

Witnessed by:

Jimmy Carter
Jimmy Carter, President
of the United States of America

JOINT LETTER TO PRESIDENT CARTER FROM
PRESIDENT SADAT AND PRIME MINISTER BEGIN

MARCH 26, 1979

DEAR MR. PRESIDENT:

This letter confirms that Egypt and Israel have agreed as follows:

The Governments of Egypt and Israel recall that they concluded at Camp David and signed at the White House on September 17, 1978, the annexed documents entitled "A Framework for Peace in the Middle East Agreed at Camp David" and "Framework for the conclusion of a Peace Treaty between Egypt and Israel."

For the purpose of achieving a comprehensive peace settlement in accordance with the above-mentioned Frameworks, Egypt and Israel will proceed with the implementation of those provisions relating to the West Bank and the Gaza Strip. They have agreed to start negotiations within a month after the exchange of the instruments of ratification of the Peace Treaty. In accordance with the "Framework for Peace in the Middle East," the Hashemite Kingdom of Jordan is invited to join the negotiations. The Delegations of Egypt and Jordan may include Palestinians from the West Bank and Gaza Strip or other Palestinians as mutually agreed. The purpose of the negotiation shall be to agree, prior to the elections, on the modalities for establishing the elected self-governing authority (administrative council), define its powers and responsibilities, and agree upon other related issues. In the event Jordan decides not to take part in the negotiations, the negotiations will be held by Egypt and Israel.

The two Governments agree to negotiate continuously and in good faith to conclude these negotiations at the earliest possible date. They also agree that the objective of the negotiations is the establishment of the self-governing authority in the West Bank and Gaza in order to provide full autonomy to the inhabitants.

Egypt and Israel set for themselves the goal of completing the negotiations within one year so that elections will be held as expeditiously as possible after agreement has been reached between the parties. The self-governing authority referred to in the "Framework for Peace in the Middle East" will be established and inaugurated within one month after it has been elected, at which time the transitional period of five years will begin. The Israeli military government and its civilian administration will be withdrawn, to be replaced by the self-governing authority, as specified in the "Framework for Peace in the Middle East." A withdrawal of Israeli armed forces will then take place and there will be a redeployment of the remaining Israeli forces into specified security locations.

This letter also confirms our understanding that the United States Government will participate fully in all stages of negotiations.

Sincerely yours,

For the Government of Israel:
M. BEGIN
Menachem Begin

For the Government of the
Arab Republic of Egypt:
A. SADAT
Mohamed Anwar El-Sadat

The President,
The White House

Explanatory Note

President Carter, upon receipt of the Joint Letter to him from President Sadat and Prime Minister Begin, has added to the American and Israeli copies the notation: "I have been informed that the expression 'West Bank' is understood by the Government of Israel to mean 'Judea and Samaria'." This notation is in accordance with similar procedures established at Camp David.

LETTERS REGARDING EXCHANGE OF AMBASSADORS

MARCH 26, 1979

DEAR MR. PRESIDENT:

In response to your request, I can confirm that, within one month after the completion of Israel's withdrawal to the interim line as provided for in the Treaty of Peace between Egypt and Israel, Egypt will send a resident ambassador to Israel and will receive a resident Israeli ambassador in Egypt.

Sincerely,
A. SADAT
Mohamed Anwar El-Sadat

The President,
The White House

MARCH 26, 1979

DEAR MR. PRIME MINISTER:

I have received a letter from President Sadat that, within one month after Israel completes its withdrawal to the interim line in Sinai, as provided for in the Treaty of Peace between Egypt and Israel, Egypt will send a resident ambassador to Israel and will receive in Egypt a resident Israeli ambassador.

I would be grateful if you will confirm that this procedure will be agreeable to the Government of Israel.

Sincerely,
JIMMY CARTER
Jimmy Carter

His Excellency
  MENACHEM BEGIN,
    Prime Minister of the
      State of Israel

MARCH 26, 1979

DEAR MR. PRESIDENT:

I am pleased to be able to confirm that the Government of Israel is agreeable to the procedure set out in your letter of March 26, 1979 in which you state:

"I have received a letter from President Sadat that, within one month after Israel completes its withdrawal to the interim line in Sinai, as provided for in the Treaty of Peace between Egypt and Israel, Egypt will send a resident ambassador to Israel and will receive in Egypt a resident Israeli ambassador."

Sincerely,
M. BEGIN
Menachem Begin

The President,
  The White House

LETTERS FROM PRESIDENT CARTER TO PRESIDENT
SADAT AND PRIME MINISTER BEGIN

MARCH 26, 1979

DEAR MR. PRESIDENT:

I wish to confirm to you that subject to United States Constitutional processes:

In the event of an actual or threatened violation of the Treaty of Peace between Egypt and Israel, the United States will, on request of one or both of the Parties, consult with the Parties with respect thereto and will take such other action as it may deem appropriate and helpful to achieve compliance with the Treaty.

The United States will conduct aerial monitoring as requested by the Parties pursuant to Annex I of the Treaty.

The United States believes the Treaty provision for permanent stationing of United Nations personnel in the designated limited force zone can and should be implemented by the United Nations Security Council. The United States will exert its utmost efforts to obtain the requisite action by the Security Council. If the Security Council fails to establish and maintain the arrangements called for in the Treaty, the President will be prepared to take those steps necessary to ensure the establishment and maintenance of an acceptable alternative multinational force.

Sincerely,
JIMMY CARTER
Jimmy Carter

His Excellency
Mohamed Anwar El-Sadat,
President of the Arab
Republic of Egypt

MARCH 26, 1979
DEAR MR. PRIME MINISTER:

I wish to confirm to you that subject to United States Constitutional processes:

In the event of an actual or threatened violation of the Treaty of Peace between Israel and Egypt, the United States will, on request of one or both of the Parties, consult with the Parties with respect thereto and will take such other action as it may deem appropriate and helpful to achieve compliance with the Treaty.

The United States will conduct aerial monitoring as requested by the Parties pursuant to Annex I of the Treaty.

The United States believes the Treaty provision for permanent stationing of United Nations personnel in the designated limited force zone can and should be implemented by the United Nations Security Council. The United States will exert its utmost efforts to obtain the requisite action by the Security Council. If the Security Council fails to establish and maintain the arrangements called for in the Treaty, the President will be prepared to take those steps necessary to ensure the establishment and maintenance of an acceptable alternative multinational force.

Sincerely,
JIMMY CARTER
Jimmy Carter

His Excellency
Menachem Begin,
Prime Minister of the
State of Israel

Notes

INTRODUCTION

1. Abraham S. Becker, "The Superpowers in the Arab-Israeli Conflict, 1970–1973," Rand Paper P-5167 (December 1973), §I, discusses the importance of 1970 events.

2. Concerning the civil war in Jordan, see John K. Cooley, *Green March, Black September: The Story of the Palestinian Arabs* (London: Frank Cass, 1973); and Paul A. Jureidini and William E. Hazen, *Six Clashes: An Analysis of the Relationship Between the Palestinian Guerrilla Movement and the Governments of Jordan and Lebanon* (Kensington, Md.: American Institutes for Research, 1971) and *The Palestinian Movement in Politics* (Lexington: Heath, 1976), Chapter 3. On the Assad "coup," see the relevant issues of *An Nahar Arab Report* and Nikolaos van Dam, *The Struggle for Power in Syria: Sectarianism, Regionalism, and Tribalism in Politics, 1961–1978* (New York: St. Martin's, 1979). Good accounts of the War of Attrition appear in Lawrence L. Whetten, *The Canal War: Four-Power Conflict in the Middle East* (Cambridge, Mass.: MIT Press, 1974), and Trevor N. Dupuy, *Elusive Victory: The Arab-Israeli Wars, 1947–1974* (New York: Harper & Row, 1978).

3. R. D. McLaurin and Mohammed Mughisuddin, *Cooperation and Conflict: Egyptian, Iraqi, and Syrian Objectives and U.S. Policy* (Washington, D.C.: American Institutes for Research, 1975), pp. 228–29.

4. Cf. Itamar Rabinovich, "The Limits of Military Power: Syria's Role," *Lebanon in Crisis: Participants and Issues,* ed. P. Edward Haley and Lewis W. Snider (Syracuse: Syracuse University Press, 1979), pp. 61–62.

5. See Mohamed Heikal, *The Road to Ramadan* (New York: Quadrangle, 1975), and Anwar el-Sadat, *In Search of Identity: An Autobiography* (New York: Harper & Row, 1978), pp. 218–22, Chapter 9.

6. Charles Wakebridge, "The Egyptian Staff Solution," *Military Review* 55, 3 (March 1975):3–11.

7. A fourth—economic—is apparent, and a fifth—psychological—is equally significant. We are not dealing with the economic context here because its importance to this book is the political ramifications of economic change, which we shall treat on political terms and because the postwar petroleum price increase, although sudden, was the product of discrete processes already under way before the October War (changing concession terms, changing ownership patterns, changing demand curves,

157

increased role of OPEC, determination of OPEC governments to enter downstream operations). The embargo, by contrast, would probably have been impossible without the war. Yet, again, it is not the economic hardship resulting from the embargo that is germane to this paper, but, rather, the political leverage conferred by *threatening* the embargo.

Psychological outcomes of the war have been significant and, in several cases, are directly relevant to this study. They have, however, been dealt with here in terms of their political manifestations, especially in Chapters 2 and 3.

8. Labor's power has traditionally been based upon the voting strength of the generally older Ashkenazi Jews. The demographic realities are that this constituency has less and less numerical strength. *Likud,* by contrast, and to a lesser extent Yadin's DMC, are attractive to the younger and less European Jews who make up an ever-increasing portion of the Israeli electorate.

9. See Steven Rosen and Martin Indyk, "The Temptation to Pre-empt in a Fifth Arab-Israeli War," *Orbis,* 20, 2 (Summer 1976):265–85. The argument in favor of preemption derives from the widespread belief that Israel could have destroyed most of the Arab surface-to-air missile sites had preemption been permitted; ibid., pp. 271–72.

10. We do not mean to leave the impression here that either Egypt (and Syria) before the war or Israel afterwards sought "peace at any price." Indeed, although the shock of the personnel losses to Israel caused an immediate postwar interest in settlement, popular attitudes on the *retention* of eastern and northern territories captured in 1967 seems to have hardened somewhat within five years. The point we are making here is simply that many in Israel considered the status quo both acceptable and *stable*—hence desirable—before the October War. Few could argue persuasively for that view in retrospect.

11. Among the many books on the war, the reader may wish to consult the following: Hassan al Badri et al., *The Ramadan War* (Dunn Loring, Va.: T. N. Dupuy Associates, 1978); Trevor N. Dupuy, *Elusive Victory,* "Book Five"; Mohamed Heik-al, *The Road to Ramadan*; Chaim Herzog, *The War of Atonement* (Boston: Little, Brown, 1974); International Symposium on the 1973 October War, *Proceedings, I: The Military Sector* (Cairo, 1976); London Sunday Times Insight Team, *The Yom Kippur War* (London: Times of London, 1974); Edgar O'Ballance, *No Victor, No Vanquished: The Yom Kippur War* (San Rafael: Presidio Press, 1978); Riad N. El-Rayyes and Dunia Nahas, eds., *The October War: Dcouments, Personalities, Analyses, and Maps* (Beirut: An-Nahar Press Services SARL, 1974); Zeev Schiff, *October Earthquake* (New York: Transaction Books, 1974); Lawrence Whetten, *The Canal War*; Louis Williams, ed., *Military Aspects of the Israeli-Arab Conflict* (Tel Aviv: University Publishing Projects, 1975).

12. See, e.g., Steven Rosen, "What the Next Arab-Israeli War Might Look Like," *International Security* 2, 4 (Spring 1978):149–74; Anthony H. Cordesman, "The Arab-Israeli Balance: How Much Is Too Much?" *Armed Forces Journal International* 115, 2 (October 1977):32ff.

13. Whether the "effect" was psychological or physical it was real. There is a persistent argument—supported by some substantial supply data—to the effect that the

embargo was *not* effective in reducing supplies of oil to the embargoed countries but that it was *very* effective in changing consumer purchase and storage behavior and in inducing cóntrol interventions. These changes taken together, it is averred, produced the "oil shortage" phenomenon, an appearance brought about by recipient-caused disruptions rather than a reality caused by supplier behavior.

14. It should not be inferred from the text that Faisal dictated foreign policy. Rather, foreign policy in Saudi Arabia evolved from a consensus of royal family views. However, even on subject areas that captured the attention and activity of princes as senior as Fahd and Sultan, Faisal's voice in intrafamily discussions was dominant and persuasive. See M. Graeme Bannerman, "Saudi Arabia and the Lebanon Crisis," *Lebanon in Crisis,* ed. Haley and Snider, pp. 113–16.

15. See Edward R. F. Sheehan, *The Arabs, Israelis, and Kissinger: A Secret History of American Diplomacy in the Middle East* (New York: Reader's Digest Press, 1976); Matti Golan, *The Secret Conversations of Henry Kissinger* (New York: Quadrangle, 1976); and William B. Quandt, *Decade of Decisions: American Policy Toward the Arab-Israeli Conflict, 1967–1976* (Berkeley: University of California Press, 1977).

16. Cf. Haley and Snider, *Lebanon in Crisis,* passim; Adeed I. Dawisha, "Syria in Lebanon: Assad's Vietnam," *Foreign Policy,* no. 33 (Winter 1978–79), pp. 135–50.

17. See Paul A. Jureidini and R. D. McLaurin, "The Hashemite Kingdom of Jordan," *Lebanon in Crisis,* ed. Haley and Snider, p. 153; and Fehmi Saddy, *The Eastern Front* (Alexandria, Va.: Abbott Associates, 1976).

18. Cf. el-Sadat, *In Search,* Chapter 9.

19. See below and Lewis W. Snider and R. D. McLaurin, *Saudi Arabia's Air Defense Requirements in the 1980s* (Alexandria, Va.: Abbott Associates, 1979).

20. Israel has received substantial amounts of grant military support from the United States over the last several years. U.S. security assistance to Israel has taken a unique form: virtually 100 percent "loan" with half of the loan "forgiven." Technically, this is not, then "grant" aid; in fact, it is just that.

21. See, generally, Don Peretz, *The Government and Politics of Israel* (Boulder: Westview, 1979), for a discussion of social change in Israel and its political ramifications.

22. R. D. McLaurin and James M. Price, "OPEC Current Account Surpluses: Assistance to the Arab Front-Line States," *Oriente Moderno* 58, 11 (Novembre 1978):533–46.

23. R. D. McLaurin, "The Transfer of Technology to the Middle East," *The Political Economy of the Middle East,* ed. R. Kaufman and J. Wooten (Washington, D.C.: U.S. Library of Congress, 1980).

24. Paul A. Jureidini, R. D. McLaurin, and James M. Price, "Arab Reactions to the Egyptian-Israeli Peace Treaty," Abbott Associates, SR46 (March 26, 1979), pp. 3–5.

25. Some of the documents relating to the U.S.-Egypt-Israel summit are included in the appendices to this volume.

26. The text of the treaty and some related documents are included in the appendices to this volume.

27. See below.

28. On November 4, 1979, following days of demonstrations near the U.S. embassy, a number of "militants" entered the compound and seized the building, the grounds, and more than sixty U.S. diplomats and others then in the embassy. Although professing support for Ayatollah Khomeini, the captors acted independently from, and somteimes in conflict with, the wishes of the Iranian government, the Revolutionary Council (the nominal supreme authority in Iran), and the ayatollah.

29. In the aftermath of the embassy seizure in Tehran and the subsequent attack by Saudi dissidents on the Grand Mosque in Mecca (falsely attributed by broadcast media in Iran to the United States), several U.S. embassies and other buildings in Muslim countries stretching from Libya to the Philippines came under attack.

30. On December 27, 1979, Soviet forces moved into Afghanistan, deposed the president, Hafizullah Amin, and installed a new regime under Babrak Karmal which then "requested" Soviet assistance. This military intervention had a significant psychological effect in Washington, D.C., and in the Middle East region as well. In addition to an immediate and bloody purge, the regime's image was adversely affected by the magnitude of the Soviet military presence, estimated at between 85,000 and 100,000 troops, many of whom were deployed along the border with Iran.

31. The American retreat can be traced to the Vietnam period and has its roots even further back in history, around 1960 when the decolonization movement had gathered substantial momentum and a Western military presence, or ties between Western and third world regimes, were viewed as *prima facie* evidence of neocolonialism.

1—ACTORS AND FORCES

1. Lawrence L. Whetten, *The Canal War: Four Power Conflict in the Middle East* (Cambridge, Mass.: MIT Press, 1974), and Trevor N. Dupuy, *Elusive Victory: The Arab-Israeli Wars, 1947–1974* (New York: Harper & Row, 1978), provide good accounts of the War of Attrition, the former providing more of the diplomatic and the latter more of the military detail.

2. For a more Egyptian—but ultimately personal—view, see Mohamed Hassanein Heykal's books, *The Road to Ramadan* (New York: Quadrangle/New York Times Book Company, 1975), *The Cairo Dcouments* (New York: Doubleday, 1973), and *The Sphynx and the Commissar* (New York: Harper & Row, 1979). For differing views, cf. Alvin Z. Rubinstein, *Red Star Over the Nile* (Princeton: Princeton University Press, 1977) and "The Soviet-Egyptian Influence Relationship Since the June 1967 War," *Soviet Naval Policy: Objectives and Constraints,* ed. Michael MccGwire, Ken Booth, and John McDonnell (New York: Praeger, 1975), pp. 153–81; Hélène Carrère d'Encausse, *La Politique soviétique au Moyen-Orient* (Paris: Presses Universitaires de France, 1975); Jon D. Glassman, *Arms for the Arabs: The Soviet Union and War in*

the Middle East (Baltimore: Johns Hopkins University Press, 1975); R. D. McLaurin, *The Middle East in Soviet Foreign Policy* (Lexington: D. C. Heath, 1975); and Galia Golan, *Yom Kippur and After: The Soviet Union and the Middle East Crisis* (Cambridge: Cambridge University Press, 1977).

3. Sadat was considered a laughing stock when 1971—which he had proclaimed as the "Year of Decision"—passed without Egypt's having made appreciable progress toward military action.

4. The recognition of this fact has driven much of Syrian policy since the Sinai II accords in September 1975. Syrian leaders have been forced to try to reconstitute a viable military threat without Egypt—in vain. But Iraq cannot replace Egypt, and the absence of a real front in the south to force Israel to conduct a two-front war guarantees the futility of the Syrian effort, even though Israel will still be forced to keep some personnel deployed on the Sinai front.

5. James M. Price, "A Country Profile of Egypt," mimeographed (Abbott Associates, 1978), pp. 1–5, provides a detailed treatment of Egyptian economic planning; U.S. Embassy, Cairo, "Foreign Economic Trends and Their Implications for the United States: Egypt" (Washington, D.C.: U.S. Department of Commerce, June 1977), p. 8; U.S. Department of State, "Discussion Paper on the Egyptian Economy," 1977, p. 3; "Sadat's Mood Clearer Than His Intentions," *An Nahar Arab Report and Memo* 2, 21 (May 22, 1978):3–4; and "The 1978 Budget and Defense Spending," ibid. 1, 35 (December 19, 1977), p. 2.

6. Price, "A Country Profile of Egypt," p. 3.

7. R. D. McLaurin, Mohammed Mughisuddin, and Abraham R. Wagner, *Foreign Policy Making in the Middle East* (New York: Praeger, 1977), Chapter 3. There, we discuss at greater length the groups identified in the text.

8. Cf. R. D. McLaurin, Paul A. Jureidini, and Preston S. Abbott, "Political Leadership and Strategic Decision," Abbott Associates SR36 (September 1978); Shlomo Aronson, "Sadat's Initiative and Israel's Response: The Strategy of Peace and the Strategy of Strategy" (UCLA: Center for Arms Control and International Security, ACIS Research Note no. 4, May 1978).

9. "Sadat Shrugs Off Attacks," *An Nahar Arab Report and Memo* 2, 26 (June 26, 1978):3; and "Critic Asks Sadat to Face Inquiry," *New York Times,* June 21, 1978, p. 3.

10. E.g., former editor of *al Ahram,* Mohammed Heikal; senior editor of the same paper, Mohammed Sid Ahmed; Abdul Ezz al Hariri; the Leftist Party's representative in Parliament, Abdul Fattah Hassan; a Parliament representative for the New Wafd, Hussein Fahmy; leader of the National Unionist Progressive Party, Ahmed Hamroush of *Rose al Youssef* magazine; Saleh Issa of *al Akhbar;* and Fuad Nugem, a poet.

11. In his early years at Egypt's helm, Sadat carefully avoided castigating his predecessor, but even then he was in the process of dismantling many programs and concepts of Nasser. In the foreign policy field the new opening toward the West and the expulsion of most Soviet advisors in mid-1972 reflected an approach to international problems distinctly different from Nasser's. Criticism of Nasser's Arab Socialist path has been more open since 1973, but most of Sadat's public statements

carefully stress his own views and methods rather than highlighting failings of the past.

12. Avigdor Haselkorn, R. D. McLaurin, and Abraham R. Wagner, *Middle East Net Assesement Volume I: Regional Threat Perceptions* (Marina del Rey: Analytical Assessments Corporation, 1979), p. 38.

13. McLaurin, Mughisuddin, and Wagner, *Foreign Policy Making,* pp. 55–56.

14. Ibid., Chapter 3, passim.

15. The Egyptian people are not oriented toward revolution. Nasser noted (with frustration) that their inclination was to tolerate and adapt to their burdens rather than to attempt to bring about change.

16. Before 1953 the shah was not as actively engaged in ruling Iran.

17. The shah for years labored to create the impression that he was restored to power in Iran on the strength of a great, popular uprising. In fact, a small group of conspirators—no more than a handful—constituted the cabal that led to his return. See Kermit Roosevelt, *Countercoup: The Bloody Struggle for the Control of Iran* (New York: McGraw, 1979).

18. See Lewis W. Snider, "Minorities and Political Power," *The Political Role of Minority Groups in the Middle East,* ed. R. D. McLaurin (New York: Praeger, 1979), Chapter 10.

19. John K. Cooley, "Iran, the Palestinians, and the Gulf," *Foreign Affairs* 57, 5 (Summer 1979):1017–34, is an excellent discussion of the new Iranian regime's relations with the PLO and the implications for the Persian Gulf.

20. Another field affected by the change is intelligence. SAVAK and Mossad, the shah's and Israel's intelligence arms, respectively, worked closely together. See, e.g., Tad Szulc, "Shaking Up the C.I.A.," *The New York Times Magazine,* July 29, 1979, pp. 16–17.

21. Cf. Kenneth Freed, "Iran's Once-Proud Army Reduced to Motley Crew," *Los Angeles Times,* June 2, 1979, pp. 1, 6.

22. Ibid.

23. A real danger is that in their inexperience the ayatollah's group may choose issues designed to rally domestic opinion or threaten foreign governments without the discrimination in these matters that experience provides. For example, the recent exploitation of the Shi'a issue in Iraq is clearly too sensitive; such an effort led to hostilities the Iranian government was ill prepared to meet.

24. Don Peretz, *The Government and Politics of Israel* (Boulder: Westview Press, 1979); Lee E. Dutter, "Eastern and Western Jews: Ethnic Divisions in Israeli Society," *Middle East Journal* 31, 4 (Autumn 1977):451–68.

25. It must, of course, be noted that despite its tenuous and exclusive grip on political legitimacy for many years, Labor never had the strength to form a majority cabinet.

26. That is, if, as some Israelis seem to believe, Jordan should become a Palestinian state, Israel might no longer be forced to confront the issue of the occupied

territories in terms of the creation of a Palestinian homeland. However, it may be argued with equal ease that the emergence of a Palestinian state in the East Bank might give a stronger, territorial base to irredentist claims on the West Bank.

27. For an overview of these problems see Ann Crittenden, "Israel's Economic Plight," *Foreign Affairs* 47, 5 (Summer 1979):1005–16.

28. Ian Steven Lustick, "Arabs in the Jewish State: A Study in the Effective Control of a Minority Population," Ph.D. diss. (University of California, Berkeley, 1976), pp. 131–32.

29. Ibid., p. 133.

30. Abraham R. Wagner, *The Impact of the 1973 October War on Israeli Policy and Implications for U.S. Defense Policy* (Washington, D.C.: American Institutes for Research, 1975), pp. 24–25, 55–58.

31. Ibid., pp. 13, 29.

32. R. D. McLaurin, Mohammed Mughisuddin, and Don Peretz, *Middle East Foreign Policy: Issue and Process* (New York: Praeger, 1981), Chapter 7.

33. McLaurin, Mughisuddin, and Wagner, *Foreign Policy Making*, p. 222.

34. Rejectionists oppose the concept of peaceful settlement with Israel. They "reject" Security Council Resolution 242 which Syria has explicity accepted.

35. See McLaurin, Mughisuddin, and Peretz, *Middle East Foreign Policy*, Chapter 7; and Nikolaos van Dam, *The Struggle for Power in Syria: Sectarianism, Regionalism, and Tribalism in Politics, 1961–1978* (New York: St. Martin's, 1979). Assad developed an effective 'Alawi shadow C^3 in Syria's armed forces; placed 'Alawis in key positions throughout the bureaucracy; used Sunni figureheads; and attempted to legitimize 'Alawism as a form of Shi'ism.

36. The best social and political analyses of the Lebanese conflict are P. Edward Haley and Lewis W. Snider, eds., *Lebanon in Crisis: Participants and Issues* (Syracuse: Syracuse University Press, 1979); for an analysis of Syrian strategy see Adeed I. Dawisha, "Syria in Lebanon: Assad's Vietnam," *Foreign Policy*, no. 33 (Winter 1978–79), pp. 135–50, and Paul A. Jureidini and R. D. McLaurin, "External Intervention in Internal Conflict: Syrian Strategy in the Lebanese Vortex," Abbott Associates SR28 Rev-3 (August 1978). The best military analysis of the principal battles is Paul A. Jureidini, R. D. McLaurin, and James M. Price, *Military Operations in Selected Lebanese Built-Up Areas, 1975–1978* (Aberdeen, Md.: Aberdeen Proving Ground, 1979).

37. See R. D. McLaurin and Mohammed Mughisuddin, *Cooperation and Conflict: Egyptian, Iraqi, and Syrian Objectives and U.S. Policy* (Washington, D.C.: American Institutes for Research, 1975).

38. Cf. van Dam, *The Struggle for Power*, passim.

39. McLaurin, Mughisuddin, and Peretz, *Middle East Foreign Policy*, Chapter 7.

40. An excellent study of the Ba'th role in political mobilization is Raymond A. Hinnebusch, "Local Politics in Syria: Organization and Mobilization in Four Village Cases," *Middle East Journal* 30, 1 (Winter 1976):1–24.

41. Peter A. Gubser, "Minorities in Power: The Alawites of Syria," *The Political Role of Minority Groups*, Chapter 2; McLaurin, Mughisuddin, and Peretz, *Middle East Foreign Policy*, Chapter 7; and van Dam, *The Struggle for Power*, passim.

42. McLaurin and Mughisuddin, *Cooperation*, Chapter 6.

43. E.g., on June 16, 1979, more than seventy-five cadets were killed or wounded at the Syrian military academy in Aleppo. While the confessional affiliations of the victims were not officially provided, most of the cadets were 'Alawis.

44. This was characteristic of Syrian behavior in Lebanon after the parameters of Syrian effectiveness were established. At times, however, the result was miscalculation of the magnitude of the incident with consequences that periodically exceeded expectations and approached the onset of another war.

45. See, generally, Michael C. Hudson, *Arab Politics: The Search for Legitimacy* (New Haven and London: Yale University Press, 1977), pp. 267–80, and passim, for an extended discussion of this problem in the Arab world.

46. Claudia Wright, "Iraq—New Power in the Middle East," *Foreign Affairs* 58, 2 (Winter 1979/80):257–58.

47. The best English language studies of Ba'thism remain Kamal Abu Jaber, *The Arab Ba'th Socialist Party* (Syracuse: Syracuse University Press, 1966), and John Devlin, *The Ba'th Party: A History from Its Origins to 1966* (Stanford: Hoover Institution Press, 1976).

48. There are in fact two Ba'ths in Syria. At its highest levels, the Syrian Ba'th operates as the creature of Hafez Assad's government—it iş preeminently an agent to legitimize government policies. Its highest officers individually and as a group are totally coopted by the regime. However, the party also lives a relatively independent life below these levels. It has served as an effective channel of communications between the government and the people in both directions. (Hinnebusch, "Local Politics," pp. 1–24.) Moreover, Ba'thist dogma's highly theoretical nature continues to be inculcated in and employed by lower and middle echelon Ba'thist functionaries.

49. See above and van Dam, *The Struggle for Power*, passim, for an excellent in-depth look at Syrian subnationalisms.

50. Assad's control over the Syrian armed forces was established through the careful assignment of 'Alawis to key communications points and command positions. Even in units where commanders are Sunni, a subordinate 'Alawi is frequently in real command of the unit and in direct contact with other 'Alawi-controlled units or with the presidential palace. Key units—armor and strike forces—are 'Alawi-dominated and staffed.

51. William E. Hazen, "Minorities in Revolt: The Kurds of Iran, Iraq, Syria, and Turkey," *The Political Role of Minority Groups*, passim.

52. Ibid., pp. 63–64.

53. Charges by Iraqi government officials of CIA and Iranian infiltration have recurred since the 1960s and have been repeatedly denied. See for example, "Iraq Executions Total 36 in Coup Plot," *New York Times*, January 22, 1970, p. A3; and "Two Iraqi Fighters Downed in North," ibid., December 11, 1974, p. C6. In 1975 the House Intelligence Committee disclosed that several times the CIA, working through

Iran, has supplied arms to Kurdish rebels. See "Kurdish Rebels in Iraq Gave Rugs to Kissinger," ibid., January 26, 1976, p. C44.

54. See S. Akhtar, "The Iraqi-Iranian Dispute Over the Shatt el-Arab," *Pakistan Horizon* 22, 3 (1969):213–21.

55. Despite repeated pleas by General Barzani, the Kurdish rebel leader, CIA support was terminated in early 1974 with the resulting reported loss of thousands of Kurdish lives; see "Kurdish Rebels in Iraq."

56. Some observers divide the north into two areas—the region between the Tigris (north of Samarra) and Euphrates (north of Hit), and the region east of the Tigris. The latter is Iraq's Kurdish area.

57. Uriel Dann, "The Iraqi Officer Corps as a Factor for Stability: An Unorthodox Approach," *The Military and State in Modern Asia,* ed. H. Z. Schiffrin (Jerusalem: Academic Press, 1976).

58. See Bahija Lovejoy, *The Land and People of Iraq* (Philadelphia: Lippincott, 1964); Stephen H. Longrigg, *Iraq, 1900 to 1950: A Political, Social, and Economic History* (London: Oxford University, 1956).

59. Cf., e.g., our paper on recruitment and promotion in the Lebanese army— Paul A. Jureidini, "The Politics of the Lebanese Army," Abbott Associates SR49 (September 1979).

60. See Michael H. Van Dusen, "Political Integration and Regionalism in Syria," *Middle East Journal* 26, 2 (Spring 1972):123–36.

61. See Adeed I. Dawisha, "Internal Values and External Threats: The Making of Saudi Foreign Policy," *Orbis* 23, 1 (Spring 1979):129–43; and M. Graeme Bannerman, "Saudi Arabia," *Lebanon in Crisis,* pp. 113–32.

62. Ba'thism is at base secular, and grew in fact as a secular response to the rivalry and mutual mistrust of divers religious communities in Syria.

63. Census data in the Middle East are sparse, selective, and notoriously inaccurate.

64. The new upsurge precipitated reaction by Arab and Muslim leaders throughout the region whose countries included significant Shi'a populations. See for example, John K. Cooley, "Armed Khomeini Cells Found in Arab States," *Christian Science Monitor,* January 22, 1979, p. 3; William Branigin, "Arab Leaders Reassessing Their Power After Shah's Fall," *Washington Post,* January 31, 1979, p. A16; and Ned Temko, "Iran Fallout Prods Arab Reform," *Christian Science Monitor,* February 6, 1979, p. 1.

65. See, for example, James M. Markham, "Arab Countries Fear Spread of Iran's Shiite Revolt," *New York Times,* January 29, 1979, p. 3, and Marvine Howe, "Iraq Discounts Religious Element in Iran Uprising," ibid., February 26, 1979, p. A11.

66. The concern over neighboring Iran's revolution led to a general tightening of control in Iraq in the months following the Shah's departure. See Alan Cowell, "Iraq Again Cracks Down on Communists," *Los Angeles Times,* April 20, 1979, p. 5; and "Unrest in Iraq," *Washington Post,* June 13, 1979, p. 24. The July coup attempt further provoked Saddam to purge the government ranks of opposition elements; see

Ronald Koven, "French See Sectarian Feud Behind Iraq Shake Up," *Washington Post,* August 2, 1979, p. 23; "A Sweeping Purge in the 'New' Iraq," *New York Times,* August 5, 1979, p. 4; and William Casey, "Iraq Executes 21 Convicted in Coup Trial," *Washington Post,* August 9, 1979, p. 1, Col. 6.

67. See, for instance, Geoffrey Godsell, "One Man Rule in Iraq: Hussein Executes His Political Foes," *Christian Science Monitor,* August 16, 1979, p. 4; and Claudia Wright, "Iraq, Tasting Prosperity, Weathers a Gruesome Purge," *Washington Star,* August 26, 1979, p. 11. See, however, the comments of Wright, "Iraq," p. 267.

68. Ranging from propagandist radio and television broadcasts across the border to active support of Kurdish rebels, Khomeini has attempted to stir up religious and Kurdish unrest against Saddam's government. See, for example, "Unrest in Iraq"; Jonathan C. Randal, "Iraq Moves to Sever 1975 Border Accord with Iran," *Washington Post,* November 1, 1979, p. 29 and especially, "Arrest of Iraqi Religious Leader Sadr Condemned," *Foreign Information Broadcast Service* (FBIS), June 14, 1979, p. R5–6.

69. Dawisha, "Internal Values," pp. 131ff.

70. See, e.g., Bannerman, "Saudi Arabia," p. 116.

71. For an estimate of U.S. nationals in Saudi Arabia, see Robert Brodkey and James Horgen, *Americans in the Gulf: Estimates and Projections of the Influx of U.S. Nationals into the Persian Gulf, 1975–1980* (Washington, D.C.: American Institutes for Research, 1975).

72. Accurate figures on adherents of Shi'ism are unavailable at this time. A reasonable estimate is 400,000, most in the eastern province.

73. See "Palestinians Trained Extremists Who Held Grand Mosque," *Washington Star,* December 6, 1979, p. 15; Roberta Hornig, "Mosque Seizure Political, Saudi Says," ibid., December 20, 1979, p. 1; and, more fanciful, Helena Cobban, "A Growing Opposition in Saudi Arabia?" *Christian Science Monitor,* November 30, 1979, p. 6.

74. Despite the authoritarian nature of his rule, Qaddafi "has no official title or post in the Libyan state or government, and he has never allowed himself to be promoted above colonel. He prefers to be addressed as 'Brother Muammar' by fellow Arabs." Strobe Talbott, "An Interview with Qaddafi," *Time,* April 9, 1979, p. 45.

75. Qaddafi has made extra efforts to develop an educated class that will consolidate Libya's development. Each year Libya sends 5,000 students to study in the United States and a much smaller number to Western Europe. It is interesting to note that almost no Libyans are studying in Eastern Europe. J. P. Smith, "U.S.-Libya: A Peculiar Relationship," *Washington Post,* July 29, 1979, p. A20.

76. Many of the reports of Libya's involvement in Uganda are contradictory. According to the U.S. Department of State, Libya sent between 1,000 and 2,000 troops to Uganda and took over 400 casualties. According to the State Department, the casualties were treated at Malta to conceal from the Libyan people the extent of Libya's involvement.

One official Libyan explanation was that the only Libyans in Uganda were civilian technicians, teachers, and medical workers. Later Libya stated that the only Libyan troops in Uganda were "part-time home guards."

Regardless of the level of Libyan involvement, however, the intellectuals were disturbed due to the loss of prestige Libya suffered by its involvement with Amin, particularly at such a hopeless stage, as well as by any loss of Libyan lives that ensued. See John Darnton, "Pullout of Libyans in Uganda Reported," *New York Times,* April 8, 1979, p. 9; "Qadhafi Faces Growing Opposition," *An Nahar Arab Report and Memo* 3, 31 (July 30, 1979), p. 5; and Claudia Wright, "Maybe It's Time to Take Libya More Seriously," *New York Times,* July 8, 1979, pp. 4, 17.

77. "Qadhafi Faces Growing Opposition," p. 5.

78. Ibid. In fact, Libya has gone to extremes to at least appear to be investing the people with authority. Not only has Qaddafi given up all official posts, he has also dissolved the Revolutionary Command Council which he governed after the revolution, and has named Libya a "Jamahiriyah"—a republic of the masses. He has also instituted the election of local popular congresses, some of whose members also sit on the General Peoples' Congress, a national body. However, these congresses are empowered to make laws or elect an executive, although the system is theoretically empowered to determine domestic policies. The extent to which the electoral bodies can operate in opposition to Qaddafi's will appears to be minimal, although Qaddafi appears to some to be serious in his desire to establish people's rule. See Hugh Pain, "Khadafy Green Book Maps Libya Future," *Los Angeles Times,* June 21, 1979, §1-A, p. 8.

79. "Improved Relations with Sudan but Rumblings of Internal Dissent," *An Nahar Arab Report and Memo* 3, 20 (May 14, 1979), p. 7.

80. Both the Algerian political and technocratic elite are highly sophisticated by third world standards. This is partly due to Algeria's very close ties with France which have resulted in a constant influx of ideas and technology. In fact, many Algerian officials speak only halting Arabic but are fluent in French. James M. Markham, "Algeria's Fast Return to Routine Belies Undercurrent of Ferment," *New York Times,* January 2, 1979, p. 2.

81. Louis Wiznitzer, "Unfamiliar Face Rises in Algeria," *Christian Science Monitor,* January 16, 1979, p. 3.

82. Although Algeria's involvement in the Saharan dispute is costly, most of the food shortages are probably caused by Algeria's inefficient socialist agrarian system. Markham, "Algeria's Fast Return"; Marvine Howe, "Algeria's Neglected Consumers Speak Out," *New York Times,* February 14, 1979, p. 13.

83. Little progress has been made on the issue of the Western Sahara, however. Chadli's attempts to bolster the economy are expected to include encouragement of free enterprise, although the socialist character of the state will be maintained. Howe, "Algeria's Neglected" and "Algeria's New Rulers Favor Slow Change and Unity," ibid., February 6, 1979, p. 2.

84. For example, Algerian citizens no longer need to obtain permission for foreign travel; income taxes, which were especially hard on the middle class, have been lessened; and restrictions on the private construction of homes have been eased. Chadli has also taken some actions that affect the political nature of the country which will also tend to ease the president's tendency to appear autocratic. For example, the appointment of a prime minister is now mandatory, and the president now has the

power to nominate one or more vice presidents. James M. Markham, "New President Acts for Eased Rule," ibid., May 11, 1979, p. 5; "Ex-President Ben Bella is Freed," *An Nahar Arab Report and Memo* 3, 28 (July 9, 1979):2.

85. In order to prevent a Khomeini-style overthrow, Kuwaiti Emir Sheik Jaber al-Ahmed al-Sabah is considering reinstituting the Kuwaiti Parliament that was abolished in 1976. Such a move could provide a safe channel for political dissent. James M. Markham, "Kuwait is Calming Down After Jitters About Iran," *New York Times*, June 28, 1979, p. 18.

86. By this we certainly do not mean these groups avoid pressing their own views; nothing could be further from the truth. Rather, the PLO has avoided *making* final decisions on issues that are highly salient to its groups where the groups have divergent attitudes. When the groups are willing to make compromises, Fatah and Saiqa work assiduously to persuade decision-makers of the superiority of their positions when solidarity is not endangered as a result.

87. The different groups are discussed in Riad N. El-Rayyes and Dunia Nahas, eds., *Guerrillas for Palestine: A Study of the Palestinian Commando Organizations* (Beirut: An-Nahar Press Services SARL, 1974). See also Bard O'Neill, *Armed Struggle in Palestine* (Boulder: Westview, 1978), for a less systematic but more current discussion.

88. Cf. Paul A. Jureidini and William E. Hazen, *The Dissolution of Lebanon: Futures and Consequences* (Alexandria, Va.: Abbott Associates, 1976) and Jureidini, McLaurin and Price, *Military Operations*. Syria by no means battled all the Palestinians in Lebanon. Most of the refugees took no part in the fighting, and the PDFLP and some PFLP-GC members frequently cooperated with Syria, Saiqa, and the PLA. The principal victims of the Syrian offensive were the ALF and PFLP, but Fatah constituted the bulk of the opposition to Syria.

89. See Paul A. Jureidini and William E. Hazen, *The Palestinian Movement in Politics* (Lexington: D.C. Heath, 1976).

90. Ibid.; William B. Quandt, Fuad Jabber, and Ann Mosely Lesch, *The Politics of Palestinian Nationalism* (Berkeley: University of California Press, 1973); John K. Cooley, *Green March, Black September: The Story of the Palestine Arabs* (London: Frank Carr, 1973).

2—BILATERAL, MULTILATERAL, AND REGIONAL PRESSURES

1. Cf. Lewis W. Snider, "Minorities and Political Power in the Middle East," *The Political Role of Minority Groups in the Middle East*, ed. R. D. McLaurin (New York: Praeger, 1979), Chapter 10; Iliya Harik, "The Ethnic Revolution and Political Integration in the Middle East," *International Journal of Middle East Studies* 3, 3 (July 1972):303–323.

2. Gamal Abdel Nasser, *Egypt's Liberation: The Philosophy of the Revolution* (Washington, D.C.: Public Affairs Press, 1955).

3. The best examples are Egypt's frustrating war in the Yemen, 1962–1967, and the poor showing in the recent brief skirmishes with Libya.

4. For an example of the sensitivity of the Nile issue in Egypt see *An Nahar Arab Report and Memo* 2, 25 (June 5, 1978):3.

5. The precise amount of total support or economic support is unknown, given the Saudi ability to transfer funds through informal channels. For estimates, see R. D. McLaurin and James M. Price, "OPEC Current Account Surpluses: Assistance to the Arab Front-Line States," *Oriente Moderno* 58, 11 (Novembre 1978):543.

6. For a good detailed analysis see Abdel R. Omran, ed., *Egypt: Population Problems & Prospects* (Chapel Hill: Carolina Population Center, 1973).

7. For the strategic nature of these considerations, cf. Paul Jureidini, "The Abating Threat of War," *International Interactions* 3, 3 (1977):225–26.

8. See, for example, R. D. McLaurin and Mohammed Mughisuddin, *Cooperation and Conflict: Egyptian, Iraqi, and Syrian Objectives and U.S. Policy* (Washington, D.C.: American Institutes for Research, 1975).

9. Iran used its naval power to violate the treaty on the division of the Shatt al-Arab in order to force renegotiation. Within Iraq, the Kurds received arms and financial aid from the shah. And Iraqi nationals resident in Iran were subject to forced emigration at the hands of the populace, the police, and others (as were their Iranian counterparts in Iraq).

10. The poor quality of the Iraqi ground forces was attested to by the Israelis after the October War and has been widely reported and acknowledged in the Middle East. See, e.g., Trevor N. Dupuy, *Elusive Victory: The Arab-Israeli Wars 1947–1974* (New York: Harper & Row, 1978), pp. 469, 536.

11. See Jon Cozean et al., *The Arab Elite Worldview* (Washington, D.C.: American Institutes for Research, 1975), pp. 21–23.

12. In particular, Saudis were concerned that an Iran whose oil was depleted might decide to take over the nearby Saudi oil fields. Dale R. Tahtinen, *National Security Challenges to Saudi Arabia* (Washington, D.C.: American Enterprise Institute, 1978), p. 5.

13. United States, National Security Council, National Security Study Memorandum (NSSM) No. 66 report, July 12, 1969 and United States, Executive Office of the President, National Security Decision Memorandum (NSDM) No. 92, reported in Michael T. Klare, "Arms and the Shah," *The Progressive* 43, 8 (August 1979):15–16; James H. Noyes, *The Clouded Lens: Persian Gulf Security and U.S. Policy* (Stanford: Hoover Institution Press, 1979), pp. 53–59.

14. See, generally, Mohammed Mughisuddin, ed., *Conflict and Cooperation in the Persian Gulf* (New York: Praeger, 1977).

15. Klare, "Arms," pp. 16ff; also, see Abul Kasim Mansur, "The Crisis in Iran: Why the U.S. Ignored a Quarter Century of Warning," *Armed Forces Journal International* 116, 5 (January 1979):26–33.

16. Kenneth Freed, "Iran's Once-Proud Army Reduced to Motley Crew," *Los Angeles Times*, June 2, 1979, pp. 1, 6; Jonathan Kandell, "Many in Iran Seek the Revival of an Effective Army," *New York Times*, June 26, 1979, p. 2.

17. Iran was one of the key regional countries—"regional influentials," as Brzezinski calls them—because of both its military power and its economic power.

Many senior U.S. officials throughout the 1970s gave particular emphasis to the fact that our relations with regional key powers were uniformly good to excellent, and this situation was often used as a justification for the absence of positive policy.

18. Helena Cobban, "Iranian Volunteers for PLO Pose Problem for Syria," *Christian Science Monitor,* January 14, 1980, p. 12, and Cobban, "Assad Steers Syria toward Harder Line," ibid., January 15, 1980, p. 7.

19. Shirin Tahir-Kheli, "Iran and Pakistani Cooperation in an Area of Conflict," *Asian Survey* 18, 5 (May 1977):474–90, discusses the relationship between Iran and Pakistan. However, Pakistan's relationship with other Middle East countries is also close, and should current attempts to develop a nuclear military capability succeed, the political fallout will certainly have serious implications for the Middle East. See, generally, M. G. Weinbaum and Gautam Sen, "Pakistan Enters the Middle East," *Orbis* 22, 3 (Fall 1978):595–612, for a general review of the Pakistani relationship to the Middle East. For a detailed description of Pakistani attempts to develop a nuclear capability see Philip Knightly and Anthony Bambridge, "Pakistan Deceived the West in Feverish Pursuit of H-Bomb," *Washington Star,* June 24, 1979, pp. A-1, A-12. Implications are discussed in Zalmay Khalilzad, "Pakistan and the Bomb," *Survival* 21, 6 (November/December 1979):244–250. (A similar article by Khalilzad appears under the same title in the *Bulletin of the Atomic Scientists* 36, 1 [January 1980].) John K. Cooley ("Iran, the Palestinians and the Gulf," *Foreign Affairs* 57, 5 [Summer 1979]:1017–34) has discussed the question of Iranian-Palestinian relations in some detail.

20. The most careful catalog and analysis of this feeling is Yehoshafat Harkabi, *Arab Attitudes to Israel* (Jerusalem: Israel Universities Press, 1972). Although feelings have evolved substantially since Harkabi compiled and wrote this book it remains the clearest study of the subject. The effects of the 1973 war permitted diffusion of acceptance beyond the elites which had recognized—albeit reluctantly— the inevitability of Israel's existence by about 1970.

21. By this it is meant only that "perfect security" is unavailable to any nation. The attempt to create it undermines others' security and breeds conflict. Although the urge in Israel to guarantee security is understandable it is also destabilizing.

22. Harkabi, *Arab Attitudes.*

23. The historical dimensions of this sympathy are made clear in Hazel Erskine, "The Polls: Western Partisanship in the Middle East," *Public Opinion Quarterly* 33, 4 (1969):627–40.

24. Egypt, in the Sinai II accords, effectively removed itself from the conflict for a limited period.

25. The accords themselves, as well as the treaty resulting therefrom, state that the parties are "convinced that the conclusion of a treaty of peace between Egypt and Israel is an important step in the search for comprehensive peace in the area and for the attainment of the settlement of the Arab-Israeli conflict in all its aspects." (Preamble, Treaty of Peace, March 26, 1979). However, until additional Arab countries espouse the Camp David basis, the treaty establishes a peace that is *prima facie* "separate."

26. There is a substantial debate over the effects of nuclearization (which must mean proliferation of nuclear weapons to Arab countries) of the Arab-Israeli conflict.

It is not our purpose here to enter, much less pass judgment on the outcome of, this debate. Without discussing the advisable strategy for Middle East countries with respect to "explicit nuclearization," we believe it is evident, given the objectives of the various Middle East states, that nuclear proliferation will not substantially change the *military* balance. Most, if not all, Arab leaders already credit Israel with nuclear capability. Though there are major differences in geography that expose the parties unequally to the effects of nuclear weapons, the technological balance (including delivery) compensates for this imbalance in large measure for the near and medium (5–10 years) term. We do not suggest that this will continue indefinitely, but there is no reason to believe nuclear weapons will have more effect on the balance than other advanced technologies. See Shlomo Aronson, "Nuclearization of the Middle East," *The Jerusalem Quarterly,* no. 2 (Winter 1977); Robert J. Pranger and Dale R. Tahtinen, *Nuclear Threat in the Middle East* (American Enterprise Institute, 1975); Steven Rosen, "Nuclearization and Stability in the Middle East," *Jerusalem Journal of International Relations* 1, 3 (Spring 1976); Robert Tucker, "Israel and the United States," *Commentary* 60, 11 (November 1975); Albert Wohlstetter, Henry Rowen, and Richard Brody, "Middle East Instabilities and Distant Guarantors (and Disturbers) of the Peace: The Arab-Israeli Case," mimeographed, California Seminar on Arms Control and Foreign Policy, Santa Monica, California, 1978.

27. United States Central Intelligence Agency, "Prospects for Further Proliferation of Nuclear Weapons," Memorandum DCI/NIO 1945–74, September 4, 1974, p. 1. (This document, originally classified SECRET, was publicly released in 1977.)

28. Major steps of symbolic importance were the appearance of Yasser Arafat before the United Nations General Assembly in 1974 and the statement of Harold Saunders before the Committee on International Relations of the U.S. House of Representatives on November 12, 1975. (See Marwan R. Buheiry, "The Saunders Document," *Journal of Palestine Studies* 8, 1 [Autumn 1978]:28–40.)

29. See, e.g., Sidney Zion and Uri Dan, "Israel's Peace Strategy," *The New York Times Magazine,* April 8, 1979, p. 21. General Ariel Sharon was explicit on this point.

30. See the discussions following rumors of an invitation by King Hussein to Shimon Peres, Labor Party leader: interview with Shimon Peres broadcast by Jerusalem radio, January 9, 1980, reprinted in Foreign Broadcast Information Service, *Daily Report,* Middle East and North Africa, (January 10, 1980), pp. N1–N6. See also Arthur H. Samuelson, "Israeli Expansionism," *Harper's* (February 1980), pp. 26–34, as well as issues of *New Outlook* for 1975–1980.

31. Private discussions with Syrians and with American diplomats who talked with Assad in late 1975 indicate that Assad became convinced in the autumn of that year that Israel would not compromise on the Golan.

32. R. D. McLaurin, Mohammed Mughisuddin, and Abraham R. Wagner, *Foreign Policy Making in the Middle East* (New York: Praeger, 1977), pp. 254–57.

33. There is some question today as to the military power of Iraq as a replacement for Egypt in an Arab alliance against Israel. On paper, Iraq poses a potent offensive threat. Increasingly mechanized and equipped with very modern arms, Iraqi ground forces are larger and much more mobile than in 1973. While relatively little is

known about training standards, Iraqi forces have had combat experience in the extensive Kurdish campaigns as well as in the October 1973 war (in which they were reported to have performed very poorly). Iraqi military power is discussed briefly below (Chapter 3), but because of both its location and its size, Iraq cannot replace Egypt as an equal threat. Moreover, Egypt poses the important strategic dimension of a second front.

34. Cf Itamar Rabinovich, "The Limits of Military Power: Syria's Role," *Lebanon in Crisis: Participants and Issues,* ed. P. Edward Haley and Lewis W. Snider (Syracuse: Syracuse University Press, 1979), pp. 55–74; Adeed I. Dawisha, "Syria in Lebanon: Assad's Vietnam," *Foreign Policy,* no. 33 (Winter 1978–79), pp. 135–50; and Paul A. Jureidini and R. D. McLaurin, "External Intervention in Internal Conflict: Syrian Strategy in the Lebanese Vortex," Abbott Associates SR28-Rev 3 (August 1978).

35. Thus Assad's response to the confessionally motivated murder of 'Alawi cadets at the Syrian military academy was a major Syrian Air Force-IAF dogfight.

36. Cf. sources in n. 34 above.

37. See Chapter 1 and R. D. McLaurin, ed., *The Political Role of Minority Groups in the Middle East* (New York: Praeger, 1979), passim.

38. Military analyses of the Lebanese conflict may be found in Lawrence L. Whetten, "The Military Dimension," *Lebanon in Crisis,* pp. 75–90; and Paul A. Jureidini, R. D. McLaurin, and James M. Price, *Military Operations in Selected Lebanese Built-Up Areas, 1975–1978* (Aberdeen, Md.: Aberdeen Proving Ground, 1979).

39. Syria's once Spartan army succumbed to the temptations of Lebanese society, openly accepting bribes and accommodating itself to the corruption and venality encountered in Lebanon. At the same time, the nature of the Lebanese conflict deflated Syrian morale both because Palestinians and Christians were more effective vis-à-vis the Syrians than expected and because Syrian army personnel did not feel comfortable about fighting Palestinians rather than Israelis.

40. Dawisha, "Syria," passim.

41. Sectarian violence had reached alarming levels with unknown assailants murdering leading 'Alawis. For a time the killings were thought to be the work of Iraqi intelligence, but by mid-1978 murders were believed to be confessionally inspired.

42. See Paul A. Jureidini, R. D. McLaurin, and Abraham R. Wagner, *Middle East Conflict Scenarios and United States Defense Options* (Alexandria: Abbott Associates; Marina del Rey: Analytical Assessments Corporation, 1978), passim.

43. See, e.g., Jim Hoagland, " 'War of Annihilation': Israeli Contingency Plan Readied," *Washington Post,* October 26, 1977; Dial Torgerson, "Armies are Basic Israeli Targets: 'Annihilation War' is Key to Strategy, Officials Confirm," *Washington Star,* October 27, 1977.

44. Among the many works on Kissinger's approach to the Middle East problem the best remains Edward R. F. Sheehan's *The Arabs, Israelis, and Kissinger: A Secret History of Diplomacy in the Middle East* (New York: Reader's Digest Press, 1976). See also William B. Quandt, *Decade of Decisions: American Policy Toward*

the Arab-Israeli Conflict, 1967–1976 (Berkeley: University of California Press, 1977).

45. Most recently in John Devlin, *The Ba'th Party: A History of Its Origins to 1966* (Stanford: Hoover Institution Press, 1976).

46. R. D. McLaurin, Mohammed Mughisuddin, and Don Peretz, *Middle East Foreign Policy: Issue and Process* (New York: Praeger, forthcoming), Chapter 7, passim.

47. Paul A. Jureidini and R. D. McLaurin, "The Hashemite Kingdom of Jordan," *Lebanon in Crisis,* p. 153.

48. Ibid., p. 298 (n. 26 and sources listed therein).

49. Lewis W. Snider and R. D. McLaurin, *Saudi Arabia's Air Defense Requirements in the 1980s: A Threat Analysis* (Alexandria: Abbott Associates, 1979), p. 16.

50. U.S. Congress, House of Representatives, Committee on International Relations, *Review of Recent Developments in the Middle East,* Hearings Before the Subcommittee on Europe and the Middle East, 95th Congress, 1st session, June 8, 1977, p. 58.

51. After late 1976, the "butter" materially suffered as a result of the Lebanese operation.

52. For a slightly more extensive discussion of Syrian perceptions of Saudi power, cf. Avigdor Haselkorn, R. D. McLaurin, and Abraham R. Wagner, *Middle East Net Assesement, Volume I: Regional Threat Perceptions* (Marina del Rey: Analytical Assessments Corporation, 1979), p. 51.

53. R. D. McLaurin, *The Middle East in Soviet Policy* (Lexington: Heath, 1975), discusses Arab feelings toward the Soviet Union and the Russian people. See also Mohammed Mughisuddin, "Arab Reaction to Communism and Soviet Policies," *Conflict and Cooperation in the Persian Gulf,* ed. Mohammed Mughisuddin (New York: Praeger, 1977), pp. 140–65.

54. R. D. McLaurin, "The Soviet-American Military Balance: Arab Elite Views," *International Interactions* 3, 3 (1977):236–37.

55. Indeed, the Soviets were not pleased when Assad successfully outmaneuvered his predecessor, because one of the principal differences separating Assad and Salah Jadid was the nature of Syrian relations with the USSR. Assad was seen at that time as anti-Soviet. Avigdor Levy, "The Syrian Communists and the Ba'th Power Struggle, 1966–1970," *The U.S.S.R. and the Middle East,* ed. Michael Confino and Shimon Shamir (Jerusalem: Israel Universities Press, 1973), pp. 406–408. By contrast, Rifaat has generally been described as pro-Soviet. His doctorate was received from the Soviet Academy of Sciences, and he wrote for some years with a stridently ideological tone. "Rifaat Suleiman Assad," *An Nahar Arab Report* 6, 32 (August 11, 1975), Profile. In fact, however, both Assads distrust Moscow in spite of what they perceive to be situationally required reliance on the Soviet Union.

56. An excellent overview of Syrian-Soviet relations is Galia Golan, "Syria and the Soviet Union Since the Yom Kippur War," *Orbis* 21, 4 (Winter 1978):777–801.

57. Cf. James F. Collins, "The Soviet Union," *Lebanon in Crisis*, pp. 209–223.

58. McLaurin and Mughisuddin, *Cooperation and Conflict*, pp. 283–92.

59. Ibid.

60. Sheehan, *The Arabs*, passim.

61. "Ba'ath Warns Leftists," *An Nahar Arab Report and Memo* 2, 23 (June 5, 1978):5. According to Iraqi Ba'th officials, Ba'th-ICP relations are not indicative of the state of Iraqi-Soviet affairs. However, Iraqi leaders see the ICP as influenced by Moscow and have in the past stated that executions of communists in Iraq were a signal to the Soviets to tread warily on Iraqi soil. See "A Fresh Warning," *Newsweek*, July 17, 1978, p. 4-F.

62. Iraq has demanded rescinding of the 1975 agreement between the two countries as regards the Shatt al-'Arab boundary, and moreover, claims much of Khuzistan ("Arabistan").

63. William Branigin, "Iran Charges New Iraqi Air Raid, Reviews Bahraini Claim," *Washington Post*, June 16, 1979, p. A18.

64. Iraq's desire for security and power necessitated a rapprochement with its bitterest Middle Eastern rival, Syria. Syria, the nation most concerned about Egypt's separate peace with Israel, needed to improve relations with Iraq for reasons we discuss elsewhere in this chapter. The Iraqis' motive behind the reconciliation was their desire to end the conflict between the two countries and the resulting threat to Iraq at a time when ties to the Soviets were undergoing renewed strains, when instability to the east (Iran) posed major implications for Iraqi unity, and when domestic problems in Iraq appeared to be surfacing. In fact, Iraq's population advantage over Syria (the ratio is three to two) and its economic strength relative to Syria could have led to Iraq's dominating the union, making it the leading nation in the Arab Middle East apart from Egypt. On the other hand, the twelve-year-old rift between the Syrian and Iraqi Ba'th parties is based upon deep ideological and personal rivalries complicated further by each regime's power designs. Neither country's leaders would allow themselves to be maneuvered into a position of subservience to the other, as happened to Syria during the 1958–1961 "union" with Egypt.

65. R. D. McLaurin, Mohammed Mughisuddin, and Don Peretz, *Middle East Foreign Policy: Issue and Process* (New York: Praeger, 1981), Chapter 7; van Dam, *The Struggle*, passim.

66. Cf. Peter Gubser, "Minorities in Power: The Alawites of Syria," *The Political Role of Minority Groups*, Chapter 2.

67. See note 18 above.

68. The talk of Syrian-Iraqi political union which was heard in the summer of 1979 (see note 64 above and Helena Cobban, "Iraq Bids for the Role of Mideast Power Broker," *Christian Science Monitor*, June 21, 1979, p. 4) was quickly hushed after talks had stalled due to intractable problems and after allegations of Syrian involvement in the July 1979 coup attempt which occurred after the resignation of Ahmed Hassan al-Bakr. See for instance Jim Hoagland, "Iraqi Leader Moves to Strengthen Rule," *Washington Post*, July 31, 1979, p. A14; and Marvine Howe, "Iraq

Now Has Powerful Claim to Leadership of Arab World," *New York Times,* July 22, 1979, p. 4.

69. Iraq, for example, took an active role in the May 1979 Islamic summit and has worked diligently at the development of good relations with Saudi Arabia.

70. Currently, the Iranian Army is in a state of complete chaos and is in no position to invade Iraq. See William Claiborne, "Many Iranians Express Discontent," *Washington Post,* July 27, 1979, p. A14; and Kenneth Freed, "Iran's Once-Proud Army." Nor is the Iranian Army capable of defeating Iraqi forces in border-type engagements. However, Iraq's ability to *sustain* an invasion within Iranian territory is believed to be minimal. Armed conflict between the two countries at any time in the foreseeable future would probably be in the form of border warfare.

71. Devlin, *The Ba'th Party.*

72. Cooley, "Iran," treats this issue more extensively.

73. James Buchen, "Saudi Concern Over Security," *Financial Times,* January 12, 1979, p. 3; Henry L. Trewhitt, "U.S. Fears Unrest in Saudi Arabia," Baltimore *Sun,* January 23, 1979, p. 4. The events of late 1979, as we have pointed out in Chapter 1, were an even more painful and pointed lesson.

74. Snider and McLaurin, *Saudi Arabia's Air Defense,* pp. 40–41. We discount the possibility of an attack on Mecca for obvious reasons.

75. Ibid.

76. McLaurin and Price, "OPEC Current Account Surpluses."

77. See U.S. General Accounting Office, *Perspectives on Military Sales to Saudi Arabia,* Report to the Congress by the Comptroller General of the United States (Washington, D.C.: October 26, 1977).

78. Snider and McLaurin, *Saudi Arabia's Air Defense,* passim; Tahtinen, *National Security,* pp. 24–25; Steven J. Rosen and Haim Shaked, "Arms and the Saudi Connection," *Commentary* 65, 6 (June 1978):33–38.

79. Snider and McLaurin, *Saudi Arabia's Air Defense,* passim.

80. Ibid., pp. 14–15, 35–39.

81. Cf. Drew Middleton, "Fall of Shah in Iran Unnerving to Saudis," *New York Times,* June 14, 1979, p. 5; Ned Temko, "Saudis See Drift to Left in Area as Iran Falters," *Christian Science Monitor,* January 26, 1979, p. 4.

82. Adeed I. Dawisha, "Internal Values and External Threats: The Making of Saudi Foreign Policy," *Orbis* 23, 1 (Spring 1979), pp. 129–44.

83. Graeme Bannerman, "Saudi Arabia," *Lebanon in Crisis,* pp. 114–15.

84. Dawisha, "Internal Values," pp. 139–41; Middleton, "Fall"; Temko, "Saudis."

85. Stephen Page, *The U.S.S.R. and Arabia: The Development of Soviet Policies and Attitudes Towards the Countries of the Arabian Peninsula* (London: Central Asian Research Centre, 1971), Chapter 1.

86. A good, contemporary overview of U.S.-Saudi relations is Jim Hoagland and J. P. Smith, "Saudi Arabia and the United States: Security and Interdependence," *Survival* 20, 2 (March/April 1978):80–83.

87. The West Bank was not originally part of the Transjordan mandate. Cis-Jordan, or the West Bank, was occupied in 1948. Israel claims that the West Bank never was part of Jordan legally.

88. With the possible exception of Habib Bourguiba and other Tunisian leaders.

89. In the wake of the destruction of the Jordanian armed forces resulting from the war, the Palestinian commandos aligned with the PLO gained strength, constituting a virtual "state within a state."

90. Cf. R. D. McLaurin, "Majorities as Minorities: The Arabs in Israeli Occupied Territory," *The Political Role of Minority Groups,* Chapter 9.

91. These negotiations did not include Jordan to any appreciable extent. Prior to the October War, Jordan had been deeply involved in the negotiations—both those concerning the Jarring Mission and those resulting from U.S. initiatives such as the Rogers Plan. Moreover, the king had secretly met with Israeli leaders only to have the meetings revealed by the latter. The negotiations after October included, first, the "step-by-step" disengagement negotiations between each of the principal Arab confrontation states, Israel, and the United States; then, briefly, wider talks on the structure of future negotiations, talks in which the king was consulted; and finally the Sadat initiative and Camp David series, during which Jordan was not kept informed. For the Jarring Mission, see United Nations, "Report of the Secretary-General Under Security Council Resolution 331 (1973) of April 20, 1973," May 21, 1973; Quandt, *Decade,* passim; and Malcolm H. Kerr, ed., *The Elusive Peace in the Middle East* (Albany: State University of New York, 1975). The Rogers Plan period is discussed in the latter two sources as well. Quandt, *Decade,* and Sheehan, *The Arabs,* describe the Kissinger period. The Sadat initiative and Camp David accords have not yet been fully analyzed, although Sadat's views are recorded in his autobiography, el Sadat, *In Search of Identity* (New York: Harper & Row, 1978), pp. 298–313.

92. Ronald Koven, "New Attempts Seen to Enlist Jordan in Mideast Talks," *Washington Post,* June 27, 1978, p. B1.

93. Anwar Sadat made it clear that he, too, foresaw an important role for Jordan with respect to the future of the occupied West Bank. Sadat's *volte-face* was symbolic, for he had been critical in persuading Hussein to renounce West Bank claims in 1974, and he is not known, moreover, as one of the king's most avid fans.

94. The Rabat Conference decided unanimously that the PLO should be the sole legitimate representative of the Palestinian people, meaning both those in the Palestinian diaspora and those in (Israel and) the West Bank.

95. See, for example, James H. Markham, "Despite Diplomatic and Battle Scars, PLO is the Palestinians Only Voice," *New York Times,* February 21, 1978, p. 14; Helena Cobban, "What PLO Wants from Talks with Jordan," *Christian Science Monitor,* May 12, 1977, p. 5; Thomas W. Lippman, "Palestinians: Resigned to Mideast Deal," *Washington Post,* March 15, 1977, p. A13.

96. Indeed, it would be far easier for the king to accept the decision of the other Arab states that some territory should be conceded to Israel and that Jerusalem need not be under Arab sovereignty than to agree himself on such provisions with Israel.

97. The old rivalry between the Saudi and Hashemite houses has been interred at least for the present partially because Jordan is weak, constituting a buffer rather than a threat on Saudi Arabia's border. As it is, Saudi leaders feel comfortable about Jordan's pattern of seeking close ties with Egypt, Syria, or Iraq only because Jordan's capabilities add little to these powerful countries and because the pattern has tended to support regional balance rather than preponderance.

98. See Paul A. Jureidini and James M. Price, "The Structures and Parameters of U.S.-Jordan Relations," Abbott Associates SR 52 (1979).

99. Jureidini and McLaurin, "The Hashemite Kingdom," p. 158.

100. This paragraph should not be interpreted to mean perfect stability or agreement. Sovereign states have different interests, and predictably relations vacillate within what Azar calls the "normal relations range" (NRR), which is unique to each dyad, or pair, of states. Even when two countries maintain a NRR that is both cooperative and relatively stable there are periods of *more* and *less* cooperation.

Perhaps the most difficult period in U.S.-Jordan relations occurred in 1979 when King Hussein was among the most active Arab opponents of the Camp David peace process. (He had acted with ambivalence toward Sadat's original initiative and the Sadat trip to Jerusalem. Only after the Camp David talks did he assume an active opposition role.) With characteristic pragmatism, however, Hussein began to modulate his criticism, talk more tolerantly of the process, and repair his relations with the United States by early 1980.

101. Jordan's internal security apparatus is highly regarded in the Middle East.

102. Especially vis-à-vis Egypt, Libya's primary external threat. Libya's armed forces contain approximately 40,000 troops, about one-tenth the size of Egypt's.

103. "Can Qadhafi Survive," *An Nahar Arab Report and Memo* 3, 22 (May 28, 1979):1.

104. This is especially true in the area of oil production. "The U.S.-Libyan oil connection will mean more than $5 billion to Qaddafi this year and has engendered an intricate web of relations between American companies and banks and Libya's maverick government." However, oil is not the only area in which the United States has economic ties with Libya. Major American companies such as Boeing and General Electric, along with various agricultural companies, did more than $400 million in business with Libya in 1979, and the trend is increasing. J. P. Smith, "U.S.-Libya: A Peculiar Relationship," *Washington Post,* July 29, 1979, pp. A1, A20.

105. Libya has gone a long way in supporting radical elements in the PLO as part of its attempts to exert influence in the Middle East. In fact, it is United States' fear of the possibility that Libya will use military or transportation equipment to assist in terrorist operations that prevents the United States from delivering eight C130 transport jets paid for by Libya. The jets were purchased by Libya five years ago at a cost of $45 million; however, no U.S. administration has granted an export license for the jets. William Safire, "Libya and Idaho," *New York Times,* February 15, 1979, p. 27.

106. Libya is purchasing more Soviet weapons per capita than the Shah of Iran did from the United States. By the end of 1980 Libya will have taken delivery on 400

war planes, 10,000 armored vehicles (including 3,000 tanks), and 24 missile boats. Arnaud de Borchgrave, "Libya's Arms Depot," *Newsweek*, July 9, 1979, p. 43.

107. Ibid.

108. Colonel Qaddafi's statement in May that Libya may allow the Soviet Union to use Libya's ports is a case in point. Nor are states such as Syria, Iraq, and Algeria pleased with Libya's efforts to assist Pakistan in developing an atomic bomb. See "Qadhafi Raises Soviet Threat," *An Nahar Arab Report and Memo* 3, 22 (May 28, 1979):4–5; and de Borchgrave, "Libya's Arms Depot," p. 43.

109. Paul A. Jureidini and William E. Hazen, *The Palestinian Movement in Politics* (Lexington: D.C. Heath, 1976). See also Bard E. O'Neill, *Armed Struggle in Palestine: A Political-Military Analysis* (Boulder: Westview, 1978), and John K. Cooley, *Green March, Black September: The Story of the Palestinian Arabs* (London: Frank Cass, 1973).

110. For a study of some of the early clashes, see Paul A. Jureidini and William E. Hazen, *Six Clashes: An Analysis of the Relationship between the Palestinian Guerrilla Movement and the Governments of Jordan and Lebanon* (Kensington, Md.: American Institutes for Research, 1971), as well as Haley and Snider, eds., *Lebanon in Crisis,* passim.

111. Some writers point out that many Syrians look upon Palestine as southern Syria in the context of a Greater Syria. Although it is technically accurate to report the existence of such views, it is quite misleading to suggest they are common or representative. Few Syrians adhere any longer to the idea of a Greater Syria.

112. The actual number of Palestinians in Lebanon is unknown. We estimate there were a total of perhaps 400,000 Palestinians in Lebanon, but perhaps as many as a quarter were Christians and have since become Lebanese citizens. (The process of citizenship acquisition in Lebanon is a highly political one.) Of the remaining Palestinians, about 300,000, a large number (est. 100,000) have in fact left Lebanon for jobs elsewhere, especially in the Gulf. In most cases these Palestinians remain registered as refugees in Lebanon for political and financial reasons. (They are also frequently counted as being in the Gulf, creating a monumental problem of double counting for those trying to determine the current size of the Palestinian population.)

113. Traditionally, Lebanon's government has been based on the sectarian balance. Because the Palestinians who have not already become Lebanese citizens are virtually all Sunnis, their formal inclusion in Lebanon would constitute a major shift in this sensitive balance.

114. And, until 1980, operations as well. By 1980 the Palestinian position in Lebanon was greatly weakened as a result of (1) growing alienation of the Sunni Lebanese; (2) a burgeoning alliance of Christians and Shi'as aimed at the Sunnis and Palestinians; (3) the debilitation of the Syrian army; (4) an enormous increase in capabilities of the Christian militias in the north; (5) Israeli support of the southern Lebanon Christian forces under Saad Haddad; and (6) a growing regional awareness that the Camp David framework was "the only game in town."

3—EMERGING ALIGNMENTS

1. Edward E. Azar, Paul A. Jureidini, and R. D. McLaurin, "Protracted Social Conflict: Theory and Practice in the Middle East," *Journal of Palestine Studies* 8, 1 (Autumn 1978):41–60, discuss the Arab-Israeli conflict as a protracted social conflict. Termination of conflicts has been little studied, but clear empirical evidence supports the hypothesis that conflict protraction is correlated with the protraction of termination processes. Cf. Michael I. Handel, "War Termination—A Critical Survey," *Jerusalem Papers on Peace Problems,* no. 24 (1978), Fred C. Iklé, *Every War Must End* (New York: Columbia University Press, 1971), and William T. R. Fox, ed., "How Wars End." *Annals of the Academy of Political and Social Science* 392 (September 1970).

2. United Nations Security Council Resolution 242 of 1967 was widely regarded as recognizing Israel. Thus the Arab confrontation states that accepted Resolution 242 were seen by some as having recognized Israel. While there is clearly a logic in this argument, given the substance of the resolution, the Arab-Israeli conflict is far more than logomachy, and the intent of the Arab governments in accepting 242 was manifestly to establish a truce not to recognize or otherwise confer legitimacy upon Israel. Thus despite the claims that Resolution 242 effectively recognized Israel, claims repeated at times even by the parties, no government acted as if acceptance of the resolution was an adequate substitute for explicit or functional acceptance of Israel.

3. Articles II and III of the Sinai agreement, signed at Geneva, September 4, 1975.

4. The appendices provide the text of the documents resulting from these meetings.

5. Thomas W. Lippman, "Sadat's Strategy Emerges," *Washington Post,* December 4, 1977, p. A1.

6. Paul A. Jureidini, R. D. McLaurin, and James M. Price, "Arab Reactions to the Egyptian-Israeli Peace Treaty," Abbott Associates SR 46 (March 26, 1979).

7. See Chapters 1 and 4; R. D. McLaurin, "Minorities and Politics in the Middle East," *The Political Role of Minority Groups in the Middle East,* ed. by R. D. McLaurin (New York: Praeger, 1979), pp. 1–14; and Lewis W. Snider, "Minorities and Political Power in the Middle East," ibid., pp. 240–62.

8. Cf. § on Saudi Arabia below.

9. In Jordan, the king's advisors, several important families, and the military generally opposed the rapprochement because it was felt Syria could not be trusted. Few Jordanians understood the nature of the regime in Damascus and how it differed from its predecessors. In Syria, both the Palestinians and the ideologues of the Ba'th were vehemently opposed to any improvement of relations with a regime they saw as anti-Palestinian and reactionary.

10. Most Syrians came to see the military value of Jordan's friendship. Many Jordanians, by contrast, still distrust Syria as a nation; they feel comfortable only about Assad as a person.

11. See, e.g., Itamar Rabinovich, "The Islamic Wave," *The Washington Quarterly: A Review of Strategic and International Issues* 4 (Autumn 1979):140; Henry Tanner, "Syria's Leadership Purged in Assad Bid to Ease Unrest," *New York Times,* January 11, 1980, p. 2.

12. Helena Cobban, "Opposition to Russian Advisors Mounts in Syria," *Christian Science Monitor,* January 31, 1980, p. 1.

13. Fehmi Saddy, *The Eastern Front: Implications of the Syrian/Palestinian/ Jordanian Entente and the Lebanese Civil War* (Alexandria, Va.: Abbott Associates, 1976), outlines the strategic role of the eastern front concept in Assad's thinking. One can, however, misunderstand the purpose of the strategy, which was aimed at influencing *Arab* rather than *Israeli* behavior.

14. King Hussein is not always an "activist," but during the late 1970s he felt that Jordan had an important role to play and that if Jordan were more visible Fate—or the other Arab nations—might call on Jordan to play that role, particularly in the West Bank.

15. The rapprochement began in mid-1978. Debates on restoring a dialog were highly visible within the PLO, less so within Jordanian councils. (For some of the PLO discussions, see FBIS autumn 1978-spring 1979 issues.) In Jordan, "debates" consisted largely of post facto representations to the king by Jordanian notables who distrusted the PLO and resented the fact that the policy change took place without any significant consultation with leading families or politicians.

16. Palestinian "memories" may be reviewed in the publicized debates reprinted in FBIS. The potency of Jordanian concern can be placed in context by recalling that Palestinians constitute over half the population of the kingdom's *East* Bank. (The West Bank is considered virtually totally Palestinian.) It is true that many Palestinians have travelled to the Gulf area and so are no longer in Jordan. Even so, the majority of the East Bank's population is probably Palestinian.

17. For more detailed treatment of this possibility see Paul A. Jureidini and R. D. McLaurin, "Political Disintegration and Conflict Reduction in the Eastern Mediterranean Area," Abbott Associates SR51 (October 1979).

18. Israel's moral basis *as a Jewish state* has been severely questioned in the Middle East—not that religious states are inherently wrong but, rather, that a specifically Jewish state was an unreasonable basis on which to usurp Palestinian land, since secular states exist already both in Syria and, especially, in Lebanon. Thus the official PLO objective of a secular, democratic state was the logical moral alternative to Israeli claims (Zionist claims) that a state *for* Jews was needed. The disintegration of secularism and subsequent "sectarianization" of the two examples of Lebanon and Syria would serve to provide a resounding confirmation of Zionism in the Middle East.

19. United States, Agency for International Development, *Regional Cooperation in the Middle East* (Washington, D.C., February 1, 1979), pp. 17–18.

20. Meir Amit, "Israel: The Bases of Economic Growth," *The Washington Quarterly: A Review of Strategic and International Studies,* Special Supplement on "Egypt and Israel: Prospects for a New Era" (Spring 1979), pp. 10–11.

21. Cf. Fred M. Gottheil, "An Economic Assesement of the Military Burden in the Middle East," *Journal of Conflict Resolution* 18, 3 (September 1974):502–513.

22. United States Arms Control and Disarmament Agency, *World Military Expenditures and Arms Transfers 1967–1976* (Washington, D.C., 1978), p. 48.

23. See William Branigin, "Iran Charges New Iraqi Air Raid, Renews Bahrain Claim," *Washington Post*, June 16, 1979, p. 18.

24. See "Arabian Gulf: Strategic Islands," *An Nahar Arab Report* 2, 22 (May 31, 1971):4; "Union of Arab Emirates: New Arab State," ibid., 2, 49 (December 6, 1971):3–4; and "Arabian Gulf: The Role of Sheikh Saqr," ibid., 2, 50 (December 13, 1971):2–4.

25. See, for instance, Emile A. Nakhleh, "Islamic Revolution: Dangerous Export," *Washington Post*, October 22, 1979, p. 16. However, the concern felt in Bahrain and in other Gulf sheikhdoms is not universally shared. Yasser Arafat was recently quoted in *Sharq al Awsat* as saying that "I will visit Iran shortly. There is no truth to the news that states that the relations between the Palestinians and Iran have cooled off." "Hani al Hassan Li *Sharq al Awsat*: Arafat Sa Yazur Iran Qarben wa la Sohat Li Anba' Futur al 'Ilaqat," *Sharq al Awsat*, December 26, 1979, p. 1.

26. Iraq's involvement in the Eastern Mediterranean differs, however, from its role in the Persian Gulf. Because it is on the Gulf littoral, Iraq is a military as well as a political power in the Gulf, while its role in the Arab-Israeli conflict is primarily political and only occasionally and secondarily military. Moreover, both roles are dependent on other countries in the immediate Eastern Mediterranean.

27. Saudi Arabia's participation in the Arab-Israeli conflict is at best reticent. The kingdom, however, already suffers Israeli occupation of some of its island territory and frequent IAF overflights. Its financial role in the conflict and its acquisition of U.S.-supplied F-15 aircraft have both had the effect of reflecting and intensifying Saudi Arabia's role.

28. See Chapter 4 of R. D. McLaurin, Mohammed Mughisuddin, and Abraham R. Wagner, *Foreign Policy Making in the Middle East* (New York: Praeger, 1977), for a more detailed description of the nature of and limits on Iraqi pragmatism.

29. In early 1977, when Syrian forces began to turn on the Christians, Iraq's leaders recognized that Syrian policy was to control Lebanon. Like Saudi Arabia, Iraq was firmly against a Syrian-dominated bloc of Jordan, Lebanon, and Syria. So, even though Iraq had aided the Palestinians earlier, Baghdad began to provide arms to the Christians.

30. See R. D. McLaurin, "The Transfer of Technology to the Middle East," *The Political Economy of the Middle East*, ed. Richard Kaufman and James Wooten (Washington, D.C.: U.S. Government Printing Office for the Library of Congress, 1980); James M. Price, "A Country Profile of Iraq," Abbott Associates report, typescript (October 1978), pp. 18–19.

31. J. P. Smith, "Oil Wealth Causing a Shift in Iraq's Foreign Policy," *Washington Post*, August 8, 1978, p. A14.

32. Robert Brodkey and James Horgen, *Americans in the Gulf: Estimates and Projections of the Influx of U.S. Nationals into the Persian Gulf, 1975–1980* (Washington, D.C.: American Institutes for Research, 1975), p. 46.

33. We do not, however, wish to overlook or discount the *domestic* impact of the Arab-Israeli issue. Public government positions on the conflict in general and on

the Palestinian issue in particular are usually taken *primarily* for *domestic* political purposes.

34. Paul A. Jureidini and R. D. McLaurin, "The Hashemite Kingdom of Jordan," *Lebanon in Crisis,* ed. P. Edward Haley and Lewis W. Snider (Syracuse: Syracuse University Press, 1979), p. 158. Redeployments were in June–July 1976.

35. E.g., cf. Marwan Iskander, "The Jordanian Example," *An Nahar Arab Report & Memo* 4, 4 (January 21, 1980):1–2.

36. "Le Jeu d'Irak," *L'Express,* December 1, 1979, p. 68.

37. The dimensions of this support are provided in R. D. McLaurin and James M. Price, "OPEC Current Account Surpluses: Assistance to the Arab Front-Line States," *Oriente Moderno* 58, 11 (Novembre 1978):533–46.

38. There are, for example, persistent rumors that some Saudi money continues to reach Cairo through secret channels.

39. In fact, the rapprochement was precipitated first by Iraqi interest in Gulf security and specifically in the creation of an antiterrorist bloc in the Gulf.

40. In a religious showdown in Syria, the Saudis must support the Sunnis.

41. While Brotherhood membership in Syria remains largely unknown, many of the leaders of at least the major branches are believed to operate subject to Saudi influence. (Several—at least four—branches of the *Ikhwan* exist in Syria, a traditional home of Sunni fundamentalism.)

42. Leading Jordanian tribes extend beyond the borders of modern Jordan. Because the Jordan Arab Army has maintained a large measure of its Bedouin Arab base, it is at least conceivable that JAA elements, Jordanian tribes, and part of their territory would come under the control of Saudi Arabia. Despite latent dynastic rivalries, either kingdom's armed forces might find themselves fighting for the other kingdom in some circumstances.

4—REGIONAL LEADERSHIP CHANGES

1. From 1962 to 1967 Nasser actively supported republican forces in the Yemen against the royalists who, though deposed in 1962, were supported by and aligned with Saudi Arabia.

2. It must be recognized that we are considering defensive or at most nonborder roles. The ability of the Egyptian armed forces to project power more than a few miles outside Egypt is still negligible unless virtually unopposed or provided with substantial outside support.

3. William E. Hazen, "Minorities in Revolt: The Kurds of Iran, Iraq, Syria, and Turkey," *The Political Role of Minority Groups in the Middle East,* ed. R. D. McLaurin (New York: Praeger, 1979).

4. Edward E. Azar and R. D. McLaurin, "Demographic Change and Political Change: Population Pressures and Territorial Control in the Middle East," *International Interactions* 5, 2 (1978):267–87.

5. Cf. Rupert Emerson, *Self-Determination Revisited in the Era of Decoloniza-*

tion (Cambridge, Mass.: Harvard University, Center for International Affairs, 1964): "What is striking . . . is the uncompromising assertion of the universality of the right of all dependent peoples to full and free self-determination set starkly side by side with the equally uncompromising denial of such rights to groups within the new countries or cutting across their frontiers." (p. 32) As then-President Tsiranana (Malagasy Republic) stated it, "It is no longer possible, nor desirable, to modify the boundaries of Nations on the pretext of racial, religious or linguistic criteria." (p. 34)

6. Although the respective population figures are an important factor in this issue they are not conclusive. In South Africa, for example, a black majority is ruled by a small, white minority, and while the situation there will probably change eventually, it has already endured a very long time. In Syria, however, the ruling minority is less well educated than the majority; geographically concentrated away from the heart of the country; too small to provide adequate security throughout the country; and is a religious minority with few intermediary groups to exploit. Moreover, the relative economic well-being and development that have assisted the white minority in South Africa can hardly be compared with the much smaller improvement in economic conditions under Assad.

7. It should be noted that although 'Alawis constitute a majority in Latakia and Tartus, they are minorities in the *cities* of Latakia and Tartus. There are also substantial numbers of Christians in Latakia.

8. Syrian Christians, numbering over 800,000, have been associated by the Sunni majority with the 'Alawis. This association is less for theological reasons—although it is true that the 'Alawi faith is influenced by Christianity—than because the Christians have cooperated with, benefitted from, and been coopted by 'Alawi control of Syria. Assad's original strength was the air force, and the Syrian Air Force is primarily Christian. Moreover, the Christians in Syria live close to the 'Alawis—most inhabit the Latakia, Tartus, and Damascus areas.

9. "Alaouites" (Alawiya), later Latakia, was separated from the rest of the then-French mandated territory of Syria in 1920. In 1926 it was reunited with Syria but retained its autonomy until World War II.

10. See Paul A. Jureidini, "The Politics of the Lebanese Army," Abbott Associates SR49 (September 1979). Franjieh was close to the Syrian 'Alawi leadership and was Syria's principal Lebanese apologist before the rapprochement.

11. The Druzes also had an autonomous state, Djebel Druze, that was, like Latakia, reuinted with Syria during World War II.

12. See Peter A. Gubser, "Minorities in Isolation: The Druze of Lebanon and Syria," *The Political Role*, Chapter 5.

13. The scenarios sketched here are developed more fully in Paul A. Jureidini and R. D. McLaurin, "Political Disintegration and Conflict Reduction in the Eastern Mediterranean Area," Abbott Associates SR51 (October 1979).

14. Prominent among the dissidents were members of the 'Utayba tribe, an important tribe sweeping from Jordan through Saudi Arabia to the Gulf, and a major source of personnel for security forces in a number of these countries.

15. Cf., for some examples, Walter S. Mossberg, "Guarding the Wells," *Wall Street Journal*, January 21, 1980, p. 1; Lewis W. Snider and R. D. McLaurin, *Saudi*

Arabia's Air Defense in the 1980s: A Threat Assessment (Alexandria, Va.: Abbott Associates, 1979).

16. "Iraq: East or West," *An Nahar Arab Report and Memo* 31, 24 (June 11, 1979). Not only has Iraq been working to hold down OPEC price increases, Iraqi oil fields have recently increased production to help lessen the world oil shortage. See Ronald Koven, "Iraqi Oil Output Reported Rising, May Ease Crisis," *Washington Post,* July 13, 1979, and "Eye to Eye with France on Oil," *An-Nahar Arab Report and Memo* 30, 29 (July 16, 1979):5. It is interesting to note that these reports stress France is the major direct beneficiary of increases in Iraqi oil production due to France's willingness to sell to Iraq almost any modern weapons France is capable of producing. Negotiations on increased oil supplies are also being carried out by Iraq with Italy and Japan.

17. By 1973, the 'Alawi future had become identified with Hafez Assad. Virtually no 'Alawis wished his brother to become Syria's strongman—and Rifaat Assad is the likely 'Alawi successor to Hafez, although it is not clear that he would assume the presidency itself. Thus all 'Alawis supported Hafez, and the potential for organized violence was almost totally controlled by 'Alawis. With the deterioration of security, a change in loyalties out of sheer desperation cannot be ruled out, although it remains unlikely. Certainly, there is enormous pressure to bring about an end to the assassinations and sabotage taking place in Syria, and this pressure is found *within* the 'Alawi community as well as *upon* the government.

18. See Herbert Goldhamer, "Perceptions of the U.S.-USSR Balance: Problems of Analysis and Research," *International Perceptions of the Superpower Military Balance,* ed. Donald C. Daniel (New York: Praeger, 1978), Chapter 1, for a useful and thoughtful discussion of the perceptual basis of power. Cf., however, R. D. McLaurin, "Perception, Persuasion, and Power," *International Persuasion,* ed. R. D. McLaurin and Marilyn Houston (New York: Praeger, forthcoming).

19. We have described the Arab-Israeli conflict as a "protracted social conflict," with the properties and implications peculiar to such conflicts. See Edward E. Azar, Paul A. Jureidini, and R. D. McLaurin, "Protracted Social Conflict: Theory and Practice in the Middle East," *Journal of Palestine Studies* 8, 1 (Autumn 1978):41–60.

5—U.S. POLICY IN THE EMERGING MIDDLE EAST

1. Cf. e.g., the remarks of James E. Akins, "Saudi Arabia, Soviet Activities, and Gulf Security," *The Impact of the Iranian Events upon Persian Gulf & United States Security* (Washington, D.C.: American Foreign Policy Institute, 1979), p. 92.

2. See R. Hrair Dekmejian, "The Anatomy of Islamic Revival: Legitimacy Crisis, Ethnic Conflict and the Search for Islamic Alternatives," *Middle East Journal* 34, 1 (Winter 1980):1–12. Dekmejian does not discuss anti-Americanism, and we are not arguing, for our part, that the Islamic resurgence is truly anti-American in nature; only that it *appears* to have such a tone. Much of this image is only the result of the high level of activity of the United States in the Muslim world, and more than a little derives from events peculiar to the situation in Iran.

3. We are not suggesting that it is a particularly *salient* issue, however. Because of its recency the intervention may have high visibility, but it takes no great insight to forecast that the issue will have less staying power as a mobilizing force than the Palestinian issue.

4. See, e.g., Cheryl Bernard and Zalmay Khalilzad, "Secularization, Industrialization, and Khomeini's Islamic Republic," *Political Science Quarterly* 94, 2 (Summer 1979):229–41; and William E. Griffith, "The Revival of Islamic Fundamentalism: The Case of Iran," *International Security* 4, 1 (Summer 1979):132–38.

5. Dekmejian, "The Anatomy," discusses the several roots and the general evolution of Islamic revival.

6. Increased attention to the traditional prohibitions of Ramadan, greater restrictions on liquor sales and displays, the invocation of religious phraseology in government decrees, even the increased prominence of beards among the middle-aged and older—all these were symbols of growing religiosity across the region.

7. R. D. McLaurin, *The Middle East in Soviet Policy* (Lexington: Heath, 1975), p. 65.

8. Failure of the opposition does not imply success of the process in terms of achieving a regional settlement, however.

9. Even in the face of some Egyptian popular resistance to normalization at the people-to-people level.

10. R. D. McLaurin, "The Soviet-American Strategic Balance: Arab Elite Views," *International Interactions* 3, 3 (1977):241.

11. *Toward Peace in the Middle East: Report of a Study Group* (Washington, D.C.: The Brookings Institution, 1975), pp. 1–2. Reprinted with the permission of The Brookings Institution.

12. The settlement *must* be that of the parties. The United States, or the great powers generally, cannot literally impose a settlement, because the complex dynamics of the Middle East provide ample opportunity to unravel such an externally imposed agreement. The settlement must be that of the parties to the conflict.

13. William B. Quandt, *Decade of Decisions: American Policy toward the Arab-Israeli Conflict, 1967–1976* (Berkeley: University of California Press, 1977), p. 299.

14. Edward E. Azar and R. D. McLaurin, "Power Projection," forthcoming article.

15. Lord Palmerston's famous speech in the House of Commons, March 1, 1848.

16. See p. 28 above.

Bibliography

Akhtar, S. "The Iraqi-Iranian Dispute Over the Shatt el-Arab," *Pakistan Horizon* 22, 3 (1969):213–21.

Amit, Meir. "Israel: The Bases of Economic Growth," *The Washington Quarterly: A Review of Strategic and International Studies.* Special Supplement on "Egypt and Israel: Prospects for a New Era" (Spring 1979).

Aronson, Shlomo. "Sadat's Initiative and Israel's Response: The Strategy of Peace and the Strategy of Strategy." Los Angeles: University of California at Los Angeles, Center for Arms Control and International Security, ACIS Research Note 4 (May 1978).

Azar, Edward E., Paul A. Jureidini, and R. D. McLaurin. "Protracted Social Conflict: Theory and Practice in the Middle East," *Journal of Palestine Studies* 8, 1 (Autumn 1978):41–60.

Azar, Edward E. and R. D. McLaurin. "Demographic Change and Political Change: Population Pressures and Territorial Control in the Middle East," *International Interactions* 5, 2–3 (1978):267–87.

el Badri, Hassan, Tahel el Magdoub, and Mohammed Din el Din Zohdy. *The Ramadan War, 1973.* Dunn Loring, Va.: T. N. Dupuy Associates, 1978.

Becker, Abraham S. "The Superpowers in the Arab-Israeli Conflict, 1970–1973." Santa Monica: Rand Corporation, 1973 (offset).

Brodkey, Robert and James Horgen. *Americans in the Gulf: Estimates and Projections of the Influx of U.S. Nationals into the Persian Gulf, 1975–1980.* Washington, D.C.: American Institutes for Research, 1975.

Buheiry, Marwan R. "The Saunders Document," *Journal of Palestine Studies* 8, 1 (Autumn 1978):28–40.

Carrère d'Encausse, Hélène. *La Politique soviétique an Moyen-Orient.* Paris: Presses Universitaires de France, 1975.

Confino, Michael and Shimon Shamir, eds. *The U.S.S.R. and the Middle East.* Jerusalem: Israel Universities Press, 1973.

187

Cooley, John K. *Green March, Black September: The Story of the Palestinian Arabs*. London: Frank Cass, 1973.

————. "Iran, the Palestinians, and the Gulf," *Foreign Affairs* 57, 5 (Summer 1979):1017–34.

Cordesman, Anthony H. "The Arab-Israeli Balance: How Much Is Too Much?" *Armed Forces Journal International* 115, 2 (October 1977):32ff.

Cozean, Jon et al. *The Arab Elite Worldview*. Washington, D.C.: American Institutes for Research, 1975.

Crittenden, Ann. "Israel's Economic Plight," *Foreign Affairs* 57, 5 (Summer 1979):1005–1016.

Dann, Uriel. "The Iraqi Officer Corps as a Factor for Stability: An Unorthodox Approach," *The Military and State in Modern Asia*, ed. H. Z. Schiffrin. Jerusalem: Academic Press, 1976.

Dawisha, Adeed I. "Internal Values and External Threats: The Making of Saudi Foreign Policy," *Orbis* 23, 1 (Spring 1979):129–43.

————. "Syria in Lebanon: Assad's Vietnam," *Foreign Policy,* no. 33 (Winter 1978–79), pp. 135–50.

Devlin, John. *The Ba'th Party: A History of Its Origins to 1966*. Stanford: Hoover Institution Press, 1976.

Dupuy, Trevor N. *Elusive Victory: The Arab-Israeli Wars, 1947–1974*. New York: Harper & Row, 1978.

Dutter, Lee E. "Eastern and Western Jews: Ethnic Divisions in Israeli Society," *Middle East Journal* 31, 4 (Autumn 1977):451–68.

Glassman, Jon D. *Arms for the Arabs: The Soviet Union and War in the Middle East*. Baltimore: Johns Hopkins University Press, 1975.

Golan, Galia. *Yom Kippur and After: The Soviet Union and the Middle East Crisis*. Cambridge: Cambridge University Press, 1977.

Golan, Matti. *The Secret Conversations of Henry Kissinger*. New York: Quadrangle, 1976.

Gottheil, Fred M. "An Economic Assessment of the Military Burden in the Middle East," *Journal of Conflict Resolution* 18, 3 (September 1974):502–513.

Haley, P. Edward and Lewis W. Snider, eds. *Lebanon in Crisis: Participants and Issues*. Syracuse: Syracuse University Press, 1979.

Harik, Iliya. "The Ethnic Revolution and Political Integration in the Middle East," *International Journal of Middle East Studies* 3, 3 (July 1972):303–323.

Harkabi, Yehoshafat. *Arab Attitudes to Israel*. Jerusalem: Israel Universities Press, 1972.

Haselkorn, Avigdor, R. D. McLaurin, and Abraham R. Wagner. *Middle*

East Net Assessment I: Regional Threat Perceptions. Marina del Rey: Analytical Assessments Corporation, 1979.

Heikal, Mohamed. *The Road to Ramadan*. New York: Quadrangle, 1975.

———. *The Sphynx and the Commissar*. New York: Harper & Row, 1979.

Herzog, Chaim. *The War of Atonement*. Boston: Little, Brown, 1974.

Heykal, Mohamed. *The Cairo Documents*. New York: Doubleday, 1973.

Hinnebusch, Raymond A. "Local Politics in Syria: Organization and Mobilization in Four Village Cases," *Middle East Journal* 30, 1 (Winter 1976):1–24.

Hudson, Michael C. *Arab Politics: The Search for Legitimacy*. New Haven and London: Yale University Press, 1977.

Jureidini, Paul A. "The Abating Threat of War," *International Interactions* 3, 3 (1977):223–30.

———. "The Politics of the Lebanese Army," Abbott Associates SR49 (September 1979).

——— and William E. Hazen. *The Dissolution of Lebanon: Futures and Consequences*. Alexandria, Va.: Abbott Associates, 1976.

———. *The Palestinian Movement in Politics*. Lexington: D.C. Heath, 1976.

———. *Six Clashes: An Analysis of the Relationship Between the Palestinian Guerrilla Movement and the Governments of Jordan and Lebanon*. Kensington, Md.: American Institutes for Research, 1971.

Jureidini, Paul A. and R. D. McLaurin. "External Intervention in Internal Conflict: Syrian Strategy in the Lebanese Vortex." Abbott Associates SR28 Rev-3 (August 1978).

———. "Political Disintegration and Conflict Reduction in the Eastern Mediterranean Area." Abbott Associates SR51 (1979).

——— and James M. Price. "Arab Reactions to the Egyptian-Israeli Peace Treaty." Abbott Associates SR46 (March 26, 1979).

———. *Military Operations in Selected Lebanese Built-Up Areas, 1975–1978*. Aberdeen, Md.: Aberdeen Proving Ground, 1979.

Jureidini, Paul A., R. D. McLaurin, and Abraham R. Wagner. *Middle East Conflict Scenarios and United States Defense Options*. Alexandria, Va.: Abbott Associates: Marina del Rey, Ca.: Analytical Assessments Corporation, 1978.

Kerr, Malcolm, ed. *The Elusive Peace in the Middle East*. Albany: State University of New York, 1975.

Klare, Michael T. "Arms and the Shah," *The Progressive* 43, 8 (August 1979).

Longrigg, Stephen H. *Iraq, 1900 to 1950: A Political, Social, and Economic History* London: Oxford University Press, 1956.

Lovejoy, Bahia. *The Land and People of Iraq*. Philadelphia: Lippincott, 1964.

Lustick, Ian. "Arabs in the Jewish State: A Study in the Effective Control of Minority Population." Ph.D. diss., University of California, Berkeley, 1976.

Mansur. Abul Kasim (pseud.) "The Crisis in Iran: Why the U.S. Ignored a Quarter Century of Warning," *Armed Forces Journal International* 116, 5 (January 1979):26–33.

Ma'oz, Moshe. "Syria Under Hafiz al-Assad: New Domestic and Foreign Policies." Jerusalem: Hebrew University of Jerusalem, Jerusalem Papers on Peace Problems, 15 (1975).

McLaurin, R. D. *The Middle East in Soviet Policy*. Lexington: D.C. Heath, 1975.

————, ed. *The Political Role of Minority Groups in the Middle East*. New York: Praeger, 1979.

————. "The Soviet-American Military Balance: Arab Elite Views," *International Interactions* 3, 3 (1977):231–42.

————. "The Transfer of Technology to the Middle East," *The Political Economy of the Middle East: Changes and Prospects Since 1973*, ed. Richard Kauffman and James Wooten (Washington, D.C.: U.S. Government Printing Office, 1980).

———— and Marilyn Houston, eds. *International Persuasion: Political and Military Persuasive Communications*. New York: Praeger, forthcoming.

McLaurin, R. D., Paul A. Jureidini, and Preston S. Abbott. "Political Leadership and Strategic Decision." Abbott Associates SR36 (1978).

McLaurin, R. D. and Mohammed Mughisuddin. *Cooperation and Conflict: Egyptian, Iraqi and Syrian Objectives and U.S. Policy*. Washington, D.C.: American Institutes for Research, 1975.

———— and Don Peretz. *Middle East Foreign Policy: Issue and Process*. New York: Praeger, 1981.

McLaurin, R. D., Mohammed Mughisuddin, and Abraham R. Wagner. *Foreign Policy Making in the Middle East*. New York: Praeger, 1977.

McLaurin, R. D. and James M. Price. "OPEC Current Account Surpluses: Assistance to the Arab Front-Line States," *Oriente Moderno* 58, 11 (Novembre 1978):533–46.

Mughisuddin, Mohammed, ed. *Conflict and Cooperation in the Persian Gulf*. New York: Praeger, 1977.

Nasser, Gamal Abdel. *Egypt's Liberation: The Philosophy of the Revolution*. Washington, D.C.: Public Affairs Press, 1955.

Noyes, James H. *The Clouded Lens: Persian Gulf Security and U.S. Policy.* Stanford: Hoover Institution Press, 1979.

O'Ballance, Edgar. *No Victor, No Vanquished: The Yom Kippur War.* San Rafael: Presidio Press, 1978.

Omran, Abdel R., ed. *Egypt: Population Problems and Prospects.* Chapel Hill: Carolina Population Center, 1973.

O'Neill, Bard. *Armed Struggle in Palestine.* Boulder: Westview, 1978.

Page, Stephen. *The U.S.S.R. and Arabia: The Development of Soviet Policies and Attitudes Towards the Countries of the Arabian Peninsula.* London: Central Asian Research Centre, 1971.

Peretz, Don. *The Government and Politics of Israel.* Boulder: Westview, 1979.

Pranger, Robert J. and Dale R. Tahtinen. *Nuclear Threat in the Middle East.* Washington, D.C.: American Enterprise Institute, 1975.

Price, James M. "A Country Profile of Egypt." Unpublished ms., 1978.

Quandt, William B. *Decade of Decisions: American Policy toward the Arab-Israeli Conflict, 1967–1976.* Berkeley: University of California Press, 1977.

———, Fuad Jabber, and Ann Mosely Lesch. *The Politics of Palestinian Nationalism.* Berkeley: University of California Press, 1973.

el-Rayyes, Riad N. and Dunia Nahas, eds. *Guerrilas for Palestine: A Study of the Palestinian Commando Organizations.* Beirut: An-Nahar Press Services, 1974.

Roosevelt, Kermit. *Countercoup: The Bloody Struggle for the Control of Iran.* New York: McGraw-Hill, 1979.

Rosen, Steven. "Nuclearization and Stability in the Middle East," *Jerusalem Journal of International Relations* 1, 3 (Spring 1976):1–32.

———. "What the Next Arab-Israeli War Might Look Like," *International Security* 2, 4 (Spring 1978):149–74.

——— and Martin Indyk. "The Temptation to Pre-empt in a Fifth Arab-Israeli War," *Orbis* 20, 2 (Summer 1976):265–85.

Rosen, Steven and Haim Shaked. "Arms and the Saudi Connection," *Commentary* 65, 6 (June 1978):33–38.

Rubinstein, Alvin Z. *Red Star Over the Nile.* Princeton: Princeton University Press, 1977.

el-Sadat, Anwar. *In Search of Identity: An Autobiography.* New York: Harper & Row, 1978.

Saddy, Fehmi. *The Eastern Front: Implications of the Syrian/Palestinian/Jordanian Entente and the Lebanese Civil War.* Alexandria, Va.: Abbot Associates, 1976.

Sheehan, Edward R. F. *The Arabs, Israelis, and Kissinger: A Secret History of American Diplomacy in the Middle East.* New York: Readers Digest Press, 1976.

Snider, Lewis W. and R. D. McLaurin. *Saudi Arabia's Air Defense Requirements in the 1980s.* Alexandria, Va.: Abbott Associates, 1979.

Tahir-Kheli, Shirin. "Iran and Pakistani Cooperation in an Area of Conflict," *Asian Survey* 18, 5 (May 1977):474–90.

U.S. Agency for International Development. *Regional Cooperation in the Middle East.* Washington, D.C., February 1, 1979.

U.S. Congress. House. Committee on International Relations. *Review of Recent Developments in the Middle East.* Hearings before the subcommittee on Europe and the Middle East, 95th Cong., 1st sess., Washington, D.C.: Government Printing Office, June 8, 1977.

U.S. Department of State. Embassy of the United States of America, Cairo, Egypt. "Foreign economic Trends and Their Implications for the United States: Egypt." Washington, D.C.: U.S. Department of Commerce, June 1977.

van Dam, Nikolaos. *The Struggle for Power in Syria: Sectarianism, Regionalism, and Tribalism in Politics, 1961–1978.* New York: St. Martin's Press, 1979.

Van Dusen, Michael H. "Political Integration and Regionalism in Syria," *Middle East Journal* 26, 2 (Spring 1972):123–36.

Wagner, Abraham R. *The Impact of the 1973 October War on Israeli Policy and Implications for U.S. Defense Policy.* Washington, D.C.: American Institutes for Research, 1975.

Wakebridge, Charles. "The Egyptian Staff Solution," *Military Review* 55, 3 (March 1975):3–11.

Weinbaum, M. G. and Gautam Sen. "Pakistan Enters the Middle East," *Orbis* 22, 3 (Fall 1978):595–612.

Whetten, Lawrence L. *The Canal War: Four-Power Conflict in the Middle East.* Cambridge, Mass.: MIT Press, 1974.

Williams, Lewis, ed. *Military Aspects of the Israeli-Arab Conflict.* Tel Aviv: University Publishing Projects, 1975.

Wright, Claudia. "Iraq—New Power in the Middle East," *Foreign Affairs* 58, 2 (Winter 1979/80):257–77.

Index

BEYOND CAMP DAVID

was composed in 10-point Mergenthaler Linotron 202 Times Roman
and leaded two points, with display type in Fantail,
by Eastern Graphics;
printed offset on 50-pound acid-free Warren Antique Cream paper,
Smyth-sewn and bound over 70-point binder's boards in Columbia Atlantic Vellum,
also adhesive bound with 10-point Carolina covers,
by Maple-Vail Book Manufacturing Group, Inc.,
and published by

SYRACUSE UNIVERSITY PRESS

SYRACUSE, NEW YORK 13210